DICTATORSHIP

DICTATORSHIP

Its History and Theory

by

ALFRED COBBAN M.A., PH.D.

HASKELL HOUSE PUBLISHERS LTD.
Publishers of Scarce Scholarly Books
NEW YORK. N. Y. 10012
1971

First Published 1939

HASKELL HOUSE PUBLISHERS LTD.
Publishers of Scarce Scholarly Books
280 LAFAYETTE STREET
NEW YORK, N. Y. 10012

Library of Congress Catalog Card Number: 76-122979

Standard Book Number 8383-1111-3

Printed in the United States of America

CONTENTS

CONTENTS

PREFACE

THE aim of this book is to make a general survey of dictatorship, taking into consideration both its theoretical sources and its actual historical development, analysing its principles as they can be observed in operation, and indicating its prospects so far as they can be deduced from experience. For comparison an appendix has been added on medieval and classical tyranny, though for practical reasons I have preferred the term *dictatorship*, which is now generally used, rather than the strictly more correct *tyranny*.

The plan of the book can, I hope, easily be grasped from the section headings, so of this it is not necessary to say more here than that the early chapters endeavour to trace the development of the idea of sovereignty up to the French Revolution and Napoleon, here taken as the first modern dictator. After a study of the rise of the contemporary dictatorial movement there follows an analysis of the elements which have contributed to the making of the modern totalitarian state, with which the dictatorial form of government is so intimately connected. Finally, a fairly long chapter is given to the attempt to sum up such conclusions as seem legitimately to flow from the previous history and analysis of totalitarianism and dictatorship.

Obviously it is not possible for one writer to speak with authority on so many different historical periods as are perforce included in the scope of this book. It would be equally impossible, even if it were a profitable task, for a single student to exhaust the immense bibliography that has already grown up around the contemporary dictatorships. Two subjects of which I have made some detailed study — French history in the eighteenth and nineteenth centuries, and the development of modern political thinking — occupy a considerable place in the material to be discussed. As for the other periods into which I have been driven, I can only plead that I have tried to behave in these with appropriate caution and decorum. In these fields I have attempted merely to utilize accepted ideas: I should be surprised and shocked to find that I had said on medieval or classical history anything original. The political scientist who is examining dictatorship cannot, however, afford to neglect the evidence that these earlier periods provide.

A serious difficulty involved in the subject under discussion arises from the fact that it necessarily includes a considerable amount of present-day material. Attempts to write contemporary history are seldom successful, and it has indeed been argued, on general considerations, that the events of current politics are not susceptible of historical treatment. Not only is it difficult at best for a contemporary to see the facts of his own day in a reasonable proportion, but so far as concerns dictatorship they have to be groped for in the midst of an opaque cloud of propaganda. Our defence for venturing into this field would be that, though much of the material is historical in nature, this book professes primarily to be a contributon to political science. The analysis — which must be distinguished from a history — of the contemporary situation, however difficult, is essential to its theme.

That any study bearing so largely on our own times is in serious danger of reflecting mainly the author's own political bias, I am well aware; and I am prepared to find that those who do not like my facts will attribute them to my opinions. I am reluctant, however, to accept the modern view that because perfect impartiality is unattainable, therefore there is no point in struggling to maintain even a moderately impartial outlook. Admittedly, not merely old-fashioned bias, but floods of consciously mendacious propaganda dictate the intellectual climate of the day, and the attempt to preserve intellectual independence may be neither easy nor popular. But if there is any virtue in an academic approach, it should lie in a willingness to see things free from a cloud of ephemeral passions. For those taking an active part in political life there is an excuse if the heat of party struggles and the compulsion of day-to-day decisions obscures the true shape of things. Perhaps, however, too many of those who profess to offer an impartial analysis of causes and effects are themselves also at the mercy of a noble admiration for what they believe to be good, or a generous indignation at what they regard as ignoble and hateful.

How far an impartial outlook on the particular political problems studied has been achieved here, it is of course for the reader to judge. I have no doubt that some, not finding the views they would have wished to find, will prefer to attribute their disappointment to the writer's bias rather than to their own. Many may not like the conclusions indicated in the latter part of the book: I cannot say that I like them myself, but I did not find in that any reason for rejecting them.

There is no branch of history so controversial as the history of dictators. From Caesar and Napoleon downwards their historians have tended to alternate between 'white-washing' and 'de-bunking'. The former has on the whole prevailed. Except for a stern moralist like Lord Acton, for whom 'nearly all great men are bad men', there has been a disinclination to admit that a man as great as, say, Napoleon, could be a bad man. Even in the history of our own time we have seen how quickly after 'the strong man with the dagger' has come 'the weak man with the sponge'. In idealized versions of the rise and rule of a Hitler, a Stalin, or a Mussolini, all that is unfit to be related to children has been removed, and the result is an idyll or a *conte moral*. The story of post-war Italy or Germany or Russia, to name only the great exemplars, is often written as though to prove that, taken on a large enough scale, 'all the good people ended happily, and the bad people ended unhappily'. 'That', said Oscar Wilde, 'is the meaning of fiction.' It is also the meaning of some of what passes as contemporary history.

In this study of dictatorship I have attempted to draw no moral lessons. While I have not sat in moral judgment on the dictators, past or present, I have equally tried to avoid being dazzled by their splendour and success. Where it has been necessary to choose between conflicting views, I have followed what seemed to me the soundest historical opinion. When I did not feel that there was sufficient evidence to come to any conclusion, I have not attempted to give one.

The object, although the subject is in part contemporary, has not been to add one more to the host of political polemics, neither to denounce nor defend, but to attempt to understand modern totalitarian dictatorship, and to put it in its place in the development of modern history, as a natural and in an historical sense necessary development. Too often modern dictatorship is treated as a mere piece of atavism, an incomprehensible freak, a reaction against the whole trend of civilization. Such, indeed, it might have seemed before 1914. But the student of modern history is like the solver of a jig-saw puzzle: while many of the pieces are missing he can only guess at the general picture, and concentrate on those individual parts of the design where something coherent can be detected. But so much has happened since 1914, so many missing pieces have dropped into position, that at last something like the pattern of the whole may be said to be emerging — and the picture revealed is as different from that imagined by our predecessors as a modern painting may differ from a Landseer or an Alma Tadema. The pity is that not a few are still pathetically struggling away, with the rosy unrealities of the once-dreamed pattern yet in their mind's eye.

At the same time, I have not put forward any pretence that the trend towards totalitarian dictatorship is the only development to be observed in modern times, nor even that it will necessarily prove in the end the dominant one. Rival tendencies in Western civilization exist, though they are not the topic of this book; the drama of our day lies in the conflict between various forces, only one group of which receives treatment here.

Upon these various forces I have not attempted to pass any judgment on moral grounds. But if moral judgments are eschewed here, it must not be assumed that this implies any acceptance of the view that the sphere of politics is somehow exempt from ordinary morality. Arguments derived from ethical considerations are omitted, not because their possibility is denied, but because they would be a disturbing influence in a study that attempts to preserve a scientific spirit. Moreover, they could not be included without including also a statement and justification of the fundamental principles in political philosophy on which they were based, and this book does not provide the appropriate occasion for that. This does not mean that I have passed no judgments, but those I have ventured to suggest are on matters such as the appropriateness of means to end or on the self-consistency of a political system. Moreover, without drawing morals I have tried to indicate consequences, and leave any judgment on these to the reader.

This study of dictatorship makes no pretence at being an exhaustive treatise. Many more examples might have been submitted to examination, and many parallels or developments which I have not had space to include will occur to readers. Most of the subjects upon which I have touched are capable of, and indeed in themselves demand more extensive discussion. But as the object was to study dictatorship in general, and not any individual example as such, I have restricted the treatment of details to what the main theme required, without expanding any individual point beyond this. I have also tried to avoid the temptation of aiming at an artificial completeness by pushing the argument of the book farther than it will logically go.

Two sections of this study, which, although they seemed desirable in the interests of academic students of the subject, may have less appeal to the general reader, and which also did not fit very easily into the history of the development of dictatorship in modern times, have been relegated to appendixes.

PREFACE

The principle on which notes are given should perhaps be explained. They are included for three purposes — first, as an acknowledgment of indebtedness; secondly, when it seemed desirable to support a statement by quoting its source; and thirdly, for the sake of students with a special interest in some particular section of the general argument. I have not thought it necessary to multiply notes by giving references for statements or facts which are commonplaces of history. Finally, a bibliography, in a book covering so extensive a field, seemed out of the question.

ALFRED COBBAN

University College
University of London
January 1939

To

MY FATHER

DICTATORSHIP

CHAPTER I

INTRODUCTORY: A DEFINITION OF DICTATORSHIP

Our object being the study of a specific form of political behaviour, the first problem is necessarily one of definition. When Aristotle said that man was a political animal, he meant that he was an animal living in societies. Politics in the modern sense has a narrower scope: it refers only to a certain class of these societies, those which we call states. It has been argued that this limitation is unjustified, and that the student of politics should be as much concerned with so-called non-political societies, such as trade unions, churches or tennis clubs, as with states, because the peculiar function of the politician, the art of government, can be practised in all these. This is doubtless true; at the same time one can hardly deny the uniqueness of the state, which, in its modern form, is in fact differentiated from all other human societies by two fundamental characteristics. The state is, in the first place, an association of neighbours, of all persons permanently settled in a given territory. It was not always so: in the beginning kinship was the bond of society, and a hypothetical racial tie is still a strong element in the mentality of many of the politically less mature communities. But since man needed from society above all mutual aid and defence, utilitarian considerations dictated the change from the principle of kinship to that of neighbourhood. Even after the Greeks had firmly established the political basis of our civilization there were periods in the history of Europe, such as the centuries which followed the decline of the Roman Empire, when ideas of kinship and the blood-tie partially ousted the Graeco-Roman idea of the state; but the primary political conceptions of Aristotle and Pericles, Cicero and Augustus, somehow survived the competition from the political ideas of Visigoths and Vandals, Slavs and Saxons, in the first Dark Age, and they may well survive a re-birth of tribal politics.

A second characteristic of the state is that it is sovereign. In the years following the war we were all told that the state, even without active assistance from those enemies of political authoritarianism, the Marxists, was withering away before our eyes. Sovereignty was an old tale, 'told by an idiot,[1] full of sound and fury, signifying nothing'. The wish was father to the thought. Faced with a challenge to his authority, Leviathan has roused himself and devoured his enemies and made the air hideous with his broadcast bellowings, for he can still be the most awful monster that the world has seen. The sovereign state is still sovereign.

What do we mean by this in plain language? We mean that the state recognizes as binding over it no other authority. It may of course, voluntarily or compulsorily, accept some external bond in the form of a treaty obligation; but history shows that modern states will only endure such a restriction while it remains to their interest, or so long as they are afraid of the consequences of repudiating it. The difficulty of maintaining the principle of absolute state sovereignty in a world that until recently was becoming economically more and more a unit, is

[1] Generally AUSTIN, formulator of the legal theory of sovereignty.

evident; but so too is the increasing disposition in practically all states to assert that principle, regardless of economic penalties, in a more and more extreme form. If we are concerned, not with what ought to be, but with what is, the territorial, sovereign state must be accepted as our primary political fact.

Given agreement on the basic characteristics of the state, the next problem for the student of politics is to find some principle by which to classify states and distinguish one from another. Here an internal analysis of the state is called for, and from it a third universal characteristic emerges. In all states there is a division at any given time between the government and the governed, though the actual attribution of the powers of government to one or another individual or group of individuals may vary from time to time. One method of classifying states is according to the form of government they possess, and this is the most usual criterion, though not, of course, the only possible one.

Aristotle's classification of forms of government may conveniently provide our starting point. He distinguishes them in the simplest way possible — numerically, according as the powers of government are exercised by one person, by a few, or by the many. He further introduces a principle by which to distinguish between good and bad governments. Good governments are those in which power is exercised in the interests of the community as a whole, bad are those in which it is exercised in the interests of the government. Thus he arrives at three good forms — monarchy, aristocracy and polity or constitutional government, and three bad forms — tyranny, oligarchy and democracy or mob rule. In making this distinction, however, Aristotle is taking us into the realm of moral philosophy. Now it may well be that sooner or later the political scientist is bound to be brought up against such considerations; but in politics, at least while it is a descriptive science, his object should be to keep clear of morals as long as possible. He must be willing to accept the limitation Spinoza imposes on himself — 'That I might investigate the subject matter of this science with the same freedom of spirit as we generally use in mathematics, I have laboured carefully, not to mock, lament or execrate, but to understand human actions'.[1] Such historical indifference is not frequent, and is liable to be perverted into a base pseudo-morality of success; but without it the student of politics is inevitably exposed to the criticism of Hobbes, who very pertinently remarks of Aristotle's bad forms, 'They are not the names of other forms of government, but of the same forms misliked. For they that are discontented under *monarchy* call it *tyranny*; and they that are displeased with *aristocracy* call it *oligarchy*; so also they which find themselves grieved under a *democracy*, call it *anarchy*'.[2]

If we wish for a means of distinguishing between forms of government that goes beyond the purely numerical distinction and yet at the same time is not ethical in nature, we must ask such questions as, How does the government obtain power? What is the extent of its power? And in what way is it exercised? Considering, for example, the government of one man, we can see that he may obtain power in three ways — by inheriting it, by

[1] SPINOZA, *A Political Treatise*, I §4; *Works*, ed. R. H. M. Elwes, 1883, vol. I, p. 288.

[2] HOBBES, *Leviathan*, ed. A. D. Lindsay, 1914, chap. xix, p. 97.

force, or by the free consent of the governed or of such among them as make any claim to political rights. These three methods are not mutually exclusive. Thus Henry VII claimed the throne of England by hereditary right, he won it on the battlefield, and his title was ratified by Parliament.

Again, we may consider how far the power of the government extends. This is, naturally, a matter of degree; but we may safely distinguish between absolute or despotic governments and others, if we are careful to base our test on practical and not on theoretical considerations. Legally, the British Parliament is as absolute as any government in the world; practically, we know that there are many fields of social life which it seldom or never invades, and that there are many other authorities of all kinds in the country whose competence it rarely if ever challenges. When we speak of an absolute government we mean one which both claims the right to interfere and does in fact regularly interfere in every branch of social life; and further, one which tolerates no authority which does not emanate from its own will.

Finally, we may distinguish between those governments which rule, except in rare emergencies, by general laws, laid down in a manner established by precedent and applying impartially to all cases, and those which govern habitually by decrees — the immediate expression of the will of the ruler applied to individual cases, executive acts, in fact, rather than rules of law.

With the aid of these further criteria it is possible to produce a classification of governments based on objective and not on ethical tests. Before doing so, however, it is necessary to observe that in the great states of the modern world no form of government can be entirely pure and unmixed with other forms. The government of one man for instance, taken absolutely literally, would be quite impossible in any large state. There must at least be subordinates, assisting him and possessing a greater or smaller share of governmental authority. With this qualification we may proceed to define the sub-class which we propose to study in this book and which we are calling Dictatorship. This is the government of one man, who has not *primarily* obtained his position by inheritance, but by either force or consent and normally by a combination of both. He must possess absolute sovereignty, that is, all political power must ultimately emanate from his will, and it must be unlimited in scope. It must be exercised, more or less frequently, in an arbitrary manner, by decree rather than by law. And, finally, it must not be limited in duration to any given term of office; nor must the dictator be responsible to any other authority, for such restrictions would be incompatible with absolute rule.

Variability of terminology is one of the great difficulties in political science, and this definition differs both from that given by some modern writers, such as Carl Schmitt, and from the actual institution of dictatorship as it existed under the Roman Republic. It is admittedly an arbitrary definition. It seems, however, to express with reasonable precision what is normally understood to-day by the term; and it provides a definition which enables us to distinguish clearly one class of government, without introducing the ethical implications involved in Aristotle's tyranny. To the definition could of course be added secondary characteristics, but it will be better to allow these to emerge from a study of dictatorship in action.

CHAPTER II

DIVINE RIGHT MONARCHY AND THE IDEA OF SOVEREIGNTY

§ I THE NEW MONARCHY

THERE is a common belief that dictatorship represents a new and untried form of government. It has on this account been hailed as a panacea, the greatest of modern political inventions, a pillar of fire in the obscurity of night, if to its critics more like a smoke cloud of propaganda in the cold light of day, to lead the tribes of humanity out of the wilderness of nineteenth-century Parliamentarism. On the other hand, it is as frequently condemned for its novelty as a reckless experiment, a wild expedient of latter-day barbarians destined to bring about the destruction of civilization. Both of these judgments would be passed a little less frequently if it were realized that dictatorship, even as limited by the definition we have given, is an old and well-tried form of government, that there is hardly any other form in the contemporary world about which we know as much, or the course of which we can anticipate with greater chance of proving correct. In classical, medieval and modern times, dictatorship has regularly appeared, and nearly every time it has appeared it has run singularly true to type. These, however, are assertions, to the proof of which this book is in part devoted.

We propose, however, to direct our attention mainly

to the modern world. Even here it will not be difficult to show that dictatorship is no mere post-war phenomenon. To understand its rise, indeed, it is necessary to go back to the beginnings of the modern age, since one essential ingredient in dictatorship — the idea of sovereignty — has been present from the very beginning of the modern state. The characteristic feature of modern times in politics is the prevalence of the nation state, regarded as a sovereign power — one, that is, acknowledging no authority superior to its own either within or without its borders. It is a commonplace that a political conception of this kind was impossible during the Middle Ages proper, when the feudal baron and the universal Catholic Church — to name only two of the rival authorities — 'cabined, cribbed, confined' the power of the king, and when the idea of the state as something different from the authority of the king can hardly be said to have existed.

But the fourteenth and fifteenth centuries are marked by the gradual breaking up of the ideas and institutions which we regard as typically medieval, and with the sixteenth century the modern state was born, for then rulers such as the Tudors in England, the Valois in France and the Hapsburgs in Spain, successfully asserted the supremacy of the secular state and embodied it in the person of the monarch. When Henry VIII or Francis I was on the throne the modern state seemed to have sprung fully armed from the brow of the Middle Ages. Among the confusion of ideas that was characteristic of the later Middle Ages had been rising the idea of sovereignty. A ruler like Henry VIII put it into practice with such thoroughness, with such a modern technique, and such mastery of *real politik*, that the parallel has inevitably been drawn between the sixteenth-century New Monarchy and twentieth-century dictatorship.

It is difficult to decide whether Henry VIII or Adolf Hitler would be the more shocked by the comparison. But though there undoubtedly are many points of similarity, an essential difference is to be found in the fact that the authority of the New Monarch was based not merely on divine right — modern dictators sometimes claim that for themselves — but on divine hereditary right. Further differences result from the absence in the sixteenth century of the complicated and powerful machinery of state control that exists to-day, and the presence then of imperfectly subjected ecclesiastical and feudal powers. The New Monarch, moreover, was limited up to a point by medieval constitutional survivals, such as the English Parliament, the Spanish Cortes and the French États Généraux and Parlements. His authority had to be exercised in the form of law and not by mere enunciation of the royal will. This is true even of Henry VIII, for it has been shown that the famous Statute of Proclamations of 1539, apparently giving the king's will the force of law, does not bear the interpretation formerly put upon it.[1] Neither in theory nor in practice, then, is the New Monarchy comparable with dictatorship in its primary characteristics. Many secondary features they may have in common, but these need not detain us.

It was, however, on the basis provided by the New Monarchs that a state in which dictatorship is possible has been built, because with them emerged into practical politics the idea of sovereignty. This idea was not

[1] This attempt to revive the prestige of royal proclamations has, indeed, been taken as evidence of the growing importance of statute law.

absent from the later Middle Ages, but it was framed in the terms dictated by the rivalry of Empire and Papacy, and when a similar claim to sovereignty was put forward on behalf of the national kings it did not at first involve a generalized theory of the state. Jean Bodin, the first modern writer to achieve a real theory of the state, by his *Six livres de la république*, printed in 1576, can justly be regarded as the founder of the modern theory of sovereignty. For him the sovereign power is 'absolute and perpetual',[1] and comprised particularly in the right of the sovereign to impose laws upon his subjects without their consent;[2] and sovereignty is so sacred a thing, according to Bodin, that the person of the Sovereign must be inviolable; even if he is the most atrocious tyrant the subject should 'suffer death rather than attack his life or honour'.[3]

Such statements are not essentially novel. The originality of Bodin lies in the purely secular basis of his political thinking; this is what justifies us in looking on him as one of those who laid the foundations of the modern theory of the state. Professor Allen has pointed out the significance of a work by Bodin which was only printed three centuries later, the *Heptaplomeres*, in which he deals scathingly with the claims of most orthodox forms of religion to possess the absolute truth, and concludes with an expression of general scepticism.[4] The consequence is that for him the Church ceases to be the depository of God's will on earth, and therefore the necessary intermediary between God and the State. The

[1] J. Bodin, *Les six livres de la république*, Lyon, 1580, Liv. I, chap. 8, p. 85.
[2] id., p. 99.
[3] id., Liv. II, ch. 5, p. 213.
[4] J. W. Allen, *A History of Political Thought in the Sixteenth Century*, 1928, pp. 399-402.

state itself becomes the manifestation of God's will,[1] and the prince is the image of God on earth.[2] But, as Allen points out, this is not all: there is in Bodin also an attempt to derive sovereignty from the will of society, a human and not a divine will, and in this respect he was more modern, not only than his contemporaries, but also than most of his successors, for a long time to come.[3]

Holding these views, it is evident that Bodin has already gone far towards that conception of a single, indivisible and absolute source of authority in the community, which is the essence of the theory of sovereignty. But we must not read our own assumptions into his theory. Sovereignty, according to the modern view, is by definition unlimited. Bodin, on the other hand, reiterates the limitations imposed on his sovereign. He does not regard himself thereby as sacrificing the absolute character of sovereignty, because these restrictions seem to him to be part of its very nature. 'If we say that he has absolute power, who is not subject to law', he writes, 'then there will not be found a sovereign Prince on the earth, seeing that all Princes in the world are subject to the laws of God and of nature, and to several human laws common to all peoples.'[4]

In addition to this, there is a further limitation to be noted in that although theoretically he allows that the sovereign may be one man, a few, or many, Bodin exhibits a very strong preference for hereditary monarchy in practice. This preference he puts forward, he says, not

[1] J. W. Allen, *A History of Political Thought in the Sixteenth Century*, 1928, p. 604.

[2] cf. Bodin, op. cit., Liv. I, ch. 10, p. 150.

[3] Allen, op. cit., p. 423.

[4] Bodin, op. cit., Liv. I, ch. 8, p. 91; cf. pp. 92, 93, 109.

to please princes, but because such a form of government is patently that which is the most likely to ensure the security and happiness of the subjects.[1] His belief in hereditary monarchy, though he holds that this form of government is prescribed by nature, is thus primarily derived from his view of its social utility. On the other hand, for most of those who upheld it hereditary monarchy was based on the principle of divine right, and this provided a second limitation on the idea of sovereignty.

Evidently, then, the theory of the sovereign state was far from complete in the sixteenth century. Its history in modern times is the history of its emancipation from these two ideas of natural law and divine right, and to this process we must next direct our attention.

The first revolt against the New Monarchy, and therefore against the principle of divine right, came in the Netherlands, but here the object was not to extend and enfranchise, but to weaken sovereignty; and the result was the establishment of a Republic in which sovereign power was limited by being divided. With the revolt of the Netherlands re-emerged into practical politics those medieval theories of contract and natural law, which during the following centuries were to form a standing challenge to the idea of sovereignty. 'In the receiving and inauguration of a prince', said the author of the *Defence of Liberty Against Tyrants*, writing in the service of that Prince of Orange, William the Silent, who first in the modern world raised the banner of free government and toleration, 'there are covenants and contracts passed between him and the people, which are

[1] BODIN, op. cit., Liv. VI, ch. 4, p. 672; cf. pp. 673, 674, and Liv. VI, ch. 5, pp. 678, 679.

tacit and expressed, natural or civil . . . He who maliciously or wilfully violates these conditions, is questionless a tyrant by practice. And therefore the officers of state may judge him according to the laws. And if he support his tyranny by strong hands, their duty binds them, when by no other means it can be effected, by force of arms to suppress him.'[1] This was a declaration of war against the claims to sovereign power put forward by divine right monarchy, in the person of Philip II of Spain.

The next attack on the New Monarchy was the Parliamentarian struggle against Charles I in England, the object of which was again to control and not to increase governmental authority. This need not necessarily divert our attention: revolutions not seldom bring about conditions precisely the opposite of those which they were intended to produce, and indeed out of the struggle for Parliamentary supremacy emerged Oliver Cromwell, in whom we have a very promising candidate for a place in any history of dictatorship.

One can only describe his government as the rule of one man; he did not inherit his position; he exercised his authority by decrees, and that authority was very extensive. Cromwell, indeed, was for all effective purposes a dictator, only of a very peculiar kind. In the first place, as his numerous experiments with constitutions and Parliaments proved, he was a dictator in spite of himself. Secondly — and this is what essentially removes him from the category of dictator as we have defined it — he did not believe in the autonomy of politics. The sovereignty of the state was an undesigned by-product of his government. What he aimed at was a Calvinistic polity, a

[1] *A Defence of Liberty against Tyrants*, ed. H. J. Laski, 1924, p. 212.

government of the godly, which should yet at the same time be a government of the people. It was to be a theocracy that should also be, so far as the seventeenth century understood the term, a representative government. Representatives proved regrettably ungodly; the godly, when tried, proved incapable of governing, and Cromwell had to intervene with dictatorial methods. His justification showed the two authorities which he recognized: 'If my calling be from God, and my testimony from the people — God and the people shall take it from me, else I will not part with it.'[1]

The Commonwealth therefore exhibited a contradiction of which Cromwell himself was perhaps not unaware. It would be profitable to study his Protectorate to extend our knowledge of the technique of dictatorial government. But it would not be wise to commence with this, for not only was it an involuntary dictatorship, and one that conflicted in its basic principles with the true modern dictatorship, but also, beyond establishing a prejudice against the rule of one man in England, it had no historic sequel of its own kind. It certainly did not initiate the modern movement towards dictatorship, and we are left, after the Protectorate was ended, with the theory of monarchy by divine right still the first and only step taken in that path.

§ 2 ENLIGHTENED DESPOTISM

For the next stage in the rise of modern dictatorship we must pass on to the eighteenth century. The right of

[1] T. CARLYLE, *The Letters and Speeches of Oliver Cromwell*, ed. S. C. Lomas, 1904, vol. II, p. 367, speech of 12 Sept., 1654.

sovereignty had been pushed pretty well to its farthest point, both in theory and in practice, by the time of Louis XIV. But except for the speculations of Hobbes and Spinoza, who come into our argument at a later point, it had remained tied to the conception of divine right monarchy, and therefore limited by the very nature of the power that exercised it. Though in theory absolute, the monarchy in fact depended on the religious sanction, and so in practice it continued to be bound in a not always happy alliance with the Church. Similarly, the king, however much power he might take away from the aristocracy, could not altogether dispense with these 'Corinthian capitals of polished society', even when they had become a mere façade to the hidden ferro-concrete of bureaucracy that really bore the weight of government. An authority based on divine hereditary right, and maintained in the last resort by religious awe, being in the nature of things inevitably conservative, the power of the king by right divine, or at least his power of effective action, was in fact drastically limited. Not only the decisions of the so-called absolute monarchy, but even the methods by which they were applied, were largely confined to what was traditional. The benevolent despots changed all this. The history of absolute monarchy in the seventeenth and eighteenth centuries is the history of its gradual emancipation from those restrictions which were part of its own nature and essential to its existence: its ultimate disappearance from the political map of Europe was the logical consequence of its success.

In the history of political development sometimes theory leads and sometimes facts. On the whole it was the theory of enlightened despotism which led the way in the eighteenth century. This theory originated from the attempt to unite the two divergent trends in modern political thinking which we have already singled out. On the one hand, Bodin and his successors had proclaimed the principle of absolute sovereignty as the basis of the state; on the other, the author of the *Vindiciae*, and the school of Locke, upheld in various ways the tradition of natural law. Put in their extremest forms, the one school found with Hobbes and Spinoza the basis of all political power in individual will, while the other, with Montesquieu, traced all authority to the operation of the laws of nature. Partly because of the successful rising of the Netherlands and the achievement of the 'Glorious Revolution' in England in 1688, taken along with the failure of Louis XIV, the latter school predominated in the eighteenth century and embodied its discussion of the origin of political authority in various theories of the social contract, in which were summed up what were supposed to be the fundamental principles of natural law.

This adoption of a contractual form by political theory was a natural result of the long dominance exercised over political thinking by lawyers, but in the eighteenth century a new influence made itself felt. The discoveries of Newton seemed to provide a scientific basis for natural law: the embodiment of this in a social contract became somewhat superflous when it had acquired the certainty of scientific truth. The prevailing idea of law was dictated by the conceptions of mathematics; and thus Mercier de la Rivière speaks of Euclid as a 'despot' and his geometric truths as despotic laws, which rested on 'the irresistible force of the evidence'.[1] The assumed infallibility of scientific law, in combination with the juristic conception of law as a command, produced the belief that the fundamental social laws, too, were commands, having behind them not merely the force of the state and the moral authority of society, but the nature of things itself.

Scientific laws operated without human interference, but they pre-supposed for most thinkers in the eighteenth century a divine impulse behind them, of the existence of which, indeed, the laws were themselves proof. From the watch, in the words of Leslie Stephen, one argued back to the watchmaker, from the shining constellations to God. The Creator, however, had been somewhat remiss in dealing with the machinery of human society. The unpredictable, ill-disciplined spontaneity of human behaviour in politics stood in shocking contrast to the obedient movement of the planets in their appointed orbits and the regularity of the stars, for esoteric speculation concerning the perihelion of Mercury had not yet come to disturb the Newtonian heaven. Now since Nature had refrained from completing her task a human substitute, a terrestrial divinity, had to take her place and set in action the laws laid down by nature for the proper regulation of social relations — a Legislator in the language of Rousseau or Mably, an enlightened despot for the Physiocrats.

The rival ideas of natural law and sovereignty were thus in a position to be united, for the despot was now regarded by the Physiocrats as the embodiment of the sovereignty of natural law. In this way the conclusion was reached

[1] LEMERCIER DE LA RIVIÈRE, *L'ordre naturel et essentiel des sociétés politiques*, 1767, ch. xxiv, p. 185.

that the government of one man was the closest to the order of nature, and that, in the words of Quesnay, 'The sovereign authority should be unique and superior to all individuals in society'.[1] The Physiocrats opposed any system of balance of powers in the state, because they believed that, 'It is the essence of authority not to be separated; to divide it, is to render it incapable of action, and in consequence to nullify it'.[2] Further, they held that sovereignty should be hereditary. This prevents disputes over succession, and has the further advantage that it unites completely the interests of the sovereigns as persons with those of their sovereignties.[3] 'All their interests', writes Dupont de Nemours, 'personal and particular, present and future, are intimately, consciously and manifestly bound up with those of their nations.'[4]

The Physiocrats distinguished between this legal despotism and the rule of a tyrant in that the former, being confined to the enforcement of the laws of nature, left no room for the exercise of arbitrary individual will. A king who governed unjustly and tyrannically, in principle ceased to be a king. Arbitrary despotism, they insisted, is by its own nature self-destructive, whereas '*despotisme légal*', 'producing necessarily the best possible condition for the nation, for the sovereignty, and for the sovereign personally, incorporates in itself the principle of its own conservation'.[5] Indeed, they held that the term despot should not be used to describe the arbitrary sovereigns

[1] Quesnay, *Maximes générales du gouvernement économique*, in *Les Physiocrates*, ed. E. Daire, 1846, p. 81.

[2] Lemercier de la Rivière, op. cit., ch. xvii, p. 129.

[3] id., ch. xliii, p. 462.

[4] Dupont de Nemours, *De l'origine et des progrès d'une science nouvelle*, 1768; in Daire, op. cit., p. 360.

[5] Lemercier de la Rivière, ch. xxiv, p. 184.

who are commonly given that designation, and who may even themselves be under the delusion that they are despotic rulers. 'They are the servants of their servants, the slaves of the vacillating opinion of their peoples, the feeble playthings of their armies.'[1] Unfortunately, they did not cease to be despots in practice, and the second generation of the Physiocrats, including writers such as Dupont de Nemours and de Chastelleux, realized that enlightenment was not so easily reconcilable with the existing kind of despotism as the founders of the school had hoped.

However, these theories of enlightened despotism fitted in so well with the ambitions of eighteenth-century rulers that, unlike most political theories, they found enthusiastic application in their own day. Benevolent despots like Catherine the Great of Russia, Frederick the Great of Prussia, and Joseph II, together with many petty German princelings, and ministers like Pombal in Portugal and Struensee in Denmark, proceeded to revolutionize their states to the best of their ability. Though they were not as successful in transforming the face of society as they had hoped, they brought about considerable changes. Private corporations, and bodies claiming independent authority or a share of political power, were everywhere suppressed — the order of Jesus throughout Catholic Europe, the Parlements in France, local institutions in the Austrian Netherlands and all the effective authority of their Estates. The nobility was as far as possible reduced to political insignificance, wherever it had not already reached this condition, and the Church was kept well under control. Social changes of the most

[1] DUPONT DE NEMOURS, Daire, op. cit., p. 364 *n*.

drastic type were attempted, sometimes genuine reforms, sometimes merely devices to increase the power or wealth of the crown, and often an admixture of both.

The justification for these wholesale innovations was found, as we have said, in the laws of nature, which the eighteenth century equated with the dictates of Reason. But neither the benevolent despots nor their 'philosophical' admirers realized the true inwardness of what they were doing. They did not see that for a divine right monarchy Reason is of all principles the most dangerous. What was happening towards the end of the eighteenth century in Europe was that the principle of sovereignty was being emancipated from its bondage to divine, hereditary right. Monarchy was trying to turn itself into dictatorship by extending its absolute authority into fields hitherto untouched, by emphasizing the arbitrary nature of its power, and by unconsciously divesting itself of its religious garb of divine right. The French Revolution is the measure of its achievement.

CHAPTER III

THE TRANSFERENCE OF SOVEREIGNTY TO THE PEOPLE

§ I HOBBES AND SPINOZA

BENEVOLENT despotism had prepared the way for great changes, but it could never become dictatorship, because it could not divest itself of its hereditary character. Moreover, as we have seen, the theory of benevolent despotism was intimately connected with the idea of natural law, and although the idea might be diverted to authoritarian ends, it could not completely deny its own nature. If it made the will of the sovereign all-powerful, theoretically this was only in so far as it was the embodiment of a higher law of nature or reason. Sovereignty thus was robbed of most of its arbitrariness. A benevolent despot who is merely the voice of universal law is no tyrant. Some means of escape both from the principle of divine hereditary right and from the natural law system of thought had to be devised, some source of authority other than the will of God or the law of nature had to be found, before the idea of sovereignty could reach its final extension and dictatorship become theoretically possible.

The idea of sovereignty having never been very happily united with the principle of natural law, the various theories of contract had arisen in the attempt to reconcile these two divergent elements in political thought; but, except in Hobbes, these theories all in the last resort reduced the sovereign to a mere executive agent for natural law. The rival doctrine of divine right bound the king even more effectively by divine law, interpreted by the traditions of the dominant religion and of his office. To enfranchise sovereignty from both these restraints a thinker was needed who would accept neither the religious view of the world nor the rationalistic, who would reject at the same time the law of God and the traditional law of nature, and base politics purely on human will, for the only alternative to law is will. Machiavelli might have done this, but Machiavelli was a historian and not a philosopher. The significance of Hobbes is that with him originates the philosophical justification of this point of view in modern Europe, and for this reason he demands particular attention in any study of the dictatorial idea.

Hobbes, as Dr. Leo Strauss has so ably shown,[1] is an heir to the humanist thought of the Renaissance. He comes to politics by way of history and not from philosophy or law, and therefore he does not put the question asked by classical philosophy, 'What is the end of the state?' but rather the historical problem, 'How did the state originate?' To answer this question historically was hardly possible in the seventeenth century unless one relied mainly on Biblical evidence, and Hobbes's views on religion did not permit him to do this, though he was always ready to cite scripture for his purpose. Moreover, history shows success and failure, not right and wrong:

[1] L. STRAUSS, *The Political Philosophy of Hobbes*, 1936. It is only right that I should acknowledge my debt to Dr. Strauss's scholarly analysis of the sources of Hobbes's political ideas.

it does not give 'norms'. Now Hobbes desired to establish a 'norm' for the state, but at the same time he was anxious to base this strictly on the facts and not on philosophical or religious theories. It is not for us to argue here whether or not this is possible. At any rate, since history failed him, Hobbes had to find some other factual basis for his theory of the state. He therefore turned from history to psychology, incidentally changed the question from 'How was the state founded?' to 'Why was it founded?' and deduced his answer from the nature of man. In consequence his starting-point becomes the human will and not *a priori* law of any kind, and the effect of this is to re-orientate his thought, and in the end all European political thinking.

The will, with the study of which Hobbes begins his analysis of the political psychology of man, is that of the individual, since for him man is naturally an anti-social individual, whose self-will and vanity are limitless. 'Men', says Hobbes, 'have no pleasure, but on the contrary a great deal of grief, in keeping company, where there is no power able to overawe them all.'[1] So radically anti-social is his individual that in the judgment of Vaughan no juggling with contracts will ever make him otherwise.[2] But there is in human nature one principle — the fear of death, or rather of violent death at the hands of other men — which explains why such an anti-social individual is found living in societies.[3] It is fear, and the desire for self-preservation, which unites men. In human nature, Hobbes argues, the only two imaginable motives

[1] HOBBES, *Leviathan*, ch. xiii, p. 64.

[2] C. E. VAUGHAN, *Studies in the History of Political Philosophy*, 1925, vol. I, p. 32.

[3] STRAUSS, op. cit., pp. 15-18.

for keeping the covenant by which society is formed are fear of the consequences of breaking it, and a glory in keeping one's word. 'This latter is a generosity too rarely found to be presumed on, especially in the pursuers of wealth, command, or sensual pleasure, which are the greatest part of mankind. The passion to be reckoned upon is fear; whereof there be two very general objects; one, the power of spirits invisible; the other, the power of those men they shall therein offend. Of these two, though the former be the greater power, yet the fear of the latter is commonly the greater fear.'[1] In these considerations Hobbes finds the psychological explanation of the foundation of the state.

The state may, of course, be established also by pure force, and such is the natural state based on patriarchal power or conquest. But Hobbes is not content with this: he wishes to found the state on a more permanent basis — on agreement, and in the principle of fear he finds in the individual wills of those composing it the motive for agreement. Thus the primary form of the state is democratic. Wishing to show the superiority of the government of one man, Hobbes begins by admitting the democratic origins of the state,[2] and then goes on to show that if the state is to be really successful in its task of defending the individual from the aggressiveness of all other individuals it has to transform itself into absolute monarchy.[3]

This change from popular government to monarchy must not be interpreted as one from freedom to absolutism, because for Hobbes all government is in the nature

[1] *Leviathan*, ch. xiv, p. 73.

[2] STRAUSS, op. cit., p. 66.

[3] *Leviathan*, ch. xix, pp. 97-100.

of things despotic; there is no half-way house between absolutism and anarchy. The peculiar feature of his political system is not that he prefers the government of one man — many political thinkers have done so, for a variety of mutually contradictory reasons — but that the power of government, the right of sovereignty, whoever holds it, is necessarily absolute, 'as great as man can be imagined to make it', and knows no superior authority and no law higher than its own will. And this great power, says Hobbes, is no artificial creation; it arises out of the very nature of man, 'whose pride and other passions have compelled him to submit himself to government: together with the great power of his governor, whom I compared to *Leviathan*, taking that comparison out of the two last verses of the one-and-fortieth of Job; where God, having set forth the great power of *Leviathan*, calleth him king of the proud. "There is nothing", saith he, "on earth to be compared with him. He is made so as not to be afraid. He seeeth every high thing below him; and is king of all the children of pride".'[1]

This brings us back to the point from which we started our consideration of Hobbes — that he is the first effectively to reject both natural law and divine law, and base the state purely on self-interest and individual will. He does not do this in so many words; indeed he has several chapters on Natural Right and the Laws of Nature. But Natural Right, he says, is 'the liberty each man hath, to use his own power, as he will himself, for the preservation of his own nature; that is to say, of his own life';[2] while Hobbes's Natural Law is devoid of content beyond the corollaries to this right of self-preservation. Further, not

[1] *Leviathan*, ch. xxviii, p. 170. [2] id., ch. xiv, p. 66.

only does he reject the traditional theory of Natural Law, he equally denies divine providence; because, disbelieving in immortality, he rejects the conduct of life upon considerations of the next world.

The conclusion would seem to be that might is right, and admittedly Hobbes's whole object is to find some method of uniting the two. This is not done merely by making them synonymous: for him only the might of the sovereign, made such by the acceptance of his subjects, is right. But once the sovereign loses his absolute physical power, he loses his right; and it is the duty of the subjects to transfer their obedience to whosoever holds that absolute power. Thus it may seem that in actual fact Hobbes has only proceeded by a circumlocution to the practical equation of might and right.[1] Strauss insists that Hobbes, unlike Spinoza, does not equate might with right, and we would admit that it is not quite fair to sum up his argument as a mere circumlocution. At the same time, his theory is only separated from this by a very fine shade of meaning. What is more important is that, emancipating sovereignty from both divine hereditary right and natural law, he bases it on individual will alone, to the exclusion of all laws of God or of Nature, other than the law of self-preservation.

To England, and to Europe in the seventeenth century, these ideas were inexpressibly shocking. Both parties in England denounced their author, and Locke, by providing a more acceptable explanation, effaced for a time the uncomfortable impression that Hobbes's theory had left. On the continent his influence was more persistent, but not until we come to the end of the eighteenth century do his basic ideas re-emerge and become of practical

[1] STRAUSS, op. cit., p. 28.

political importance. For all this, we must agree that, 'there is no possible doubt that Hobbes, and no other, is the father of modern political philosophy. For it is he who, with a clarity never previously, and never subsequently attained, made the "rights of nature", i.e. the justified claims (of the individual) the basis of political philosophy, without any inconsistent borrowings from natural or divine law'.[1]

The full implications of Hobbes's ideas, however, had been realized, and stated with greater clearness than he himself ever achieved, by one who was almost his contemporary, Spinoza, whose naturalistic view of politics completely eliminates the traditional conception of the laws of nature. For Spinoza the rights of nature are merely those conditions inherent in the nature of any individual being, which determine it to act in a given way, and their scope is limited only by the power of the individual.[2] 'Every natural thing has by nature as much right, as it has power to exist and operate;'[3] — a principle which applies to states as well as everything else. Inside the state a system of law may be imposed by the will of the sovereign,[4] but the state itself is above all law. 'For the maxims and motives of fear and reverence, which a commonwealth is bound to observe in its own interests, pertain not to civil jurisprudence, but to the law of nature, since they cannot be vindicated by civil law, but by the law of war. And a commonwealth is bound by them in no other sense than that in which in the state of nature a man is bound to take heed, that he preserve his independence

[1] STRAUSS, op. cit., p. 156.
[2] SPINOZA, *Tractatus Theologico-Politicus*, ch. xvi; *Works*, 1883, vol. I, p. 200.
[3] id., *A Political Treatise*, ch. ii, § 3; *Works*, vol. I, p. 292.
[4] id., ch. iii, § 5; vol. I, p. 302.

and be not his own enemy, lest he should destroy himself.'[1]

According to Spinoza, therefore, for the state, right is equated with might, and natural law with natural will; moreover this will, he insists, is far from being the rational will of the philosopher.[2] 'Such as persuade themselves, that the multitude or men distracted by politics can ever be induced to live according to the bare dictates of reason must be dreaming of the poetic golden age or of a stage play.'[3] Men are ruled not by reason but by their desires and passions, and so are states; and as men are naturally enemies, so also are states.[4] The sovereign will of the state is completely free from any superior right or law: it cannot even with its own consent be bound. 'Every commonwealth', writes Spinoza, 'has the right to break its contract, whenever it chooses, and cannot be said to act treacherously or perfidiously in breaking its word, as soon as the motive of hope or fear is removed.'[5] No student of international relations will find anything very novel in these observations; but it is necessary to remember that we are listening not to the unscrupulous Machiavelli — he merely says that this is how states do behave — but to the sweet-dispositioned, almost saintly philosopher of Amsterdam, who says that this is how they ought to behave.

One final argument with which Spinoza underlines and extends the conclusions of Hobbes is to be noted. Taken logically, as the English royalists saw, this reason-

[1] SPINOZA, ch. iv, § 5; vol. I, p. 311.
[2] *Tractatus*, vol. I, p. 204.
[3] *Political Treatise*, ch. i, § 5; vol. I, p. 289; cf. *Tractatus*, vol. I, pp. 201, 204.
[4] cf. *Political Treatise*, ch. ii, § 14; vol. I, p. 296.
[5] id., ch. iii, § 14; vol. I, p. 307.

ing is fatal to the principle of hereditary monarchy. Here again Spinoza is so explicit that we need only quote his words: 'Those who, from the fact that the king is master of the dominion, and holds it by absolute right, infer that he can hand it over to whom he pleases, and that, therefore, the king's son is by right heir to the dominion, are greatly mistaken. For the king's will has so long the force of law, as he holds the sword of the commonwealth; for the right of dominion is limited by power only . . . the king's will is the civil law itself, and the king the commonwealth itself. Therefore, by the death of the king, the commonwealth is in a manner dead, and the civil state naturally returns to the state of nature, and consequently the supreme authority to the multitude.'[1]

Summing up the whole argument of Spinoza — that there are no natural laws except that might is right, that the right of the sovereign is despotic and limited only by the limits on his power, that will rules in politics and not reason, and that there is no hereditary right, since the only source of political right is power — we have some of the basic elements of dictatorial government laid down a century, or perhaps two and a half centuries, ahead of their time. Spinoza was indicating a station, perhaps a terminus, at which European political thinking had not yet arrived, and while Machiavelli's *Prince* was read almost as widely as it was reprobated, Spinoza was most often condemned unheard. The execration with which his other works were unjustly received, helped to conceal the importance of his political writings. For us, they are significant because, even more clearly than the *Leviathan*, they show the political tendencies that were latent in the modern theory

[1] SPINOZA, ch. vii, § 25; vol. I, pp. 339-40.

of the state, though a long political development was still required to enable them to become manifest in practice.

§ 2 ROUSSEAU AND SIEYÈS

The conception of absolute sovereignty as a right which cannot be shared or divided, and which is derived in the last resort from the might of the strongest, is an important step towards the theory of dictatorship. But Hobbes and Spinoza had still not challenged that dualism of Ruler and People, which was inherited from medieval theory, and which, as Gierke has shown, presented a formidable obstacle to the development of the modern theory of the sovereign state.[1] Spinoza did not seriously tackle this problem. Hobbes, by substituting one contract for two, had eliminated the initial contract with God which established the personality of the People. He thus left the sovereign as the only embodiment of the unity of the state. Remove the sovereign, and society at once fell back into the disorder of the state of nature. Hobbes's *Leviathan* is at best only an artificial personality: the unity of his state is merely the product of force; the members of a commonwealth, he writes, 'cohere together, but they depend only on the sovereign, which is the soul of the commonwealth; which failing, the commonwealth is dissolved into a civil war, no one man so much as cohering to another for want of a common dependence on a known sovereign'.[2]

When Rousseau, a century later, takes the basic idea

[1] O. GIERKE, *Natural Law and the Theory of Society* 1500-1800, trans. with an Introduction by E. Barker, 1934, vol. I, p. 50.

[2] *Leviathan*, ch. xlii.

of Hobbes and breathes the life of real communal personality into it, the modern state, for good or evil, is born. The most important distinction between Hobbes and Rousseau is that, whereas Hobbes is consciously building up his theory to justify the absolute rule of one man over the multitude of individuals making up society, Rousseau is concerned to establish the conception of a unified state, including government and governed, with a single will and a single sovereign personality. For Hobbes, as we have just said, there is still a radical separation between the sovereign and the subjects, even though the latter have abandoned all their rights, save the ultimate right of defending their own lives. Rousseau is able to remove even this last dichotomy, because whereas Hobbes is content to stop short of this end, so long as he can establish the power of government beyond question, Rousseau is anxious also to find some means of reconciling governmental authority with the liberty of the individual. Unless he reverses the whole trend in the development of European political thought by abandoning the idea of sovereignty — and Rousseau has no intention of doing this — the only solution is the identification of the will of the sovereign with the will of the subject, and this he achieves through the idea of the General Will.

It is not our object to examine in detail Rousseau's political theory. Elsewhere I have attempted to give a critical account of the views which he himself actually held. Here our interest is in the single but vital point that with Rousseau we have at last a real philosophical justification for the attribution to the state of a single, unitary, sovereign will. He is able to reach this conception because, unlike his predecessors, he does not allow that any prince or government, any individual or collective ruler, can enter into the theory of the state as a primary element. Sovereignty, as absolute and unlimited as that of Hobbes's Leviathan, is the essential characteristic of political society, according to Rousseau, but it belongs to the General Will of the People alone.

Before we draw any conclusions from this idea it is necessary to note the qualifications with which Rousseau surrounds it; for his General Will, in which the corporate sovereignty of the people is embodied, is only a philosophical idea, an ideal, in fact, and one realized in practice by no actual state, nor, under the severe conditions imposed by Rousseau, likely to be realized. It is a platitude to say that for Rousseau only in so far as it is General can the Will be sovereign. But what follows from this? Surely that since, according to Rousseau, it cannot be General unless its object is the permanent well-being, both spiritual and material, of the community and of all the individuals comprised in it, so the will cannot be sovereign unless it embodies the ideals necessary for this — a qualification which implies the acceptance of a complete set of moral and political principles. Rousseau may have expelled natural law from the front door, but only to re-introduce it through the back under another description.

Furthermore, there is another essential limitation imposed by the author of the *Contrat social* on the practical exercise of sovereignty, in that he excludes executive action from its scope; he combines unity for the legislative power with separation of governmental function. The legislative power is exercised by the General Will, the executive by the government, which Rousseau treats as within its own field an independent body, and the judicial by an independent branch of the executive. Power thus divided is quite irreconcilable with dictatorship, and Rousseau's theory, which at first sight seemed to be an essential link in the chain of development we are tracing, turns out to be subject to quite a different interpretation.

Rousseau's views on dictatorship may be gathered from the commentary on the Roman constitution incorporated in the *Contrat social*. He is ready to admit that a provision allowing for a temporary suspension of the law and establishment of a dictatorship may be a feature of a constitution which would prove valuable in an emergency; but he adds that even this is a dangerous expedient, only to be permitted for a short period and with the most carefully devised safeguards.

What, however, of the union of ruler and ruled in the idea of the sovereignty of the people? Surely this is something new and something fundamental in the development of modern political theory? Even granting that there are many elements in Rousseau's political thought that are not easily reconciled with the principle of absolute sovereignty, surely, it will be said, we cannot question as a historical fact the importance of his idea of the General Will in the formation of that theory of popular sovereignty which was destined to dominate the French Revolution and the whole of subsequent history to the present day?

But this is precisely what we are questioning. The work in which Rousseau expanded his idea of the General Will, the *Contrat social*, was certainly before 1789.[1]

[1] D. MORNET, *Les enseignements des bibliothèques privées* (1750-80), in *Revue d'histoire littéraire de la France*, 1910, t. XVII, pp. 449-96; and *Origines intellectuelles de la Révolution française*, 1715-1787, 1933, pp. 95-6.

Its supposed role as a cause of the outbreak and a source of the ideology of the French Revolution is one of those historical legends copied by one writer from another, but never adequately examined. A prolonged study of the voluminous pamphlet literature, as well as the letters, memoirs and speeches of the Revolutionary period, would be necessary before one could speak with absolute certainty on the extent of the actual influence exercised by Rousseau's political writings over the revolutionaries. A partial survey of some of these sources leads one to suspect that it has been greatly exaggerated. Of a real understanding of his philosophical theory of the General Will one can hardly find a single example in Revolutionary times.

Admittedly, without being put in such abstruse terms and limited as Rousseau limits it, the idea of popular sovereignty was the dominant idea of the Revolution. But it was an idea for which the revolutionaries did not require to go to Rousseau: they could find it sown broadcast throughout the writings of the *philosophes* of eighteenth-century France. In a sense the idea of the sovereignty of the people runs back through Locke and generations of medieval thinkers to classical sources; but this sovereignty was of a restricted nature. What the speculative thought of the eighteenth century did was to emancipate the idea of sovereignty from the traditional restraints, and attribute to the people a sovereignty as absolute and unlimited as Hobbes and Spinoza had given to the Ruler. But while the sovereignty of Hobbes and Spinoza had remained a theory — for if we omit the oriental Turkish Sultan and Russian Czar, no European ruler could in fact wield a power so unbounded and so arbitrary without breaking completely with the tradition of the divine right monarchy — the sovereignty of the people was destined to receive a startling application in the realm of practical politics.

The writer who sums up these ideas on the eve of 1789, and passes them on to the Revolution, is not Rousseau but the abbé Sieyés. In no way a profound thinker, not even a brilliant writer, though with a certain Gallic gift for epigram and for giving difficult matters an illusory appearance of simplicity, Sieyés had the good fortune to write a book which expressed exactly what the politically minded French bourgeois were thinking about politics just at the time when they were on the point of putting their thoughts into practice. There is nothing in Sieyés that is not to be found in the *philosophes*, but by writing *Qu'est-ce que le Tiers État?* when he did, in the autumn of 1788, he made himself the mouthpiece of the French nation, and the real founder of the new theory of popular sovereignty in all the extension which the French Revolution was to give it.

Sieyés's object was to assert the autonomy of the national will, and one could quote passage after passage in which he reiterates this idea. 'The Nation', he says, 'exists before all things and is the origin of all things'.[1] 'A Nation is independent of all forms, it is sufficient that its will is manifested for all positive law to vanish before it.'[2] And we seem to hear Spinoza speaking when we read, 'Nations must be conceived as being like individuals outside the social bond, or, as it is said, in the state of nature. The exercise of their will is free and independent

[1] SIEYÈS, *Qu'est ce que le Tiers Etat?* 3rd ed., 1789, p. 111.
[2] id., p. 116.

of all civil forms. Existing only in the natural order of things, their will, to have its full effect, needs only to possess the natural characteristics of a will. In whatever manner a nation wills, it is sufficient that it does will: all forms are good, and its will is always the supreme law.'[1]

With this, natural law is relegated to the rubbish heap on which the eighteenth century shot so much of the heritage of the past, sovereignty is emancipated from all restraints, and the dualism of sovereign and subject, ruler and ruled, has vanished, and in Revolutionary France the new idea of the sovereignty of the people was to be put to the test of practice. It may seem that the development which we have been tracing, though approaching in the enlightened despots within measurable distance of dictatorship, had now turned into another channel altogether, that with the triumph of the idea of popular sovereignty the possibility of dictatorship had been eliminated from European history for ever. The illusion was to endure a brief five or ten years. When a king's head fell under the guillotine it was thought to be the last step necessary to achieve the rule of the people: but the blood of kings proved the seed of tyranny.

§ 3

THE AIMS OF THE FRENCH REVOLUTION

Gradually, as the Revolution evolved in France, the road leading from the assertion of popular sovereignty to the setting up of dictatorship was for the first time traced in modern history. Benevolent despotism had gone a long

[1] SIEYÈS, *Qu'est ce que le Tiers Etat?* 3rd ed., 1789, pp. 115-16.

way towards dictatorship. It had proved tyrannical, but in the last resort weak; incapable of putting either its benevolent or its despotic intentions fully into effect; inefficient because bound up with the personality of an hereditary monarch, who was unlikely to be a great administrator himself, and who, because of the traditional basis of his authority, was unable to suppress effectively the rival powers in the state.

The idea of the sovereignty of the people revolutionized the terms in which the political problem was stated. The people had none of the traditional limitations of divine right monarchy, and their despotism, being over themselves, was not considered inconsistent with freedom. Thus it was that a revolution made in the name of liberty could set up a sovereignty more absolute than that of the despots themselves. But to appreciate what this means we must turn from political theory to political practice, and attempt an analysis of the aims of the French revolution as they appeared in actual historical fact.

It is hardly fair to say, though the statement is often made, that liberty was not aimed at by the revolutionaries. The political literature of eighteenth-century France, from Montesquieu to Rousseau and Mably, shows a constant preoccupation with liberty. Even Voltaire, called by Brunetière 'the most aristocratic and the most arrogant of our great writers', for whom the people, in a well-known phrase, will always be 'barbarous fools' can yet write, 'I confess I could adapt myself well enough to a democratic government . . . I like the sight of free men, themselves making the laws under which they live'.[1] The Physiocrats, in so far as they are indifferent to political

[1] VOLTAIRE, *l'A.B.C.*; in *Œuvres*, 1869, t. XXVII, p. 347.

liberty, are not typical of French thought of the time. Nor was the idea of liberty confined to a small literary clique. On the contrary, a study of the cahiers of 1789 has shown that a free constitution was the first demand of those who drew them up in all classes.[1] The monarchy, treated as an element in a constitutional system which went back to the Middle Ages, and from which the absolutism of the seventeenth and eighteenth centuries was regarded as a divergence, was at first not attacked: Burke truly said that the Revolution was rather made against the condition of a gentleman than against the power of the crown. But this did not imply any acceptance of despotic government. The king was regarded as having indicated, by calling the *États généraux*, his willingness to take his place as the excutive agent in a constitutional government. Legislative sovereignty, however, was henceforth to be in the hands of the people.

Political liberty, then, which was assumed to go hand in hand with the establishment of the sovereignty of the people, was one prime aim of the Revolution. A second object was the abolition of privilege, and a third the introduction of efficiency into the public administration, especially the finances. There was general agreement in France, except for a few 'die-hards' of the first emigration, on the desirability of these aims. Disagreement came over the means of attaining them.

The representatives of the three estates met: a short struggle eliminated those of the nobles and upper clergy who were unwilling to co-operate in the establishment of the new order. The National Assembly which emerged from this struggle consisted of about a thousand patriotic,

[1] E. CHAMPION, *La France d'après les cahiers de* 1789, 5th ed., 1921, ch. xvi.

enthusiastic, well-intentioned individuals, with a high general level of ability and intelligence, but entirely devoid of Parliamentary experience, and lacking practical knowledge of any form of government other than bureaucracy. The king, weak but obstinate, well-meaning, slow-moving, Louis XVI, would have made an ideal constitutional monarch if he had ever been taught how to play the part, but he was quite incapable of giving the Assembly the political leadership it needed at such a time. It was not expected of him, anyhow, because jealousy of the executive had been inherited from the struggle against the *ancien régime*, and inculcated by the writings of the *philosophes*.

Both in practice and in theory royal authority was put on one side. Under the tutelage of Sieyès the *pouvoir constituant*, power to draw up a new constitution, and until it had been drawn up dictatorial authority over the whole activity of the state, was claimed for the National Assembly, as the representatives of the people. The revolutionaries failed to observe the theoretical conflict between this claim to absolute sovereignty and the ideal of political liberty, but it was to be thrust upon their notice by practical difficulties. Separation of powers, they had been taught to believe, was essential to political liberty. Now the refashioning of the political and social order in France, which as we have just said, was to be the work of the Assembly, not of the king or ministers, necessarily involved government; and so long as they drew a rigid line between executive and legislative, that was precisely what the revolutionaries could not provide. The efforts of Mirabeau, and later of Danton, to persuade the Assembly to allow its members to hold ministerial office met with overwhelming opposition. The result was that the ministers gradually became little more than mere clerks; yet the Assembly itself was incapable of efficient executive government. No wonder that the revolutionaries experienced a sense of frustration, seemed to be continually coming up against intangible but effective obstacles, found the country drifting into disorder and themselves unable to control the forces they had let loose.

The absolute authority, which they had claimed in the name of the nation in 1789, the revolutionaries would not abandon. But since the Assembly could not effectively wield executive power, it gradually passed into the hands of a small group and finally went to a single man. The traditions of the nation reasserted themselves as France drifted back, almost unconsciously, to the only form of government of which it had any experience, bureaucracy under a despot; but he was to be a despot of a new kind — one who had attained supreme power by his own ability and not by inheritance, in fact, a dictator. From the very beginning of the Revolution one observer had detected the nature of the situation. 'If the present project of a republic should fail', wrote Burke, 'all securities to a moderated freedom fail along with it; all the indirect restraints which mitigate despotism are removed; insomuch that if monarchy should ever again obtain an entire ascendency in France, under this or under any other dynasty, it will probably be ... the most completely arbitrary power that has ever appeared on earth.'[1]

[1] E. BURKE, *Reflections;* in *Works*, 1872, vol. II, p. 456.

§4 REVOLUTIONARY DICTATORSHIP: MARAT AND ROBESPIERRE

Revolutionary France did not come to dictatorship at one bound, nor did it come willingly. When imprisonment and excution had revealed the powerlessness of the king, the fear of royal power turned into a fear of the dictatorship of any prominent leader. From an early date, as outstanding men, beginning with Mirabeau, rose to pre-eminence, in turn the cry of dictatorship was raised against them and played a large part in their fall. With one exception all the early leaders of revolutionary France dreaded the charge. To Marat alone was the name of dictator something more than a weapon to use against his enemies, a menace if applied to himself.

The traditional portrait of Marat does justice neither to his scientific attainments nor to his political ability. His capacity for grasping the essentials in a man or a situation is well illustrated by his verdict of August 1790 on the unhappy king. 'He is precisely the man we need. Without schemes, without artifice, without cunning, without craft, and hardly formidable to political liberty, he would be a good prince if he had enough tact to choose wise ministers.'[1]

This moderate and judicious opinion is difficult to reconcile with Marat's customary violent invective, but we must not take the rhetoric of *l'Ami du Peuple* too literally. Marat knew what he was doing. As little as any revolutionary leader was he influenced by a blind faith in the people. It was because he took the Paris mob for what

[1] L. R. GOTTSCHALK, *Jean Paul Marat*, 1927, p. 66.

it was, that he appealed to its passions and not its intelligence. He never believed that the people could govern: as late as 1792 he wanted a change of kings, but not the abolition of monarchy.[1]

He had realized at an early stage that if the remodelling of the French state was to be carried through, the motive force would have to come from the people, by which he meant in practice the people of Paris. But the howling mob that tore the lovely Princess de Lamballe to pieces and paraded her head on the end of a pike through the streets, or the butchers of September, were incapable of giving any coherent direction to policy. The people were the source of power, and in revolutionary conditions the mob was the executive agent of the people: but their action needed to be directed, and Marat believed that the man who could direct it to the appropriate revolutionary ends was the true upholder of popular sovereignty. In the spring of 1790 he was appealing to the nation to 'name for a short period a supreme dictator, put him at the head of the public forces, and entrust him with the punishment of the guilty'.[2] Again, after the flight of the king he urged the need to 'name a military tribune, a supreme dictator'.[3] His predilection for a dictatorial system was so well known that in September 1792 he had to defend himself at the Convention from the charge, and in May 1793 he was again denounced at the Jacobin Club for having maintained that the people needed a dictator.[4]

It needs no saying who, in Marat's imagination, the dictator was to be. The dagger of Charlotte Corday

[1] L. R. GOTTSCHALK, *Jean Paul Marat*, 1927, pp. 98-99.
[2] *Appel à la nation;* in *Les pamphlets de Marat*, ed. C. Vellay, 1911, p. 155.
[3] GOTTSCHALK, op. cit., p. 111.
[4] id., p. 136.

brought a sudden end to his ambitions; but although snatched away by an avenging angel before his ideas for France had been more than roughly sketched out, of Marat we may say that he was potentially the first dictator of modern Europe.

Marat was a precursor. A clearer indication of the trend of events is given by the career of Robespierre. Faced with a triple menace of foreign invasion, domestic rebellion and administrative chaos, the people of Paris and the other large towns, and even the politicians of the Convention, felt the urgent need for a leader. The relationship which existed on a small scale between Marat and the Paris mob was now repeated by Robespierre and the revolutionary bourgeoise of France. Robespierre put himself forward as the voice of the people, as a mere agent of the popular will, devoid of self-interest or personal ambition, sea-green, in the famous phrase, incorruptible; and his near approach to a dictatorial form of government was only made possible by his constant and emphatic denunciation of would-be dictators.

The natural development of the revolution, so long as the revolutionary wave was advancing, was for moderate parties to be ousted by extremer ones, and these in turn by new parties arising farther to the left. This process in the end brought to power the group in France which was most like an organized national party — the Jacobins. The quarrel between the large but inchoate body of politicians which history has called the Gironde, and the smaller but well organized Jacobin faction, was, according to Aulard, rather a quarrel between personalities than between policies, though Mathiez has shown the significance of their differences on social policy. Although the chief reason for the collapse of the Girondins was their inability to convince France that they were capable of saving the Revolution, the Jacobins had also certain specific advantages over them. They possessed in Robespierre the leader most popular with the lesser bourgeoise, the most trusted and the most honest of the revolutionary politicians. They had the most effective demagogues, and as time was to show some of the best administrators too. In the network of clubs scattered through the towns of France they possessed a political machine for keeping in touch with the provinces and controlling local authorities. They were, in fact, the first group to realize some of the essential factors of success in modern politics.

The Jacobins came to power as the most democratic of the revolutionary parties. The Constitution which they substituted for that proposed by the Girondins, established for the first time universal and direct suffrage. It was submitted to a plebiscite — the first in modern history — and approved by a small vote of 1,801,908 to 17,610 — not bad for a first attempt at a totalitarian ballot — after which it was safely pigeon-holed to await the restoration of peace. It remains as a proof of the democratic principles of the Jacobins, just as their earlier history shows their demogogic methods, and whereas Marat had consciously seen dictatorship as the only solution to the political problems of the Revolution, the Jacobins remained in theory democrats. A dictatorial form of government was, as Mathiez says, imposed on them. 'They neither desired nor foresaw it. The Terror was a *dictateur de détresse*, in the words of Hippolyte Carnot, and the saying is profoundly true.'[1]

[1] A. Mathiez, *La Révolution française*, 1925, vol. III, p. 17.

The tyranny of the Jacobins was established in the first place in September-October 1793 for political reasons, and above all to enforce the *levée en masse*. The spirit in which it began was expressed in a decree drawn up by Carnot and passed by the Convention in August 1793: 'From this moment until that when all enemies shall have been driven from the territory of the Republic all Frenchmen are permanently requisitioned for the service of the army ... *Le peuple français debout contre les tyrans!*' A law of September established the supremacy of the Committee of Public Safety over the other committees of the Convention. The ministers were reduced practically to the condition of clerks — 'poor creatures', as Gouverneur Morris described them, 'scarcely daring to blow their own noses without an order'. For the first time since the breakdown of the monarchy France had a real government, controlling both legislative and executive in Paris, while through the establishment of the system of agents dispatched by the committee to the departments and the armies, and a decree calling on the Jacobin clubs to watch the conduct of all officials and report on them to the committee, its authority was extended to every part of France not in open rebellion.

The problem of the revolutionaries was not only political and military, but also economic. Faced with the threat of rebellion because of scarcity and soaring prices, the Jacobins passed the law of the *maximum général*, fixing a maximum for all prices and wages. Only by a rigid authoritarian government could such a law be maintained; in a revolutionary state only by terrorism. Gradually the powers of the government were extended. Robespierre defined the revolutionary government as 'the despotism of liberty over tyranny',[1] but in the name of liberty, liberty was extinguished. To save the Republic a ferocious despotism was established. In Paris the Convention became a mere shadow of the all-powerful Committee and voted the decrees it proposed almost without discussion.[2] In the provinces, the municipal elections were suspended, local bodies purged, national *procureurs* dispatched to nominate new members and guard the interests of the Republic; and a revolutionary tribunal was set up to equate justice with the will of the people.

Under the Jacobins the authority of government was extended into every sphere of social life, from petty changes like the revolutionary calendar with its *Vendémiaires* and *Brumaires*, *Floréals*, and *Fructidors*, and the attempt to introduce a ten-day week, to fundamental ones. There was a strict censorship of the press; on the stage only safe, patriotic pieces were performed. The societies where popular oratory had flourished disappeared. A close rein was kept on the tribunals of the Sections of Paris and of the Jacobin club itself: most of the time they were occupied by dutiful minions of the new 'terrorist bureaucracy'.[3] Religious liberty, guaranteed by a series of Declarations of Rights, was practically non-existent, nor was there even — as the fate of Hébert and the *enragés* showed — the liberty to be irreligious. 'The revolutionary government', says Mathiez, whom we quote because of all the leading historians of the Terror he is the most favourable to the Jacobins, 'became the dictatorship of a party, exercised for the profit of one class, the class of consumers, of artisans, of small proprietors, and of the poor, guided

[1] *Discours et Rapports de Robespierre*, ed. C. Vellay, 1908, p. 333.
[2] MATHIEZ, op. cit., vol. III, p. 166. [3] id.

by men of the middle classes who had bound their lot invincibly to that of the Revolution, and above all by those of that class who were enriched by the making of munitions of war.'[1]

Although the Committee of Public Safety undoubtedly ruled after a dictatorial fashion, however, its government cannot count as a dictatorship unless it was in essence the rule of a single man. Here we are faced with a much-discussed historical problem. Although we cannot say that Robespierre was in the strict sense of the word a dictator, yet the part he played in the government was so extensive, and his pre-eminence in the eyes of the people so great, that for a short time we can consider him as at least a dictator in the popular imagination, and many dictators are perhaps in fact no more than that. Robespierre had early realized the necessity for unified control of the revolution. 'We need a *single* will', he had written in his private note-book.[2] And his devoted follower, Saint-Just, expressed more clearly than Robespierre the ideal of strong government behind the Jacobin Terror. 'It is said that a strong government is oppressive', Saint-Just wrote, 'this is an error, because the question is badly put. The essential thing in government is justice. The government which enforces justice is not on that account oppressive, because it is only the evil that it represses'.[3] Or, more plainly, he says, 'In every revolution a dictator is necessary to save the state by force or Censors to save it by virtue'.[4] It is understandable if Robespierre and Saint-Just cast themselves for the latter role, and history has attributed to them the former.

[1] MATHIEZ, op. cit., vol. III, p. 77. [2] id., vol. III, p. 4.
[3] SAINT-JUST, *Œuvres complètes*, ed. C. Vellay, vol. II, p. 506. [4] id., p. 530.

Like Marat, the Jacobins realized the necessary implications of revolution. A revolution cannot be conducted by liberal methods: towards those who are hostile or even indifferent it must be a tyranny. But, since they all accepted the sovereignty of the people, it must be a tyranny based on the popular will. Put into practice in the early years of the Revolution, this had meant the rule of the mob of Paris and therefore anarchy. Marat had seen, and the Jacobins after him, the necessity, if the Revolution was to be saved, of reconciling mob rule with strong government, a problem for which there is only one solution. To give organization and effective purpose to its movements a mob requires a mouthpiece, an executive agent, a leader. Robespierre, the incorruptible, who had painstakingly built up his revolutionary reputation, alone had a public personality adequate to filling the gap between government and people. Europe had still far to go before the name of dictator could be proudly claimed as a title of honour, and a proof of the political wisdom of the country with the foresight to subject itself to its natural ruler; but Robespierre was in the popular mind the head of the government, which indeed could hardly have been set up or have survived without his reputation for patriotism, loyalty to the ends of the Revolution and personal honesty.

Personal dictatorship or not, the essential task of the Terrorist government was to save the Revolution by an energetic attack on the enemies of the Republic inside and outside France. Under Carnot's vigorous impulsion the *levée en masse* added huge new conscript armies to the volunteers of 1791; a crowd of brilliant young officers, from whom Napoleon later recruited his marshals, sprang to their head; and out of the Revolutionary War a new force, and one of immense moment, was born. Patriotic sentiment became increasingly strong and France began to pass unconsciously from the defensive to the aggressive. Carnot himself desired only the natural frontiers of France: in others the revolutionary crusade was already becoming mixed with imperialist ambitions. Not the goddesses of Reason, rapt from the service of a softer goddess and devoted to that austerer deity for a day, nor the Supreme Being of Robespierre, but the cult of *la patrie* was becoming the true religion of the revolutionaries. Even in the Incorruptible himself is to be found more than a slight admixture of nationalist ardour. 'Under the title of Supreme Being, as under the title of Reason, the *patrie* was the true object of adoration; and the cult of the Supreme Being, like that of Reason, was to be lost, without the people distinguishing clearly the one from the other, in patriotism.'[1]

Patriotic zeal was rewarded with military success, and this in turn made the Jacobin tyranny less necessary and helped to bring about its fall. In so far as terror was the child of fear, the disappearance of the sources of the fear removed the psychological basis of the Terror. The power of the Terrorists had been erected on too narrow a base, and the elements in the population menaced by them were too extensive for their rule to survive the panic which had called it into being. The attempt of the 'triumvirate' — Robespierre, Couthon and Saint-Just — by intensifying the Terror to enforce the economic dictatorship implied in the *maximum général* and other social laws, produced

[1] A. AULARD, *Histoire politique de la Révolution française*, 4th ed., 1909, Part II, ch. ix, § 4, p. 493.

general opposition. The success with which Robespierre had removed rival politicians alarmed those who were not of his inner circle and saw themselves next on the list for elimination. A group of intriguers, with Barras, Tallien, and Fouché at their head, began to organize secret opposition. Robespierre, had he realized the necessity, or been willing to stoop so low, could have bought over any or all of these men. But more honourable politicians like Carnot were saying openly that all was not well in a republic where the government depended on a single man, even if it was his virtues that upheld the state.[1]

Further, the practice and the principles of the Terrorists remained irreconcilable. Their consitution, liberal and democratic in its provisions, had been brought forward in a hurry as evidence of good intentions, but no attempt had been made, or could have been made, to put it into effect. Dictatorial government, at first regarded as merely a temporary expedient, showed no signs of coming to an end, and was to be maintained, Saint-Just had said as much, until virtue was triumphant in the hearts of all citizens.[2] Well might such as Barras and Tallien and Fouché be alarmed. Meanwhile, the rank and file of the revolutionaries, who had so often been roused by the cry of tyranny, were finding it difficult to stomach the appearance of dictatorship even from their chosen leader.

Robespierre himself, though he might act as a dictator, was sufficiently the victim of his own ideology to be unable to push his policy to its logical conclusions. Faced with an organized revolt of the Convention, which, however

[1] Mathiez, op. cit., vol. III, p. 195.
[2] id., vol. III, p. 147.

purged or overridden, he had always thought of as embodying — after himself — the will of the Nation, he shrunk from the necessity of suppressing it by armed force. Howled down with cries of '*A bas le tyran*', he hesitated and was lost. He fell, not because he was a tyrant, but because he was not sufficiently tyrannical. Instead of acting up to the part, he attempted to excuse himself. His eloquent speech of the 8 Thermidor was an effort to rid himself of the inculpation of tyranny. The charge of dictatorship, he said, directed at first against the Committee of Public Safety as a whole, has been concentrated on the head of one of its members.[1] The very word dictatorship, he says, is enough to degrade the institutions of the Revolution and make them odious. His retaliation is not without dignity or truth. 'They call me tyrant', says Robespierre. 'If I were one, they would crawl at my feet, I should lavish gold on them, give them impunity to commit any crime, and they would be my grateful followers.'[2]

When at last he was ready to call to his aid the armed force of the Commune of Paris and the mob, it was too late. Barras, with a body of troops, seized Robespierre and twenty-one of his closest supporters, and rushed them to the guillotine without the pretence of a trial. The terrorist dictatorship was over: the rule of the great Committee of Public Safety had lasted for just a year. During that time, Carnot had saved France, and Robespierre had saved the Revolution, but for what fate was not yet to be seen.

[1] *Discours . . . de Robespierre*, p. 389.
[2] id., pp. 395-6.

§ 5

THE SIGNIFICANCE OF THE REVOLUTION IN THE POLITICAL DEVELOPMENT OF EUROPE

We have devoted the previous section to a discussion of the attempt of Robespierre to establish a dictatorial government, because although it had been premature and on unsound lines, it held a lesson for the future and foreshadowed the rise of a different kind of dictator. Before we can pass on, however, it is necessary to pause for a moment to ask ourselves what change the Revolution had wrought in political data, and in what way this change affected the prospects of dictatorship.

In the first place the Revolution must be credited with the decisive blow it had dealt to the system of divine right. In this respect it provided the appropriate climax to a whole century of iconoclastic thought, though it was another century and more before the war which the revolutionaries had declared against divine right monarchy was finally successful in every corner of Europe. In our own time, as an aftermath of the first World War, the dynasties still effectively ruling in the more backward countries of Europe crashed in ruins, and the reign of divine right was at last brought to an end in the Western world: but the effect on human freedom has not been exactly that anticipated. Their inherited despots removed, men have sought out new tyrants of their own invention, nor were they slow in so doing: not much more than a decade after Louis XVI's head had fallen under the guillotine, Napoleon's was adorned with an imperial crown.

For half a century Napoleon was, apparently, an isolated phenomenon. When another upstart Emperor appeared, in the person of Louis Napoleon, at most it seemed a revelation of a special weakness of the French nation in politics. Only in our own time, when the process has been repeated in so many countries, has it been possible to discern the operation of more general historical causes and the working out of a development in which the French Revolution constitutes an essential stage.

The first step in this historical process is obviously the loss of faith in divine right monarchy, in which respect the French Revolution merely drew the practical conclusion to centuries of contractual and natural law thought. The attempt of the natural law theorists to establish politics on a rational basis, interpreted in the eighteenth century in terms of utilitarianism, involved the assumption that the behaviour of man as a political animal was rational, and it seemed a modest one before 1789. Politics was henceforth to be taken off its traditional, semi-religious basis, and built up on the principles of reason or utility, which were taken as synonymous.

In practice the matter was not quite so simple. Divine right monarchy fell, like the walls of Jericho, with sound; but the resistance to the rule of reason had not ended but only just begun, for the allies and dependants of the monarchy — the Church, the aristocracy, and even the wealthy bourgeoisie — were not willing to commit suicide without greater persuasion. The revolution against absolutism was therefore combined with a war against the privileged classes. The struggle for liberty became also a struggle for equality.

The idea of the equality of man is of course not new;

emerging in the ancient world, it had become an important element in the religious revival in the Roman Empire. But having achieved the abolition of slavery, the equalitarian principle of Christianity remained in suspense for a prolonged period; and indeed the serfs and peasants of eighteenth-century Europe, like the negroes shipped to America, might be excused if they were not aware of its existence. The principle of equality, however, was an important element in the natural law theory, and was inherited from it by the utilitarians and rationalists of the eighteenth century. Few, if any, of these really meant equality in an economic sense and between all men. They took for granted the class structure of society. What they desired was equality between equals — equals in education, in intelligence, in *lumières*.[1] Even thus limited the ideal of equality was sufficient to rouse the fierce hostility of the privileged classes and to produce a struggle far more formidable than that against the power of the king, especially when to it was added, as a result of developments during the Revolution, a popular hatred of the wealthy bourgeoisie. This phase of the revolutionary struggle was not at first conducted very efficiently. To carry it through ruthlessly a strong authoritative government was needed: without this even a moderate degree of economic equality was not likely to be achieved. But since the revolution was a revolt against despotism, the

[1] A considerable degree of economic equality is advocated in Rousseau's *Constitution de Corse*, but this ideal affected only some sections of the Jacobins and a few of the extremer revolutionaries. Babœuf's communism is a 'freak' in the history of the Revolution. Mathiez has shown that the *Complot des Egaux* is to be interpreted rather as a final attempt to revive the principles of Robespierre and the Jacobin Terror than as a doctrinaire communist movement. With it perished the last effort at a dictatorship of the left. – MATHIEZ, *La Directoire*, ed. J. Godechot, 1934, ch. ix.

revolutionaries could not easily set up a strong executive without doing violence to their own principles. To the conflict between the ideas of separation of powers and sovereignty was thus added a similar contradiction between the ideal of political liberty and the authoritarianism necessary to enforce even a moderate degree of social and economic equality.

The dilemma with which the Revolution was thus presented is to be detected not merely in its actual events, but also in the theoretical development which had preceded it; for the political theory of eighteenth-century France had insisted on the one hand that the liberty of the individual was the hall-mark of legitimate government, and at the same time had based on a belief in natural equality a theory of the rights of the state over privileged individuals and corporations, which amounted to an assertion of the principle of sovereignty more absolute than that claimed by any government since the fall of the Roman Empire. Burke, in the early days of the Revolution, perceived this contradiction in its theoretic foundations, though he attributed it to a deep-laid plot to make France formidable under pretence of making her free.[1] Others have said that the French, having no real desire for liberty, gladly sacrificed it in the struggle for equality, though in what sense Napoleon and his court represented equality, or Robespierre and the Jacobins liberty, it is not easy to understand. In fact neither of these explanations is tenable and we must be content simply to record the fact that the French Revolution had launched these two opposing tendencies on Europe, and that the thought of the eighteenth century, without realizing how difficult

[1] E. BURKE, *Letters on a Regicide Peace*, II, *Works*, 1868, vol. V, p. 244.

they would be to reconcile in practice, had established and handed on to posterity a belief in the intellectual validity of both.

The immediate future lay with neither liberty nor equality. They were both by-passed on the high-road of history. The principle of the sovereignty of the people was to work itself out in its own way and regardless of either. The revolutionaries had attempted a reconciliation of their liberal political principles with an assertion of the rights of the sovereign state by means of this idea of popular sovereignty. Unfortunately the 'People' as a political conception proved somewhat ill-defined: nor, when its voice was heard, was its message the one that had been expected. Though it gained the adherence of philosophers and was saluted by statesmen in eloquent speeches, the 'People' proved a singularly unattractive political ideal to the very individuals who in fact composed that huge collectivity. Even when a revolution had been made in the name of the People, other objects of political devotion rapidly ousted it. So in France, as the Revolution proceeds, we hear less and less about the People, and more and more about *la patrie*, which had all the allure which the noun of multitude lacked; for with the uprising of the People of France against her invaders was born a new and a stronger force in European politics — nationalism.

It might be argued that such a movement was an inevitable result of the general acceptance of the idea of the sovereignty of the people, for the People could only recognize itself as the Nation. But nationalism is based on emotion and not on reason; in so far as it appeals to the spirit of self-sacrifice and not of self-interest it is a direct contradiction of the rationalistic, utilitarian theory of the eighteenth century. It brought a new and a preponderating influence to bear on the development of revolutionary France, and one which was to determine for the time the result of the conflict between liberty and authoritarianism. The liberal tendencies of the revolutionaries, their desire for an executive which should be a mere agent of the will of the people, embodied in the legislative power, had waged a slowly losing battle with the desire to suppress the privileged classes and therefore the need for a strong government. The spirit of nationalism, bringing a lust for national power and glory, finally overweighted the balance and the first dictatorship of the modern world was born.

CHAPTER IV

BONAPARTISM

§ I THE FIRST MODERN DICTATOR: NAPOLEON BONAPARTE

ONE need not belittle Napoleon to hold that some form or other of dictatorship was, as Burke had prophesied, the inevitable outcome of the Revolution. The Republic, ruled after the fall of Robespierre by an increasingly narrow oligarchy of politicians, could not survive. Had the prisoner of the Temple, the little son of Marie Antoinette, lived, a monarchy might easily have been set up in his name. Had the brothers of Louis XVI shown any willingness to accept its basic social achievements, there might have been a Restoration at any time after 1795; but even moderate revolutionaries feared the return of a king tied to the *émigrés* and bent on revenge.

Although historians, wishing to draw a picture of Napoleon as the saviour of France, have exaggerated the defects of the Directory, at best it could not be regarded as a government likely to inspire popular enthusiasm. Too many of the politicians ruling France were corrupt, too many of their plans, both domestic and foreign, ended in disaster. The *jeunesse dorée* was parading the boulevards. Madame Récamier and Madame de Staël had stepped into the shoes of the great salonnières and were educating the revolutionary leaders in the ways of smart society. The bourgeois Puritanism of Robespierre had perished with him on the scaffold, sacrificed to the 'triumphant nudities' of the future Madame Tallien, *notre dame de thermidor* and reigning deity of the Directory. The demi-monde had been restored, if not the *monde*. Indulgence was replacing terrorism as the order of the day, and revolutionary ardour was a thing of the past.

In central and local government, in the law, the Church, the land, foreign relations — in none of these fields had stability been achieved. Local administration was a chaos, the national elections a fraud, the currency worthless and the Treasury bankrupt. The government, living from hand to mouth, survived only with the aid of the loot sent home by its generals from conquered cities and provinces, though if the revolutionaries made war pay for itself they were certainly cleverer or luckier than most modern governments. Idealism was dead. War profiteers flaunted their riches, while the comrades of Robespierre and Saint-Just lurked in obscure hiding places or rotted in exile. The last futile flicker of Jacobinism died when the conspiracy of Babœuf was crushed, yet the country had no confidence in the groups of intriguers who had taken the place of the Jacobins — the Barras and Talliens, Reubells and Revellières. Only the army seemed a relatively stable point.

The emergence of the army as a leading factor in the political situation justified a fear which had possessed men as diverse as Robespierre and Burke. The armies of the *ancien régime* — small in size compared with the whole population, but possessing a monopoly of military power, attached by long service and tradition to the monarchy, officered by an hereditary aristocracy, and having in their *corps d'élite* an efficient and generally reliable force for use in any civil emergency — were a strong bulwark of the *status quo*. The Revolution could not have succeeded in France if the discipline of these troops had not cracked. Under the menace of foreign invasion the revolutionaries set about building up new armies by the system of universal compulsory military service. They were well aware that a small professional army was normally an instrument of the Crown and the nobles: a citizen army, it was thought, would be the defence of the people. Only a nation in arms, they believed, could be a free nation.

The belief that conscription naturally went with democracy has ever since been held on the continent, and it is indeed on the surface plausible enough. Further consideration might have been suggested by the fact that the system was first used by Frederick the Great, no great lover of liberty. To put the manhood of a nation through a course of military discipline, always to have in the ranks and under arms a large body of young men, forming a nation apart, officered necessarily by professional soldiers, and putting loyalty to its generals above any respect it might be supposed to have for civilian leaders, is a great source of strength to a state, but not necessarily to the Parliamentary form of government, especially if to this is added a smaller body of seasoned veterans, a potential praetorian guard for any would-be Emperor. Armies are not usually politically minded, the doings of parliaments do not interest them, loyalty is their strongest emotion, and if they look for anything in politics it is for a leader.

So it was with the French revolutionary armies. They had developed a passionate attachment to their more successful generals, and especially had fallen under the sway of the irresistible Bonaparte. Moreover, the professional interest had largely replaced the political, and their hostility could easily be aroused against the politicians who left them starved of supplies and pay. It must not be thought that the armies were anti-revolutionary in spirit. Among both men and officers probably more genuine republican patriotism lingered than in any other section of the French people. But they were easily capable of identifying republican government with the rule of a great general, so long as the name of king was not breathed and royalists were not openly brought back into favour. Thus, if one general had not led them to overthrow the civil government, another would. Napoleon saw this, and at the critical moment used his hold over the army to strike a decisive blow.

The first effective intervention of the army in politics was in September 1797, when Augereau dispersed the Jacobin mob with the famous whiff of grape-shot: the echoes of his cannon were to sound through modern history. Two years later Bonaparte concerted his plans with a group of politicians, who, with the short-sighted astuteness of their kind, thought they could use him as their instrument. When he ordered his grenadiers to disperse the Five Hundred in 1799, the Revolution was over. The prestige of government, which had collapsed with the downfall of Bourbon divine right, could now, it was hoped, be rebuilt on the victories of French arms. The reign of reason had come to a premature end, and government in France was to venture on the fakir-like experiment of sitting on bayonets.

It must be granted that the support of the army was not

enough by itself to set up and maintain a new government; but along with the army went military glory, conquest and the growing spirit of imperialist aggression. Not Brumaire but Marengo gave France to Napoleon. True, military conquest ran counter to the basic principles of the Revolution, but from the pacifism of the early Robespierre to the crusading fervour of the Brissotins, and from the struggle of Carnot and Reubell for 'natural frontiers' to the imperialist wars of Napoleon, the transition was easy.[1] Bonaparte himself had taken the decisive step in this process, when he forced the preliminaries of peace with Austria, signed at Leoben in April 1797, on the Directory, in spite of the opposition of Reubell. From the system of limited annexations and natural frontiers France now passed to a policy of imperialist expansion, from the possible to the impossible, and it was the ambition of Bonaparte that largely dictated the development.[2]

French imperialism still wrapped itself in the tattered robes of revolutionary propaganda. Bonaparte was still to idealists like Revellière-lèpeaux a 'Mahomet of Liberty', in success the armed prophet of the new dispensation, in defeat the valiant defender of French independence. To the end the motive of defence was probably stronger in the French people than the lust of aggression, but that was not a fact of great political importance. It was later to be found almost a *sine qua non* of an imperialist war that it should be termed a war of self-defence. That a statement is ridiculous is no barrier to popular credence, as Napoleon rapidly discovered; for he was able to keep up the legend of the defence of France throughout

[1] A. SOREL, *L'Europe et la Révolution française*, 17th ed., 1922, vol. III, p. 144.

[2] R. GUYOT, *Le Directoire et la Paix de l'Europe*, 1911, pp. 376-8.

his career. He returned from Elba in 1815, as he came back to France from Egypt in 1799, to save the country, and he went on saving it from conquest to conquest. Every battle was to be the final victory that would bring peace. France and Bonaparte were hardly to be expected to realize that only defeat could bring that to a power claiming the hegemony of Europe.

This search for peace was, it must be admitted, a necessary pretence, for when Bonaparte came to power after Brumaire it was above all because France believed that he could give her peace, internal and external. Among all the articles, manifestos, pamphlets, rhymes, music-hall sketches, which celebrated the *coup d'état*, says Vandal, there is not a single one in which is not to be found expressed the universal desire for peace, and to it Bonaparte responded, swearing in vibrant proclamations to bring back peace to France and Europe.[1]

If the combination of military glory with the desire for peace formed the foundation of Bonaparte's authority, they were not the only elements contributing to it. France, which had not felt the hand of a master since the fall of the great Committee of Public Safety, urgently wanted a government. The demand was not yet for a leader, a chief of the state. Nowhere does one find the cry, says Vandal, 'A man, we need a man'. Modern Caesarism, he adds, is a legacy of Bonaparte.[2] One would be tempted to modify his statement. In the situation in which France found herself the demand for a leader, a saviour of society, was almost inevitable. That this desire was not consciously

[1] A. VANDAL, *L'avènement de Bonaparte*, 1907, vol. I, p. 409; vol. II, pp. 287-9.

[2] id., vol. I, p. 217.

formulated is doubtless true; it was hardly to be expected that it should be, for it was the first time that such a situation had appeared in modern history. But after ten years of revolution uncertainty had lasted too long: authoritarian government was needed to end the strain, and to restore a feeling of stability. This was the real meaning behind the meaningless maxim of Sieyès — 'Authority must come from above and confidence must come from below'. Although the internecine struggles of the earlier revolutionary period had died down, their memory was fresh, and the fear remained that they might at any time break out again.

Bonaparte came to power because his name provided a new source of authority, but at the same time the principle of the sovereignty of the people had established too firm a hold over men's minds to be abandoned. Some means of reconciling this principle with the rule of one man had to be found. Emotionally this was easy: the sovereignty of the people had become fused with nationalism, and Napoleon through his victories had come to be a living symbol of the national greatness. But to add the appearance of free choice he adopted the method used by the Jacobins in presenting their Constitution of 1793 to the country — the plebiscite. Sieyès and the men of Brumaire had themselves presented this device to Bonaparte, when they incorporated in the Constitution of the year VIII the name of the First Consul, Citizen Bonaparte; so that when it was submitted to the popular vote, it was as much a plebiscite on Bonaparte as a vote for a constitution. The votes on the life consulate in 1802 and on the establishment of the Empire in 1804 are mere sequels. By these popular votes democracy, or at least the principle that all authority is derived from the people, was to be triumphantly vindicated by the election of Napoleon to the post of supreme power in the state. In this way arose, in the modern world, the idea that one man might himself represent the will of the people, and be invested with all the authority of the most despotic ruler in the name of democracy. The idea of sovereignty, freed from all restraints, and transferred to the people, had at last given birth to the first modern dictatorship.

The Jacobin attempt at dictatorship from the left had failed. Napoleon came to power as a dictator from the right — not, of course, as a leader of the old reactionary party, but as a dictator supported by the propertied classes, the financiers and commercial men, the upper bourgeoisie, and speculators, who had made large fortunes out of the revolution and had bought up church or crown lands or the property of *émigrés* with worthless *assignats*. The financial blunders and economic incompetence of the revolutionaries had at least allowed these men to make large fortunes; but as a final bankruptcy loomed nearer and nearer, the Directory was driven to ever more desperate expedients. It even proposed to suspend the assignments on the taxes allocated to the government contractors, to deprive them of the right of collecting payment themselves, and to introduce a progressive tax.[1] The contractors and speculators, in the words of Vandal, threw themselves into the arms of Bonaparte to defend them from this blow. He returned from Egypt penniless, to face the mounting debts of Josephine; a group of bankers formed a syndicate to come to his aid, and they provided the financial resources without which the

[1] A. VANDAL, *L'avènement de Bonaparte*, 1907, vol. I, p. 283.

coup d'état of Brumaire would have been impossible.[1] Direct benefits to its financial backers followed, for the measures proposed against the contractors were dropped at once, and ten days later the progressive tax was abolished.

While Bonaparte needed the solid advantages that the support of the financiers and bankers could give, he also had to preserve the confidence of the masses. Military glory and the hope of peace went a long way towards this, but economic benefits were also required. The peasantry was fairly easily contented: the reassertion of law and order and therefore the revival of prosperity, a conservative social policy, a gradual return to Catholicism, along with a guarantee that the alienated lands and feudal dues of the Church and the *noblesse* would never be returned — and the peasantry were satisfied. The populace in the towns required more management. For this reason Bonaparte's relations with the monied men were a carefully guarded secret. Indeed, in public he declared himself the enemy of the financiers and the government contractors, and after he had become First Consul he did not hesitate to fling one of them to the wolves as evidence of his own high principles; though when the arrest and examination of this scapegoat for a whole class had received sufficient publicity, he was secretly rescued, at a price.[2] This reputation as an enemy of the speculators was an important element in the popularity which Bonaparte was winning in the poorer quarters of Paris. From General to Consul and from Consul to Emperor, he managed to keep the devotion of the Parisian working-classes: they

[1] A. VANDAL, *L'avènement de Bonaparte*, 1907, vol. I, pp. 203, 283.
[2] id., vol. II, pp. 107, 114.

loved and admired him, says Aulard, far more than they had ever admired and loved Robespierre or Marat.[1]

Bonaparte's genius lay in his capacity for combining with this popular adulation a conservative and authoritarian system of government. France as a whole demanded a government which would guarantee the country against a revival of terrorism without handing it back to the *ancien régime*. The fear of a Jacobin revival was still strong in France and it was a force which Bonaparte used to the fullest degree. It played the part which fear of Communism has played in modern Germany. With its aid he took the critical step of ordering the Grenadiers to disperse the legislative body. At the very root of his authority was the magnificent, incredible lie of the dagger attack upon him by Jacobins in the meeting of the Five Hundred. Incredible as it might be, the country believed it.

It is not true to say that Bonaparte rescued France from the rule of the extreme revolutionaries, for the Directory had already suppressed the Jacobins and the mob of Paris, and the First Consul merely inherited their success. But he certainly carried on, and even exaggerated the trend to the right, welcoming in particular any moderates or even royalists who would accept his authority. Although he won over more than a few of the leading Jacobins and incorporated them in his bureaucracy, to those who would not sacrifice their principles he remained implacably hostile. The royalists who, in December 1800, attempted to blow up Napoleon when he was driving to the Opera, were never discovered; but their conspiracy was used by the First Consul, not as a

[1] Aulard, op. cit., pp. 765-7.

reason for taking action against the many known royalists, but as a pretext for police measures against the republicans, ending in the exile to the Seychelles or French Guiana of nearly one hundred Jacobins, well over half of whom perished. The murder of the duc d'Enghien in 1804 was merely a warning to the royal family that Napoleon would stop at nothing in the defence of his regime. A carefully calculated act of terrorism against the Bourbons, it did not imply any hostility to royalists who were ready to abandon their king.

As well as ex-royalists, Bonaparte summoned the clericals to his banner. He made the most energetic efforts to win over the Church, suppressed anti-ecclesiastical societies, such as the Theo-philanthropes, withdrew the support of the government from the Constitutional Church, and as soon as he dared bought the alliance of Rome by the Concordat; subsequently, when it was too late for the Church to withdraw, passing the Ordinances, which achieved what the kings of France had struggled to gain for centuries, and made the Church in France for all effective purposes a department of the state. The Pope thought he had won a powerful supporter, but found that he had merely submitted to a master.

Taking into account all these diverse sources of support, it is comparatively easy to understand how Napoleon was able to make himself the leader of France. But if it was to be permanent his power had to have a more concrete basis. A political system capable of sustaining his authority had to be erected. This meant, first, the creation of a governmental machine dependent on his will alone, and then the occupation of all the key positions in the state by an army of personal supporters.

Here, the centralizing trend, which had struggled with the elective principle throughout the Revolution, finally triumphed in the creation of the prefectoral system with its hierarchy of officials. In the Napoleonic bureaucracy revolutionary sentiments received their due with the application of the principle of equality, interpreted as *la carrière ouverte aux talents*. Ten years of revolutionary turmoil had thrown up plenty of talent from all ranks of French society, and Napoleon had no difficulty in filling his administration and officering his army with men of ability, and men who, owing everything to him, would be his devoted followers.

Supported thus by a powerful political machine, his rule sanctioned by the will of the people, his person idolized by the army, trusted by the men of property and the peasants, and backed by the Church, Napoleon was in a position to gather the whole of France into his hand. Terrorism he used comparatively little as an instrument of government: it was hardly necessary. Marat, Robespierre and the Directory had already removed most of those who were not amenable to influence. Moreover it is only fair to credit Napoleon with an appreciation of the fact that terrorist methods are a sign of weakness rather than of strength.

Although he had risen to power by the Army, Napoleon never made the mistake of over-estimating the power of force in governing a country or of under-estimating the power of opinion, as hosts of typically Napoleonic *obiter dicta* bear witness. All the factors capable of influencing public opinion were mobilized for the maintenance of his regime — the Church inculcated obedience; the Press suffered a rigid censorship and its news was dispensed through official journals; the stage and the arts were set to the task of glorifying the Emperor; literature, rather unwillingly, was to be harnessed to his chariot; education was organized, with *lycées* and one central university, to enforce discipline in the academic world; finally, Napoleon's dispatches, comparable indeed with Caesar's, were a series of masterpieces of propaganda. The *ancien régime*, because it had neglected the people, had seldom condescended to tell them lies. Napoleon 'erected mendacity on a hitherto unparalleled scale into an art of Empire'.

We have been attempting to analyse the real reasons why Napoleon was able to gain and keep power, but though these would have been effective by themselves, it must not be supposed that he did not perform any services to France other than the rather doubtful one of winning battles and extending his sway over the greater part of Europe. The codification of the laws, even though this was only the completion of years of work by the revolutionary lawyers — the establishment of a sound financial system, presided over by the new Bank of France — the restoration of stability to land ownership, the economic activity of the *préfets*, devoted to building up the prosperity of their *départements* — all these and much more must go on the credit side of the balance. Mostly, it is true, they represent the work of the First Consul. As Emperor Napoleon took far more than he gave to France, and in the end the sum total perhaps hardly represents a great return for fifteen years of despotic rule.

More important than what Napoleon did was what he was. Of his colossal executive capacity and power of decision there can be no question. Lacking the higher forms of creative genius, he was still intellectually the superior of all his experts. It was not this side of his personality, however, which was most valuable to him as a leader of men. His intellect would never have made him an emperor without his appeal to the non-intellectual elements which are the driving forces in men and nations, — his capacity for catching and communicating emotion, his handsome appearance in youth, his charm of manner, his eloquence, and his knack of coining effective phrases. His life was a series of dramatic gestures and he was his own press agent. From the beginning of his career — take, for instance, the words with which he was supposed to have stopped a Marseillais about to butcher one of his victims — 'Man of the South, let us save this unfortunate' — to the end, when, defeated and flying, he could still turn an elegant phrase, 'I come, like Themistocles, to seat myself at the hearth of the British people' — his career is punctuated with memorable, if sometimes apocryphal, sayings.

Wellington and Castlereagh remained unmoved even at the last of these, but the theatrical disposition, the proneness to picturesque attitudes of the Corsican, was well fitted to catch the fancy of a Romantic generation, to win the admiration of the youthful Goethe, to inspire a Beethoven, or to make him the idol of a Byron, even if the melodramatic scenes which comprise his career are only the pseudo-heroics of an Ossianic hero. This association between Napoleon and the great Romantics is no mere accident: it deserves to be emphasized, because it establishes a connection at the beginning of the nineteenth century between Romantic ideas and dictatorship, which will emerge with greater effect when we come to study the origins of contemporary dictatorship.

Napoleon appealed to the Romantic imagination in part because he was a supreme individualist, a complete representative of the emancipation of the ego. If ordinary moral laws did not exist for him, that was one of his principal sources of strength. The politician who is completely emancipated from moral prejudices will naturally have an advantage over those who are liable to have their freedom of action occasionally hindered by moral considerations; whilst the people will admire a ruler in whom the absence of inhibitions gives them vicarious pleasure. Only an adventurer could have risen to fame as Napoleon did, and he remained an adventurer until the day when the *Bellerophon* carried him to an island where there was no room for more adventures. His very wars were a brigand's campaigns for loot, and diamonds, it is said, were found sewn in the upholstery of his carriage after Waterloo. He always cheated at cards. He was a worthy peer of the Renaissance Italian tyrants and the twentieth-century dictators.

Napoleon was the architect of his own greatness, and his ability alone held him on his throne. He knew it himself. 'My position', he said, 'is entirely different from that of the old sovereigns. They can live a life of indolence in their castles ... Nobody contests their legitimacy, nobody thinks of replacing them. ... Everything is different in my case ... Within and without my dominion is founded on fear. If I abandoned the system I should be immediately dethroned.'[1] A regime cannot escape

[1] H. FISHER, *Napoleon*, pp. 117-18.

from its origins: and here at least Napoleon frankly recognized that war was a necessity for him. He had come bearing pledges of peace, but that was precisely what he could never give France. War made him necessary to France, and at the same time created the psychological atmosphere in which the continuance of his rule was possible. It is arguable, of course, that the practically continuous war while Napoleon ruled France was the result of the hostility of Europe, but whichever way one looks at it, the association between Napoleon's dictatorial system of government and his continual wars is certainly no mere coincidence.

What Napoleon had won by the sword it seemed he would have to keep by the sword. Gradually he became aware that if his power was to endure and to be handed on to a successor it would have to be put on a different basis. Dictatorship, aping the *ancien régime*, would have been more than a little ridiculous, were it not for the power that Napoleon represented. All the panoply of Empire which Napoleon created, his court, with its ancient pomp and ceremony, and its new Napoleonic nobility, was directed to one end: it was an attempt to wrap his new absolutism in the old mantle of divine right, and to legitimatize himself in the eyes of Europe. Hence his increasing reliance on former royalists. They alone knew how to obey, he said. Hence too his marriage with the Austrian Archduchess. All was in vain. Not that there was yet any fear of revolution. The army remained loyal, and the Prefects held the country firmly in their grasp. Enthusiasm had waned, but there was little sign of active opposition inside France. Foreign armies were needed to overthrow the Napoleonic system.

The country as a whole seems to have accepted with extraordinary passivity his fall, the return of the Bourbons, the Hundred Days and the final defeat. Political life in France, so hectic for a few years after 1789, was dead. During the brief interlude in Paris between Elba and Waterloo Napoleon tacitly admitted the failure of his dictatorship, and attempted by re-erecting his power on constitutional bases to connect it again with its revolutionary origins. In vain: the Napoleonic essay in constitutional monarchy never had time to come to life, nor is there any evidence that it could ever have lived. The greatest dictator in modern history fell, as he had risen, by war, and dragged out his remaining years in the midst of petty squabbles on a miserable tropical island. Meanwhile Europe set about reconstituting the reign of divine right, or putting Humpty Dumpty together again.

§ 2 THE RISE AND FALL OF LOUIS NAPOLEON

In 1815 the Bourbons were restored in France and ancient potentates and princes reappeared throughout Europe, but the revolutionary principles let loose by 1789 had not ceased their work. The year 1848 again saw the collapse of the monarchy in France, and the country once more set out on the path which led from revolution to Empire. The revolution of 1848 in France has been called a '*revolution du mépris*': almost universally contemned, Louis-Philippe was easily persuaded by a few days' rioting in Paris to put his famous umbrella under his arm and seek safety across the Channel. The revolution won its victory only too easily: too many incompatible elements joined in the overthrow of the Orleanist monarchy — clericals and Voltairian rationalists, legitimists supporting the claims of '*l'enfant du miracle*', a few stray Bonapartists, doctrinaire republicans, disgruntled Orleanist politicians like Thiers, romantic liberals like Lamartine, and radicals like Ledru-Rollin, together with socialists of all hues, under leaders as united in their love of humanity and hatred of one another as Louis Blanc, Barbès, Blanqui, and P.-J. Proudhon, were fighting side by side in February 1848. The revolution was the result of the collapse of a centralized bureaucratic government in Paris. The rural masses, for France was mainly an agricultural country, accepted the revolution, since the Church, which retained most of its influence over them, approved; they shared in the initial rejoicing, but had no desire for any revolutionary change in the French social or political system.

Since the revolution was based, like that of 1789, on the principle of the sovereignty of the people, its first act had to be an appeal to the popular vote. But when on April 27th, 1848, the National Assembly met, it was found that the influence of priests, landlords and officials over a naturally conservative peasantry had returned, even in the first wave of revolutionary enthusiasm, some 400 monarchists out of 900 members, while the really revolutionary parties formed an insignificant minority.

The first three months of the revolution witnessed a sharp struggle between the socialists in Paris and a few other large cities and the conservative majority, after which the socialist leaders found themselves imprisoned, exiled and nullified as a political force. The folly of the right wing in suppressing the so-called National Workshops, without any attempt to cope with the distress of the town populations, produced a revolt in the working-class quarters of Paris and the terrible street fighting of the June days. The army, and the bourgeois National Guard of Paris, reinforced from the provinces, suppressed the revolt ruthlessly, but it was an irrelevant and unnecessary tragedy, for well before June socialism had ceased to have any control over the development of the revolution. The fighting in Paris served, however, to make socialism an effective bogy with which to frighten the peasantry and the middle-classes, and this was its active role for the remaining years of the Second Republic and long after.

The power of the populace of Paris and of the really revolutionary leaders had been overthrown in less than six months, and the Second Republic found itself now in a position that the First Republic only reached at the end of ten years of turmoil. The National Assembly was left apparently master of the situation, with a majority desiring a conservative, bourgeois republic, though a large minority would have preferred a return to monarchy. The strange fate of the French Assembly was to find that it could have neither of these forms of government: another, desired by a bare handful of representatives in the Assembly, was thrust upon it. Even stranger is the fact that the new regime arrived comparatively peacefully, by the silent pressure of the will of the people, one might almost say. Its authority was strengthened and consolidated by the usual methods of tyranny, but in the beginning the future dictator became President without any exercise of governmental authority in his favour.

Before the presidential election, which was to be held in December 1848, the republican government had been preparing the ground by the usual methods of official persuasion for the victory of the candidate of the conservative republicans, the hero of the June days, General Cavaignac — a military man, it is true, but one pledged to republicanism, and an eminently safe and moderate politician. A small group of left-wing republicans were supporting the radical lawyer, Ledru-Rollin, but he obtained a bare quarter of the votes that were given to Cavaignac, whilst the tiny polls of the various socialist candidates showed how little support they had in the country at large. The surprise of the election was the victory over Cavaignac by 5,400,000 votes to 1,400,000, of Louis Napoleon Bonaparte, nephew of the great Emperor.

There is no possibility of explaining away this four million majority. An election in which the whole influence of the government is directed against the victorious candidate cannot be suspected of representing anything but a genuine popular decision. 'Louis Napoleon', wrote Proudhon, who saw some things more clearly than most of his contemporaries, 'is indeed truly the chosen of the people. The people, you say, were not free! The people were deceived! The people were afraid! Vain excuses. Are men afraid? Can they be deceived in such a matter? Have they no liberty? We ourselves, the republicans, have repeated on the faith of our most suspect traditions:

the voice of the people is the voice of God. Well, the voice of God has named Louis Napoleon. As an expression of the people's will, he is the most legitimate of sovereigns.'[1] Louis Bonaparte was not yet an emperor, but the whole of his subsequent dictatorship is implicit in the vote of December 1848, which demands a detailed examination, because it exhibits more clearly than any episode in the rise of the first Napoleon the real nature of Bonapartism and the sources of modern dictatorship.

The new President was the son of Hortense Beauharnais and Louis Bonaparte, Napoleon's younger brother. His life up to 1848, had been that of a political adventurer. His attempts to start rebellions against Louis-Philippe at Strasbourg in 1836 and at Boulogne in 1840 had merely served to show how little support there was in the country for a Bonapartist regime. When the revolution broke out in 1848, there existed, we may safely say, no Bonapartist party in France, and hardly a single person of any consequence had thought of the possibility of a Bonapartist restoration. Among the peasantry, it is true, the tradition of Napoleonic glories lingered, while the memory of the miseries had faded. But though Louis-Philippe tried to use it for his own ends, no one in February 1848 seems to have considered that this sentiment was capable of being converted into a serious political force.

Louis Bonaparte started with an advantage in possessing a name and a tradition: most dictators have to make their own legend, whereas he inherited one. He made his own

[1] P.-J. PROUDHON, *La Révolution sociale démontrée par le coup d'état du Deux Décembre*, 1852; in *Œuvres complètes*, ed. P. Bouglé et H. Moysset, 1936, p. 169.

contribution to the development of the Napoleonic myth, however, in a famous work of imagination, *Des idées napoléoniennes*, published in 1839. A careful study of this book would have suggested already that Louis Napoleon was no fool. He begins cautiously with an attempt to establish a more positive attitude towards government, which, he says, is not 'as it has been called by distinguished economists, a *necessary ulcer*, but is rather the beneficent motive power behind every social organism'.[1] Governments, he admits, in obedience to the laws of progress, vary: there is no single good form.[2] This prepares the way for a reconsideration of Napoleon, treated as the 'testamentary executor' of the revolution.[3] His aim was liberty, but it was necessary to restore prestige to government, and re-establish order, before liberty was possible.[4] The services of Napoleon to the people are of course detailed at great length, but we need not follow the author into his account of these. His conclusion is, 'To sum up the imperial system, one can say that its basis is democratic, since all power comes from the people; whilst its organization is hierarchic, since there are in society the different grades necessary to stimulate all capacities'.[5]

It had been ten years before the first French republic had discovered that the solution to its political problems was presented by Napoleon. The Second Republic took ten months to arrive at the same conclusion, and whereas the first Napoleon obtained supreme power at a time when the revolution had for the present worked itself out, and with the support of men whom ten years of

[1] L.-N. BONAPARTE, *Des idées napoléoniennes*, 1839, p. 6.
[2] id., pp. 7-9. [3] id., p. 17. [4] id., pp. 36-8. [5] id., p. 121.

revolution had disillusioned, and who asked for nothing more than strong, efficient government, the second Napoleon was brought to power by a combination of the most heterogeneous supporters, with the most incompatible aims. The true nature of his polity was to develop and to find its permanent bases during four years of nominally republican government.

The great body of his supporters were necessarily, as we have said, the peasantry. Marx, whose 18 *brumaire of Louis Bonaparte* is still one of the shrewdest analyses of the political evolution of France at this time, rightly said that Louis Napoleon was in the first place the peasants' Emperor.[1] While tradition played its part here, a panic fear of anarchy and socialism played an even greater part. Cavaignac and his supporters, in their campaign against the socialists and the red republicans, had spread the fear of social chaos very effectively. But the alarmed population of the countryside, and the moderate bourgeois in the towns, seeking an insurance against a communist *loi agraire* and a red terror, saw a better one in a Bonaparte than in a Cavaignac. The republicans of the Assembly had over-played their hand and their propaganda merely served to recruit voters for the nephew of Napoleon.

A second force to be reckoned with was the Church, for too many of the republicans were also anti-clericals. While the Church, which had its own reasons for being glad to see the back of Louis-Philippe, had welcomed the revolution in February, it was not long before it discovered its mistake, and realized that even a moderate

[1] KARL MARX, *The Eighteenth Brumaire of Louis Bonaparte*, trans. E. and C. Paul, 1926, pp. 132-4.

republican was not very favourably disposed towards the power of the Church in politics and education. What the Church really desired was a return to divine right, in a restoration of the older line of the Bourbons, but pending that, a Bonaparte as President, dependent on clerical support and therefore favourably disposed towards the Church, was preferable to a republican, however moderate and conservative he might be. Thus, led by Montalembert, the huge clerical influence was flung into the scale on the Bonapartist side. A similar calculation was made by the monarchists, who assumed that a Bonaparte in the Presidential chair would keep the seat warm for a king when the time was ripe. Later clericals and monarchists have made similar miscalculations about later dictators.

On the other hand the left wing also provided its recruits. The working classes in Paris and the other great towns, suffering severely from the economic slump, which had appeared before the revolution, but had been intensified as a result of the social and political disorder it involved, resenting bitterly their violent suppression by the middle-class National Assembly, demanding social reform, which there seemed no hope of getting from the conservative republicans, regarding Cavaignac as their deadly enemy but disillusioned with the socialist leaders who had merely led them to disaster, turned in hope or despair to the imperial disciple of Saint-Simon, the author of the *Extinction du Pauperisme*, who at least was lavish with promises and who, while he promised order and stability to the middle classes, offered paternal government and social progress to the lower. The enmity of the bourgeois republican politicians was

Louis Bonaparte's highest qualification in the eyes of the industrial workers.

Finally, there were many individuals of influence who saw which way the wind was blowing and trimmed their sails to it – adventurers staking all on the name of Napoleon, such as de Morny and Persigny, romantic writers like Victor Hugo, carried away by the glamour and the genuine idealism of Louis Bonaparte, and professional politicians like Odilon Barrot and Thiers, true descendants of Sieyès, believing with characteristic blindness that the nephew of Napoleon would be a tool, and in the words of de Tocqueville, 'a tool that they could break'.

Once in the Presidential chair Louis Bonaparte had simply to play his cards carefully and bide his time. As President he controlled the administration of France, which he gradually filled with ex-Orleanist officials who had transferred their allegiance, or with new men who would be his personal supporters. Working with the conservative majority in the Assembly he was able to suppress socialist or red republican leaders by police action, while leaving the republican politicians to bear the brunt of the opprobrium aroused by these proceedings. At the same time the Assembly, fearing a revival of the reds and hoping to deprive Louis Napoleon of supporters, had imposed a residential qualification which greatly restricted the franchise: some three million out of ten millions lost the vote. This, and other reactionary measures, gave the President the opportunity by opposing them to maintain his reputation as a friend of the people. The continuance of the support of the Church was ensured by the *loi Falloux*, restoring the control of education to the ecclesiastical authorities, and by the Rome expedition, which suppressed the Roman Republic of Garibaldi and Mazzini and reinstated the despotic authority of the Pope.

The defeat of the revolutionary forces in France had checked the economic collapse, and Louis Napoleon was careful to associate himself with the improvement in conditions by increasing the pay of the army, offering loans to small business men and promising stability, public works and economic progress for the future. From about November 1849 onwards the influence of the Bourse was brought to bear in his favour and against the Assembly. Early in 1848 there had been some attempt on the part of the Bonapartists to raise the anti-Jewish cry, but as — perhaps because it was too patently counter to the current of fraternity then running at its strongest — this had proved a complete fiasco except in Alsace, it had been dropped, and soon afterwards Fould and other leading Jewish financiers became strong supporters of the President.

A skilfully conducted campaign of propaganda, in which a prominent feature was the carefully staged progresses of Louis Napoleon through various districts of France, won over many even of the hostile centres. At Lyon, a stronghold of the republicans, the President achieved a personal triumph in an official visit which culminated in a reception given to a thousand Napoleonic veterans. The Army was sedulously cultivated, and Bonapartist officers put at its head. The *Société du dix décembre* played its part in spreading Bonapartism, and even more in suppressing its opponents; but the excessive zeal displayed by the society seemed likely, in a period not habituated to the political persecutions of a later epoch, to bring discredit on the cause it was trying to serve, and in December 1850 it was dissolved.

When, on December 2nd, 1851, Napoleon's *coup d'état* overthrew the constitution, the ground had been so well prepared that resistance was slight, though it is interesting to note that the printing establishments and the belfries of Paris were the first centres to be seized by the Bonapartists. Revolts in the provinces were easily suppressed; the massacre of some 1200 people in the streets of Paris was a mere executive blunder. A plebiscite ratified the coup by 7,500,000 votes to 650,000, and the establishment of the Empire in 1852 was only the recognition of a *fait accompli*.

The dictatorship of Louis Napoleon was now complete. He upheld it, at first, by the persecution of opponents. Torture, beheading, assassination, castor oil, beating and concentration camps were not used. But nearly 10,000 persons were sent as compulsory colonists to Algeria, 2804 were confined to a given French town, 239 — the most unfortunate — were sent to Guiana and 1545 were exiled.[1] But most were allowed to return on accepting the new regime; there was no permanent proscription, and in 1859 an amnesty was extended to all, with the single exception of Ledru-Rollin. It is worthy of note that it was a red republican and not a socialist who had the honour of being treated by the Emperor as his deadliest enemy. Many of the socialists, indeed, accepted the new government: the Saint-Simoniens, in fact, were the group which most intimately collaborated with the Emperor after the *coup d'état*, and not

[1] F. A. SIMPSON, *Louis Napoleon and the Recovery of France*, 1923, p. 186.

merely the financiers who happened to be disciples of Saint-Simon, such as the Péreire brothers, but even the intellectual head of the movement, *père* Enfantin, himself.[1]

Judged by modern standards the mildness of the repression was its most marked feature. Even parliamentary life was not entirely suppressed under the Second Empire, though the Chamber retained little power, and methods of administrative pressure well established in France ensured that the official candidate should nearly always be successful. A strict censorship of books and periodical literature was maintained, and the Church saw to it that education preserved a due respect for the powers that were, both spiritual and temporal.

On the more positive side must be put the attempts by Louis Napoleon to live up to his promises. Great public works, like the boulevards which Haussmann drove through Paris, extensive railway building, encouraged by the state, industrial exhibitions and commercial treaties, stand to the credit of his government. While the industrial achievements of the reign are the better known, his efforts for the improvement of agriculture also deserve to be remembered. 'Sometimes', writes one of his ministers, 'he is visiting la Sologne, bringing with him engineers, chemists and agriculturalists. Sometimes he is concerned with an increase in the fertility of the *landes* of Gascony, and he has brought under cultivation 7000 *hectares* of heath-land. He drains marshes, builds farms, clears immense areas, sows the dunes, distributes farm carts, subsidizes the labours of the Trappists in the

[1] H. N. Boon, *Rêve et Réalité dans l'œuvre économique et sociale de Napoléon III*, La Haye, 1936, p. 85.

Dombes and in Algeria, and devotes 10,700,000 francs from his revenue towards fertilizing the soil.'[1]

In the field of social reform, systems of insurance, co-operative societies, credit establishments and reformed *monts de piété* were founded or encouraged by the government. Even trade unions were legalized. But Louis Napoleon was too dependent on the support of the formerly Orleanist upper bourgeoise to be able to take as effective action in defence of the growing industrial proletariat as he himself would have liked. Karl Marx had foreseen his dilemma as early as 1852. 'Bonaparte', he said, 'would fain pose as the patriarchal benefactor of all classes. But he cannot give to one class without robbing the others.'[2]

Despite the growth of a revolutionary, underground, socialist propaganda among the people and a liberal opposition among the middle classes, the Bonapartist bureaucracy managed to hold its own. True, the will of the people, which had called it into being, could not permanently tolerate its failure to cure or even satisfactorily to palliate the social ills. But it was through its foreign relations and not through domestic policy that nemesis came upon the Second Empire as on the first.

Among Napoleon's other pledges to France had been peace. Of Napoleon I he had written, 'He was no aggressor; on the contrary he was unceasingly compelled to repulse the coalitions of Europe'. If he made conquests, it was in the interests of a 'European confederation'.[3] '*L'Empire, c'est la Paix*', had been the catchword with which the second Napoleon had come to power;

[1] A. Granier de Cassagnac, cited in Boon, op. cit., p. 98.

[2] Marx, op. cit., p. 142.

[3] *Des idées napoléoniennes*, p. 173

and one need not be cynical over this, for the Emperor was himself genuinely a man of peace. An unexpected witness does justice to him in this connection. 'Personally', Treitschke says of the Emperor, 'he was perhaps more free from the dangerous passions which are the curse of modern France than any notable man among his French contemporaries; yet that necessity for self-preservation which was the very essence of his system, incessantly impelled him to goad on these passions.'[1] The passions referred to here are of course those desires for national aggrandisement and glory, which, applied to Germany, become for Treitschke 'the great patriotic idea' for the sake of which man must 'renounce his whole ego'.[2] He judges France more clearly than his own country. For our part we may confine ourselves to elucidating, without judging, the general tendency of Bonapartism. That the government of Louis Napoleon, despite the Emperor's personal inclinations, should have lurched from one foreign adventure to another, until finally it ended in irretrievable military disaster, is a certain indication that the association between Bonapartism and war is no mere accident.

The humiliation of Sedan brought with it inevitably the downfall of Louis Napoleon and the end of Bonapartism in France. There are yet monarchists: divine right is still the ghost of a political force in France; but Bonapartism is a historical memory, a twice-told tale, ending each time in disaster. The experiment will not easily be repeated for a third time. Moments when

[1] H. von Treitschke, cited in H. W. C. DAVIS, *The Political Thought of Treitschke*, 1914, p. 89.

[2] TREITSCHKE, *Die Politik*, in Davis, p. 155.

dictatorial forces have seemed to be rising again in France, as behind General Boulanger and later Colonel de la Rocque, have been marked by the strength of the popular reaction.

Perhaps the ultimate reason — apart from military defeats and domestic disillusionment — why Bonapartism has died so completely, is that it was so 'pure' a dictatorship, relying for its appeal almost exclusively on loyalty to an individual, or rather to a name. 'Napoleonic ideas' never become anything like a real ideology, despite the efforts of Louis Napoleon, and hence Bonapartism remained an exclusively French phenomenon, and passed away when France turned against it. The careers of the two Bonapartes are evidence in the realm of practical politics of the bias of the modern state towards dictatorship; but it had to receive a great ideological extension before it could become a movement of world-wide significance.

CHAPTER V

DICTATORSHIP IN THE TWENTIETH CENTURY

§ 1 THE DICTATORSHIP OF THE PROLETARIAT

FROM the standpoint of the early twentieth-century Bonapartism appeared a strange aberration, a flying in the face of the secular trend of modern history. All over the world parliaments were springing up like mushrooms. The fall of the surviving autocratic dynasties, Hapsburgs, Hohenzollerns and Romanovs, during and after the World War, seemed to put the seal on the triumph of democracy. It was not noticed, or at least was not regarded as significant, that the victory was only won by investing individuals — Woodrow Wilson, Clemenceau, and Lloyd George — with an authority which practically amounted to a dictatorship in the Roman sense of the term. Nor was it realized how fleeting the triumph would be. Already, two years after the Armistice, one of the most acute observers of politics, Lord Bryce, had pointed out the many weaknesses in the parliamentary system as it was being worked,[1] and within a few years, from left and from right the rule of parliamentary democracy was being challenged.

The opposition to it first took concrete form in Russia, where the revolutionary social democratic government,

[1] J. BRYCE, *Modern Democracies*, 1921, Part III, chs. lviii, lix.

based on Western liberal ideas, was overthrown by the bolsheviks, and what was called the dictatorship of the proletariat was set up. With this a new factor enters the history of dictatorship. Bonapartism, early and late, had been a practical response to circumstances. Any special theory of dictatorship behind it — and there was little — was an attempt to justify it after the event. But with the twentieth century definite dictatorial theories appeared, and challenged the supremacy of liberal, parliamentary doctrine. With Marxian socialism, or communism, as a general theory we are not concerned, but it must be mentioned here because it has the credit of introducing the new theories of dictatorship into practical politics: in a sense all European dictators of the present day are the children of the *Communist Manifesto*.

Das Kapital is a long book and a difficult one, and can only have been read by comparatively few, and understood by a still smaller and more select company; but the *Communist Manifesto* is short, concise, eloquent, full of brilliant and memorable phrases, and a great part of it is patently true. It effected a revolution in the attitude of large numbers to politics, because it swept away the old conception of the state as a power directed towards the common welfare and above all the struggling individuals and groups comprised within it. Marx and Engels were the political heirs, not of Robespierre, but of Marat. 'Political power', they said, 'is the organized use of force by one class in order to keep another class in subjection.'[1] Bentham had made exactly the same discovery, but he believed that the sublime machinery of universal suffrage — one man, one vote — would remedy this state of affairs.

[1] *The Communist Manifesto.*

Marx had the advantage of having seen a more or less reformed Parliament in operation and to him it seemed if anything merely a more efficient instrument of class government. Economic power, he believed, was the real force behind the façade of politics. Parliament, as he saw it, was merely 'an administrative committee of the bourgeoisie'; its rule 'open, unashamed, direct and brutal exploitation'.[1] Times have changed — at least, we manage things differently to-day — but it is hard to deny some truth to this as a description of Parliament in the age of the Chartists.

The conclusion that Marx draws is that the rule of force can only be overthrown by force, and that the dictatorship of the possessing classes can only be replaced by a dictatorship of the proletariat. It is clear that the term 'dictatorship' is here used not as we have defined it, but in the sense of a government based on the forceful suppression of one section of the community by another section. The experience of 1848 and 1871, however, showed that the proletarian masses were not ready to seize power. Hence arises the belief in the necessity for the leadership of a class-conscious minority in the proletariat, who will stir the masses to revolt when the critical moment appears, and subsequently exercise political power on their behalf.

One group of revolutionary socialists held that the revolution must be made by the revolutionary minority itself. This group, of which Auguste Blanqui was the leading representative, was influential in Paris during the early days of the revolution of 1848, and played a large part in the commune of 1871. According to Blanqui

[1] *The Communist Manifesto.*

and his disciples revolution was a skilled art, not to be entrusted to the masses, but to be practised by a small, carefully organized cadre of determined men, who would occupy the technical and administrative centres of authority by a sudden attack, and thus seize control of the machinery of the state. What the Blanquists dreamed of was in fact a *coup d'état* rather than a revolution; their tactics were put to good use by would-be dictators, but were inapplicable to the conditions of a social revolution. Their teachings were specifically repudiated by the first successful social revolutionaries, the bolsheviks. Trotsky, who made very effective use of Blanquist methods during the October revolution, quotes Lenin, who had expressly said, 'We are not Blanquists, not advocates of the seizure of power by a minority'.[1] The bolsheviks only struck when they believed that they had the support of the masses in Russia for their immediate programme. But after the revolution, as had happened in 1848, the peasant majority, which had supported the workers of the towns in the initial stages, began to show signs of breaking away. Such a development had been Lenin's greatest fear, and faced with this, to save the revolution, the minority must now, as a matter not merely of fact, but of right, seize control of the machinery of state. In this way, to the belief that the political system in all existing states is based on force and not on consent, was added a claim on behalf of a minority to the right of exercising that force.

This minority, the class-conscious proletariat, is in effect the Communist Party. Stalin has thus explained

[1] L. TROTSKY, *A History of the Russian Revolution*, trans. N. Eastman, 1932, vol. III, p. 128.

the relationship between the party and the people: 'No important political or organizational problem is ever decided by our soviets or other mass organizations, without directives from the party. *In this sense*, we may say that the dictatorship of the proletariat is substantially the dictatorship of its vanguard, the "dictatorship" of the party, as the force which guides the proletariat.'[1] He proceeds to quote from Lenin the definition of the party as 'the directly managing vanguard of the proletariat; it is the leader'.[2] In the following pages this idea of leadership is reiterated again and again. An English apologist has pointed out the difference between the parliamentary conception of a party and the party in the U.S.S.R., which he defines as 'the organized political leadership of the people'.[3] This conception of dictatorship — or leadership — by a party, from which it seems only one step further to the Führer-principle, is a new element in theory, though the rule of the Jacobins during the French Revolution approximated to it in practice.

The communist dictatorship, if not exactly dictatorship in our sense of the word, shares certain of the characteristics which have already emerged from our study of Bonapartism. It is a government set up and maintained by force. On principle it repudiates the rule of law. Like the Jacobins, it governs by means of terror, which it justifies in theory as 'a weapon utilized against a class, doomed to destruction, which does not wish to perish'.[4] Thus the communists took up the tradition of 1871 and 1793; but the authority of Lenin depended

[1] STALIN, *Leninism*, 1928, vol. I, p. 33.
[2] id., p. 36.
[3] P. SLOAN, *Soviet Democracy*, 1937, p. 210.
[4] Trotsky, cited in H. J. LASKI, *Communism*, 1927, p. 142.

more on his personal superiority in intellect and character than on the execution of opponents or rivals within the ranks of the revolutionaries, and at no stage can he really be regarded as a dictator.

It must be added, moreover, that in communist theory this dictatorship of the proletariat was only a transitional phase, necessary while the war against capitalism was still being carried on, but destined to give way in the end to a true communistic democracy, which in turn would 'wither away', as the repressive machinery of the state became less and less necessary, until the political millennium aimed at was reached. The actual historical evolution of revolutionary Russia has deviated — to use the fashionable term — from this hypothetical line. First, the most important element in the state apparatus, a standing army, had to be built up at the very beginning: it was destined to become, internally and externally, an essential bulwark of the regime.

In the second place, we must note the remarkable reaction that took place against the soviet principle in government and administration. When Lenin was struck down by illness, supreme power passed into the hands of a group of party leaders, and for some time it seemed as though government by committees or soviets was to be the peculiar characteristic of the communist political system. No feature has received higher praise: it was through the method of government by soviets, above all, that the feudal and bourgeois state was to be destroyed, because it put an end to the existence of a ruling class, distinct from the nation.[1] Trained observers, such as the Webbs, remarked on it and apparently had no suspicion

[1] A. Rosenberg, *A History of Bolshevism*, 1934, p. 87.

that 'government by committee' would not prove permanent.[1] But the Russian Revolution contained inconsistent elements and the interest in the Union of Socialist Soviet Republics was to see whether the committee system or the dictatorial tendency would prove the stronger. By 1934, in the report of the Congress of the Communist Party, the reaction against the system of collegiate instead of individual responsibility had become plain, with the demand for 'the splitting up of the commissariats', 'the abolition of depersonalization in work', 'the abolition of the functional system, increasing personal responsibility and taking the line towards liquidating collegiates'.[2]

This tendency to substitute personal for committee rule went with a great increase in the importance of the bureaucracy, and determined the constitutional evolution of the U.S.S.R. It is not necessary to trace its development from the assumption of power after Lenin's stroke by a triumvirate of Zinoviev, Kamenev and Stalin, aiming at the exclusion of Trotsky, through the gradual stages by which Stalin undermined and destroyed his enemies of the right and the left, to the trial and execution of the sixteen old bolsheviks in 1936, which proved the opening phase in the systematic destruction of all the old communist leaders, both local and national, who were unwilling to accept the supreme authority of the party secretary. It is worthy of note that this last stage went with the introduction of a nominally more democratic constitution, including such features as direct election, secret ballot, and a fairer representation of the rural

[1] S. and B. WEBB, *Soviet Communism*, 1937, vol. I, p. 436.
[2] *A Handbook of Marxism*, ed. E. Burns, 1935, pp. 949-50.

districts. Not for the first or last time democracy and dictatorship appear hand in hand. The introduction of the new constitution has been interpreted as a method of 'dissolving' the proletariat in the nation,[1] but the proletariat is after all a conception of doubtful scientific value: the party presents a more concrete objective. It is not a wild surmise to suggest that the new Russian constitution was needed not to free the people from the rule of a dictator, but to emancipate the dictator from control by the Communist Party, by making him, instead of the party, the embodiment of the dictatorship of the proletariat, the incarnation of the *vox populi*, which is also *vox dei*.

Thus up to the present it would seem as if the political implications of dictatorship, even of the proletariat, were proving more powerful than the ideology of the Communist Party. The state, which according to Marxist theory should at least have commenced to wither away with the extinction of the capitalist classes in Russia, has on the contrary swollen and become all powerful. The evolution of government in Russia has patently been following national rather than Marxist principles. Nationalism, a useful instrument in the early stages of the revolutionary struggle, a force which a communist might use against capitalist imperialism, but which those who sang the *Internationale* could never fall victims to themselves, has gone from strength to strength, until it seems as though the appeal of the government in Russia is far more to national patriotism than to the communist fervour of the masses.

The evolution of the bolshevik regime is to be

[1] L. TROTSKY, *The Revolution Betrayed*, 1937, p. 261.

explained, according to one of its founders, by the triumph of bureaucracy. There would be nothing strange in this, for national traditions are strong and bureaucracy has been the established government of Russia for centuries. But the bureaucracy could not function without a head — 'an inviolable super-arbiter, a first consul if not an emperor.'[1] Hence what Trotsky calls Soviet Bonapartism. We should prefer to suggest that with the re-birth of a new Holy Russia may be coming the reappearance of a Little Father of all the Russians, terrible in his wrath to the enemies of his country, yet at heart benevolent and kind, the protector of his adoring subjects, the head of a great bureaucracy, an all-powerful state machine, supported by a mighty army and a dreaded secret police, the autocrat of all the Russias, Stalin — a true heir to the Czars in all except the non-hereditary nature of his power. If this interpretation of the development of revolutionary Russia be correct — and, while not put forward in any over-confident spirit, it at least appears to afford a reasonable explanation of the facts that now and then percolate to the outside world from Russia — then the third great modern revolution had at last produced its dictator.

§ 2 FASCISM

The communist revolution thus had unforeseen developments; but if it produced a Stalin, had not the French Revolution produced a Bonaparte? Revolutions have their own logic, and even a Lenin, whose inflexibility

[1] L. Trotsky, *The Revolution Betrayed*, 1937, p. 277.

of purpose controls the beginning, may not predict the end. But he who sows dragon's teeth should know what harvest to expect, and socialists, who come to bring revolution, should at least not be surprised when revolutions appear.

The 1917 revolution in Russia was in its beginnings the kind of revolution socialism had expected, and throughout Europe in the period immediately following the conclusion of the European War, the revolutionary socialistic movement was spreading, though it came to fruition nowhere outside Russia. The establishment of parliamentary and generally republican systems in place of the defunct monarchies in the defeated countries and the successor states, indicates the failure, rather than the success, of the revolutionary socialist movement. The next truly revolutionary regime to be established was of an unexpected type. Italian fascism borrowed a good deal from the technique of communism, but it found its intellectual origins in a different brand of socialist theory, and it proved that the revolutionary urge might assume forms unanticipated by those who provided its first impetus.

The doctrine from which fascism took its basic ideas was syndicalism, a branch of socialist theory which was widespread in France and Italy before 1914. Its chief prophet, Georges Sorel, wrote his *Reflections on Violence* in 1908. His justification of force as a political weapon attracted considerable attention because of the manner in which it was stated, but went no farther in this direction than orthodox Marxian Socialism. The particular contribution of Sorel to the development of socialist theory was his emphasis on the emotional elements in politics.

Socialists as a whole had accepted the belief of the early democrats in the rationality of man as a political animal. Sorel, at the end of a century's experience of democracy, or attempts at democracy, drew another conclusion, and taught the syndicalists to use other methods than the mere appeal to reason, to self-interest, or to a humanitarian idealism. He revived the Platonic idea of the myth as the ruling influence in politics, in the form of the General Strike, which he defined as 'the passage from capitalism to socialism conceived as a catastrophe'. Literally a myth and a catastrophe it has proved in practice; but for Sorel, through the General Strike and physical violence in other forms, the mystical or emotional forces in the life of the people were to be released and used to establish a condition in which the state would be reduced to a federation of self-governing industries, termed corporations or syndicates, and the ideal condition of society thus achieved.

A wave of revolutionary strikes followed the rise of syndicalism in Italian labour politics, but the influence which was to have a more permanent importance lay in another direction. The syndicalists, believing in the use of violence and of emotional forces in politics, were emancipated from the humanitarian, liberal ideology that the orthodox social democratic parties had inherited; and when the modern imperialist movement in Italy took form with the war for the conquest of Tripoli in 1911, more than a few of them drifted into the nationalist camp. One of their chief leaders, Labriola, who had broken away from the Socialist Party as early as 1906, wrote, 'Revolutionary syndicalism has well been called a form of workers' imperialism, since it reveals the same tendencies of energy and conquest as appear in capitalist imperialism, the same distrust for sentimental and humanitarian democracy'.[1] The transition from syndicalism to imperialism was less difficult than might have been supposed. Professor E. Barker has pointed out that the syndicalist belief in the real personality of groups is only a defence against the state if it is assumed not to apply to states.[2] Syndicalism, applied to the state, becomes absolutism, and so it has proved in the history of Italian politics.

The syndicalists who abandoned the internationalism of socialist theory were able to translate their new nationalist ideas into socialist phraseology without much difficulty. Transferring the idea of the class war into the international field, they began to talk of 'proletarian nations' and 'capitalist nations'; and just as, internally, for the communist, an aggression by the capitalist class was a monstrous piece of tyranny, while the use of force on the proletarian side was the mere exercise of a natural right, so in external relations, for the 'have-not' nations — to use a current term — imperialism was a sacred and irresistible duty, imposed by the dialectic of history.[3]

Along with the introduction of the idea of imperialism under a new guise into left-wing ideology went a new development in the conception of political society, with the idea of a natural aristocracy, to replace the effete hereditary one. An Italian thinker, whose kinship with

[1] Quoted in H. W. SCHNEIDER, *Making the Fascist State*, 1928, p. 140. The notes to this section will show my indebtedness to this excellent survey of Italian Fascism.

[2] E. BARKER, introduction to Gierke, *Natural Law and the Theory of Society*, trans. 1934, p. lxxxiv.

[3] L. VILLARI, *The Economics of Fascism*, in G. S. Counts, L. Villari, etc., *Bolshevism, Fascism and Capitalism*, 1932, p. 68.

Labriola and Sorel is evident, Vilfredo Pareto, expresses this belief thus — 'The use of force is indispensable to society; and when the higher classes are averse to the use of force . . . it becomes necessary, if society is to subsist and prosper, that the governing class be replaced by another which is willing and able to use force. Roman society was saved from ruin by the legions of Caesar and Octavius. And it may happen that our society will one day be saved from decadence by the heirs of the syndicalists and anarchists of our day.'[1]

A minor figure in the syndicalist movement at this time was the young socialist, Benito Mussolini, who headed a general strike at Forli in 1911 as a protest against the nationalist war in Tripoli, and subsequently became the founder of a journal, the *Popolo d'Italia*, started for the purpose of bringing Italy into the World War on the side of the Allies. Like many others he had adopted nationalist aims without abandoning his syndicalist ideas. In 1919 he was proclaiming that 'Imperialism is the eternal and immutable law of life'.[2] In 1921, internationalism has become for him 'an article of luxury, good for the aristocracies of art, banking, industry, and a snobbish imbecility; in short, for the bourgeoisie of capitalism and of socialism; but at bottom internationalism is an absurd fable; the great masses do not escape, nor can they, and it is the best of fortune they cannot escape, the insuppressible datum of race and nation. "Go home to your own country!" This is the formula that sums up the workers' internationalism'.[3]

[1] V. PARETO, *The Mind and Society* (*Trattato del Sociologia generale*), trans. and ed. A. Livingston, 1935, vol. III, pp. 1292-3.

[2] SCHNEIDER, op. cit., p. 273.

[3] id., p. 275.

After the war, in March 1919, Mussolini founded the first fascist groups. Fascism was still, of course, a revolutionary and socialist movement, hostile to the monarchy, to finance, and to parliamentary government, demanding social reform and workers' control, but separated from the other branches of the socialist movement by its intense nationalism. The extreme left-wing socialist and communist movements that had threatened — or promised — to introduce social revolution in Italy immediately after the war, had collapsed by 1920, and the resulting disorder and disillusionment left the field open for rival parties. The nationalist section of the syndicalist movement now had its opportunity; it began to grow in importance, nor were the nationalists unaware of the strength syndicalism brought them, as d'Annunzio showed when he gave a corporative system to the independent government he temporarily set up in Fiume. The nationalist syndicalists were strong enough by January 1922 to hold a congress at which they declared their alliance with the new Fascist Party.

With this exception, fascism — revolutionary national socialism, as it might well have been called — found itself at enmity with all the existing political parties, and in particular it directed its attack against the parliamentary institutions through which they ruled. It has been suggested that fascism took up the attack on parliamentary democracy because it needed an objective and therefore had to create a 'villain of the piece' to denounce as the source of all the woes of Italy. This view rather underestimates the importance of the fundamentally antidemocratic pre-suppositions of fascism, but it must be admitted that a more suitable or a more unpopular enemy could hardly have been chosen for attack. Parliamentary government was a new institution, which the greater part of Italy had only known since its union with Piedmont; and while Cavour had managed to conduct parliamentary government successfully in Piedmont, when the rest of the country, lacking any aristocracy with political training, and illiterate and backward in almost every respect, was added, the system experienced a strain under which it broke down. The fault was not exactly excess of democracy, except in relation to the political capacities of the people; indeed, parliamentarism in Italy has sometimes been accused of being little better than a euphemism for government by corruption. In this it did not differ conspicuously from the despotic regimes which it replaced, but the newest generation was not to know that.

By 1919 the really active forces in Italian politics were thus revolutionary and anti-parliamentary. Italy emerged from the war with the psychology of a defeated rather than a victorious country. She had deserted her allies and thrown in her lot with the Western Powers, who had promised her great territorial gains, but disappointment with the terms of the treaty of peace, the burden of the war, the humiliating defeat of Caporetto, and economic distress, had put a strain on the Italian political structure which it could not stand. Parliamentary liberals and socialists still controlled the majority in parliament, but those who were willing to vote were not willing to fight for them.

The new factor that was to be the determining one in the situation was the appearance of rival revolutionary parties, each appealing to force and proclaiming the need for dictatorship, but the one on a national and the other on an international basis, the one relying on the spirit of the class war, the other on national loyalties and jealousies. For a brief period the communist movement seemed to be sweeping to victory: its very success was fatal, for alarm seized the possessing classes, from the peasantry upwards. The existing parliamentary parties seemed too effete to offer a solid resistance to communism, and hence much support was given openly or secretly to the fascists.

This half-hearted backing, as the lesser of two evils, would not have been adequate to carry the fascists to victory, however, without the use of methods borrowed from their opponents. The similarities between bolshevism and fascism in their rise are striking. They both arose out of military defeat and civil strife and came to the front because they were united, closely organized, well disciplined and rigidly centralized parties, with a single pre-eminent leader, whereas their opponents were divided and practically leaderless and the government weak. Neither had any scruples about letting loose the dogs of civil war, and using revolutionary methods to undermine constitutional government. On the other hand, whereas it was fifteen years or more before the dictatorial method of government introduced in Russia brought its natural fruits in a nationalist dictatorship of one man, the fascist regime in Italy was this from the beginning; for Caesarism was a tradition which had not died out in Italy with the fall of the Roman Empire. It renewed its vitality with the Renaissance tyrants and might easily have emerged again in the *Risorgimento.* Before Mussolini became famous the career of d'Annunzio had shown that Italy was ready for a leader.

With the triumph of the Fascist Party the whole Parliamentary structure of government in Italy crumbled like a stucco façade. From top to bottom of the political system nomination by authority replaced election. The powers of the prefects were greatly enlarged, and for the elected mayors of the communes were substituted appointed officials. The country ceased to be ruled by the ordinary process of legislation, until finally in a law of 1936 decrees were given the force of law, with the rider that they must be published in the official gazette and submitted to 'Parliament', if one can call it such, within two years. It is doubtful if even these fairly simple rules have been observed.[1] During the four years 1922 to 1926 a complete dictatorial regime was gradually set up in Italy. This was a true revolution. What were its fruits?

The national, imperialist and dictatorial elements in fascism, along with the gospel of force, are manifest throughout its rise; so too is the derivation of its power from the sovereignty of the people. In the elections of 1924 fascism obtained — not without the assistance of the usual Italian electoral methods — the support of nearly five million voters, more than twice those voting for the numerous opposition parties. The plebiscite of 1929 produced an overwhelming vote in favour of the fascist list of candidates to the national Grand Council. There were, of course, no other candidates, and the authorities provided printed ballot papers, the patriotic affirmative ballot being decorated with the Italian tricolour, which was naturally absent from the negative ballot, while the envelope provided was transparent, so that those who voted against Signor Mussolini should not

[1] *New Governments in Europe*, ed. R. L. Buell, 1934, p. 65.

be able to conceal their light under a bushel. It is interesting to compare a speech of Signor Mussolini — 'This plebiscite will take place under absolute tranquillity. We will exercise neither trickery nor pressure' — with a circular from a provincial fascist administration — 'All provincial organizers shall inform the voters verbally that, on the basis of a revision of the registers of every ward, we can easily learn who has failed to fulfil his duty as an Italian, as a public official, and as a free adherent of a fascist association.'[1]

In spite of such devices, which do not wholly reflect a democratic spirit, and although fascism prides itself on the creation of a new aristocracy, its plebiscitary origins, the constant appeals to public opinion, and the omnipresent and unceasing stream of propaganda it emits, are proof that it is conscious of its dependence on the popular will. Appropriately enough, its *Duce* was first and foremost a great journalist, and fascism has been described as 'government by journalism'. Mussolini has often been compared to Napoleon Bonaparte, not unjustly, and of Napoleon Vandal writes, 'He was a journalist in his very soul'.[2]

The socialist or syndicalist element cannot at first be traced in the policy of the new government so clearly as the democratic. Fascism only conquered power by degrees and extensive economic changes were not possible in the early stages of the process. The affiliation between socialism and fascism was rather theoretical than practical; and principles have generally been the handmaid of practical politics in Italy. 'Fascism', writes Schneider,

[1] C. Haider, *Capital and Labour under Fascism*, 1930, pp. 257, 259.
[2] Vandal, op. cit., vol. II, p. 388.

'was carried along on its career by the force of events and not by any inner aims. The essence of the movement lay not in its programmes, which were subject to change without notice, nor in its ideas, which shiftily followed its shifting fortunes, but in its growing power.'[1]

Moreover, fascism had been backed by the great industrialists: their reward seemed to have come when Mussolini appointed De Stefani, a rigid *laissez-faire* individualist, as his first finance minister. De Stefani abolished death duties, reduced direct taxation on the wealthy classes, imposed additional indirect taxation on the poor, repealed such socialistic laws as existed in Italy, abolished the Ministry of Labour, and in fact seemed to be turning Italy into a paradise of the classical economy.

But the original tendencies of the movement were too strong to be permanently suppressed. After the first few years, syndicalist leaders entered the government, and by decree after decree the unwieldy machinery of the Corporative State was slowly hoisted into position. A vast and expensive bureaucracy, through which their deserved reward was given to thousands of loyal party men, was set up to man the new machinery of economic control, as it already manned the political structure. Before a decade was out the capitalists and financiers woke up to find that instead of a servant they had created a master. The new fascist *condottieri*, at first regarded as the mercenary troops of capitalism, having won the victory, revolted against their employers,[2] and a new phase began in the economic life of the country.

The syndicalist organization which was established on

[1] SCHNEIDER, op. cit., p. 111.

[2] G. SALVEMINI, *Under the Axe of Fascism*, 1936, p. 120.

paper, does not appear as yet to have functioned effectively; indeed one might suppose that a dictatorial government was by its very nature hardly likely to be able to give the Corporations any real power.

But the fascists had to persuade the masses that something was being done for them; moreover, the leader and some at least of his followers, came from the working classes or the peasantry and had socialist antecedents; so, measures of minor or local importance were sometimes taken in favour of the employed and against the employing classes. Further, Mussolini, like Napoleon, required the support of the peasantry, and therefore their interests had to be considered, as well as those of the wealthier landowners. Through the *Dopo Lavoro* organization 'games' were provided for the poor, even if bread was short. Nor should one under-estimate the positive achievements of fascism in the field of administration, not the least of which was the destruction of the Mafia in Sicily and the Camorra in Naples, secret societies which had too long ruled whole districts tyrannically and corruptly. There was no room for these rival organizations and for fascism in the same community.

Such reforms were not irreconcilable with the existing capitalist structure of society. But the decisive factor in shaping the economic development of fascist Italy was the political nature of the regime. In the end the dictatorship proved incompatible with liberal economics. Fascism meant glory, and glory is the most exigent of national gods to serve. Glory demanded great public works, *autostrada*, draining marshes — all dictators insist on draining marshes — constant and expensive public celebrations, the old Roman 'bread and games', a great multiplication of officials, a large army and navy, and finally — most costly of all — war.

Even De Stefani had found that the *lire* needed discipline. His modest attempt at this had induced Mussolini, under pressure from the bankers, to abandon him in 1925; but the fascist government was to be driven to far more extreme measures of economic control than its first finance minister had dreamed of. 'Italy', Mussolini could claim by 1933, 'is not a capitalist country in the meaning now currently given to that term.'[1] Under the stress of war in Africa and Spain, the government had gradually to take control of one branch after another of the nation's economic life, until the dictatorship was as complete in the economic sphere as in the political. The apparent contradiction here evident between origins and end must not prevent us from realizing the facts. Even as Marxian socialism had given birth to a Stalin, and the humanitarian and reforming ardour of eighteenth-century France produced a Bonaparte, so the syndicalist dream of a state which was to be a free federation of gilds led up to Mussolini's Italy, and the second great dictatorship of the contemporary world.

§ 3 NATIONAL SOCIALISM

While Italian fascism has syndicalist antecedents, the German National Socialist Movement proclaims both in title and in policy its affiliations with the older state socialism. It is notable that each of the three great dictator-

[1] Address to the National Corporative Council, November 14th, 1933; in B. Mussolini, *Fascism, doctrine and institutions*, 1935, p. 53.

ships of to-day can be traced to socialist origins. In Germany liberalism had never been a very strong growth: the body of the German people has always looked to the state for authoritative leadership. Moreover the Bismarckian state had been no merely political or military machine. Its essays in state socialism, as well as episodes such as the *Kulturkampf*, are proof of its innate tendency to assert its power in the religious and economic spheres of life. But the absolutist police-state theory of the Hohenzollerns had fallen in ruins in 1918, and for Germans, to whom a theory of the state was the first condition of its existence, the various brands of socialism seemed the only ones that remained available. Hence they practically monopolized German political thought in the post-war period, the newer forms, such as National Socialism and Communism, naturally attracting the more vigorous spirits. The great advantage these had was that they did not leave souls to wander in the wilderness of liberalism, to find their own political salvation: they each offered an infallible dogma and an authoritarian leadership such as a defeated and disorientated people naturally craved. One might have guessed, even in 1919, that some form or other of dictatorship was inevitable in Germany.

Stresemann, perhaps the only great statesman Germany has produced since Bismarck, wore himself out in vain in the attempt to create a stable political system in his country. While he was labouring to restore Germany to its rightful place in Europe, and rebuild the German economic system, his political support was gradually vanishing beneath his feet. The People's Party had sunk to insignificance before its Chancellor was dead. The blockade, Versailles, the inflation, above all the occupation of the Ruhr, were not forgotten — even though the years 1925 to 1929 were years of economic recovery — and they were to bring their nemesis when the economic slump, which began with the crash of October 1929, in Wall Street, reached Germany. In September 1930, Dr. Brüning and Dr. Schacht began the policy of deflation, which destroyed the home market, lost all the gains of the period of recovery and earned them the title of the starvation government. Unemployment grew to huge numbers. Desperate men became prepared for desperate remedies. Economic disaster completed the ruin of the middle parties in Germany; but in truth they had only continued so long in nominal authority because the forces of dictatorship were divided between the extreme right and the extreme left.

That German politics had become by 1930 a race between Communism and National Socialism is well known; it is not so commonly realized that even the Weimar Republic had strong dictatorial elements in its constitution. The men who drew up the Weimar Constitution in 1919 could no more than any other constitution makers dissociate themselves from their own past. They had abandoned the Kaiser — or he had abandoned them — but merely to put the President in his place. Modern Germany, it must be remembered, was used to a strong hand. Bismarck had established a tradition from which it was found difficult to depart. In Germany in 1919, as in France in 1848, it was believed that in face of the menace from the 'reds' the executive must retain its strength and independence, and that it could only do this in a democratic state if its power were derived directly from the people. This was the view of the principal theorist of the new Constitution, Hugo Preuss,[1] and it was accepted by the Weimar Coalition of the Catholic Centre, Democrats, and Social Democrats. The middle parties, afraid above all of the communist menace, aimed at obtaining a strong Presidency, the chief duty of which would be to nominate the Chancellor and the other ministers, who would thus by way of the President derive their authority from the people, and so be in a sense independent of the Reichstag. Subsequently the Social Democrats realized the dangers involved in the position of the President, but their partners in the Coalition upheld the famous Article 48.

The political system constituted by Hugo Preuss has been called 'parliamentary caesarism'.[2] In theory both elements in the Constitution derived their authority from the people, but in a disagreement Caesar was likely to count for more than Parliament in a country with Germany's traditions. The German President, elected by the whole people, re-eligible for office, the head of the executive government, and Commander-in-Chief of the army, was from the beginning a dictator in embryo. Enshrined in the terms of the republican constitution was a provision which made him in emergency a real dictator, the already mentioned Article 48, which demands quotation: 'If a state fails to carry out the duties imposed on it by the national constitution or national laws, the President of the Reich may compel performance with the aid of armed force. If public safety or order be seriously disturbed or threatened within the German Reich, the President of the

[1] E. GORDON, *Les nouvelles constitutions européennes et le rôle du chef de l'état*, 1932, p. 86.

[2] id., p. 257.

Reich may take the necessary measures . . . if necessary with the aid of armed force. For this purpose he may temporarily suspend in whole or in part the fundamental rights enumerated in Articles . . .' Nor was this Article a dead letter. If the period of comparative prosperity, from 1925 to 1930, saw it invoked only nineteen times, it had been used 135 times between 1919 and 1925; while 1931 was to see it applied in 42 cases and 1932 in 59. It remained only to unite the offices of President and Chancellor, generalize Article 48, and dictatorship would be complete.

The interesting problem then is not why Germany became a dictatorship, but why her dictatorship took the particular form it did. The early history of the Nazi Party, in so far as one can disentangle it from the prejudice of hostile accounts and the hagiography of its disciples, presents nothing very remarkable. It did not seem a very important occasion when in July 1919, Corporal Hitler, who had been engaged in nationalist propaganda among the troops after the Armistice, became the seventh member of the German Workers' Party, but this was a critical moment in the history of modern Europe.

The civil engineer, Gottfried Feder, provided this party with a programme of Twenty-five Points in February 1920. These are worth pausing over. Nationalism takes pride of place in the first Article, along with the demand for equal treatment for Germany, for the abolition of the Treaties of Versailles and St. Germain (2), and the granting of land and colonies to cope with surplus population (3). Then follows racialism (4 to 8), and equality for all citizens (9 and 10), and with these we may link the demand for a people's army (22). A series of articles embodies an extensive programme of state socialism: measures are to be taken against war profiteers and financiers (12), trusts are to be nationalized (13), and unearned income is to be abolished (11), for work is the first duty of every German (10). The government is to be strong and centralized (25) and is to assert its might in every field of national activity, including the press, art and literature (23); it is to promote health (21) and a reformed education (20); old age pensions are to be introduced (15); agrarian reform is proposed at the expense of the great proprietors, who are threatened with expropriation without compensation (17). Religions are given a warning, for they are promised freedom only 'so far as they do not endanger the state or oppose the customs and morals of the German race' (24). Finally, one freak clause — the old German common law is to replace Roman law (19), and one which was to be instrumental in winning the Nazi Party much support — small shopkeepers are to be protected from the competition of great multiple shops and department stores (16). The significance of many of these points will emerge in due course, but already we may note that nationalism is becoming 'racialism', that the socialist elements come only next in importance to the nationalist, and that the whole programme is built up on the conception of an immensely powerful and omni-competent state.

Captain Ernst Röhm brought the little party which had accepted this programme into association with the Reichswehr and with the volunteer corps, which had sprung up in Germany during the period of anarchy and had been of service in crushing the Spartacist revolt. But despite its ambitious programme the party seemed in no way important, and its ignominious collapse on the occasion of the Beer-house *Putsch* of November 1923 in Munich set the seal on its insignificance.

In 1925 Hitler reorganized the party; in 1926 he founded the S S; by 1928 he had twelve deputies in the German Reichstag. In September 1930 the number leaped to 107; in March, 1932, Hitler obtained 13,400,000 votes at the second ballot in the presidential election, and in February 1933, 17,200,000 votes.

The peculiar interest of post-war German history for us lies in the reasons for the rise of Hitler to supreme power. Germany, we have said, was almost bound to have a dictatorship, and it was bound to be a dictatorship based on some kind of socialist theory. But why, out of various possibilities, should National Socialism have been chosen? The first point in answer to this question is clearly that the party had at its head a potential dictator, a man with the personality requisite for making a leader of the people. As Napoleon had the intellectual power, the military genius and the dramatic qualities that appealed to eighteenth-century France, Louis Napoleon the romanticism of the mid-nineteenth century, and Mussolini the ruthlessness and the efficiency of the Machiavellian prince, so in Hitler it is not difficult to detect the semi-religious fervour, the mysticism, the emotionality necessary to win the affections of the land of Luther and Beethoven, along with the sentimentality of a Heine or a Mendelssohn, and the brutality of the robber barons. Above all Hitler possessed the power of oratory, and in a supreme degree that hypnotic element in his personality which is necessary to all great demagogic leaders. For, and this is the second point, although force was an element in the rise of Hitler, as of Napoleon or Mussolini, the popular will was a far more important factor. The para-military formations of the Nazi Party, the S A and the S S, the martial parades, the assassinations, the street warfare with the communists, all give the superficial impression of a conquest of power by force; but in fact it was by winning the support of the people, and through the ballot box and not the machine-gun, that Hitler was called to his high office.

Probably he did not even need to falsify the election returns. The Nazi mastery of the instrument of propaganda was an irresistible weapon. 'Propaganda', he had written in *Mein Kampf*, 'is not science. . . . The more modest its scientific ballast, and the more exclusively it addresses itself to the emotions of the masses, the more decisive will be its success. . . .' 'The more narrow-minded their ideas were', he said of the Marxists, 'the more easily were they taken up and assimilated by the masses, whose spiritual level corresponded well with the pasture it was offered."[1] Through a long and untiring agitation the Nazi Party carried on its propaganda, at mass meetings in the great towns and small gatherings in the villages throughout the countryside, whither political agitation had never penetrated before. With fortified headquarters, armed, drilled and more or less disciplined troops, great parades to 'show the flag', especially through opposition quarters, like the march through the communist section of Altona-Hamburg in July 1932, when fifteen were killed and seventy injured, the appearance and a good deal of the reality of a civil war was created; because under war conditions the particular appeal of the party was more likely to succeed.

[1] *Mein Kampf*, (ed. of 1935) I. 6, 12, pp. 196-8, 376.

Different classes aligned themselves behind the Führer for different reasons. In the beginning he had those who desired to see a socialistic reorganization of society, but who rejected the theoretical internationalism, and the actual subservience to Russian interests of the Communist Party, as well as a fair sprinkling of mere adventurers. The socialistic elements in the party creed continued to provide sufficient attraction to proletarian recruits to enable the Nazis to compete seriously for working-class allegiance with the communists. Into one or other of these parties the youth of Germany was flocking; whereas the average age of the Social Democrats in the Reichstag of 1930 was 51, that of the Communists and the Nazis was each about 37.[1] But while the Communists could offer world revolution and a new and somewhat speculative order of things to the poor and the disinherited youth of Germany, the Nazis made more concrete promises, appealing to the interests and passions of more varied sections. Above all they appealed to what Continental thinkers call the 'petty bourgeoisie', with its bitter memories of the inflation, resentful of a Social Democratic legislation which had seemed to protect the interests of the industrial workers at the expense of other classes, feeling themselves menaced with utter ruin by the development of great capitalist enterprises, and traditionally looking to the state for guidance and salvation. Pareto has some hard things to say about the German middle classes. He quotes from *Vorwärts* that 'force and struggle are two words that are not to be found in the dictionary of the German middle classes', and adds in comment, 'These classes are the most docile of all classes. Respectful,

[1] The exact figures are given in Buell, op. cit.

timid, they like nothing better than to be led blindfold'.[1] But the War and the inflation had ruined the German middle classes. If a bourgeois is, in the French definition, '*quelqu'un qui a des reserves*', the German bourgeoisie had lost this natural ballast; it had become a new proletariat, a new revolutionary class, destined to accomplish a new kind of revolution.

On the other hand, it should be remembered that the middle classes are also those in which above all nationalist, patriotic emotions are to be found. The aristocracy and the proletariat may be internationally minded. But nationalist sentiment and the middle classes rose side by side at the beginning of modern history, and nationalism became a dominant force when the middle classes achieved political supremacy in the nineteenth century. Thus the German middle classes were ready to support a movement which was at the same time nationalistic, and hostile to the great financial interests as well as to the older socialistic movements. The Nazi Party was ideally fitted to supply a response to their demands.

The importance to the Nazi movement of the support of the big industrialists and capitalists has perhaps received undue attention. Not, of course, that one should forget, though in the nature of the case their existence is hardly susceptible of proof, the heavy subsidies said to have been paid to the party by the big industrialists, anxious to overthrow the yoke of social democracy, fearing even more the onset of communism, and hoping through the re-armament of Germany to bring back prosperity to the heavy industries. Between 1928 and 1932 it is said that the annual Nazi budget was over 250 million marks.

[1] PARETO, op. cit., vol. IV, p. 1487 *n*.

Certainly the expenses of maintaining the party, with its huge private army and its costly publicity campaigns, must have been colossal. It was not from altruistic motives that Hitler, when he came to power, made Thyssen, the greatest of the Ruhr iron-masters, supreme state authority for Western Germany, and returned for the time to private hands the control of the great steel trusts, which Brüning had seized during the economic crisis. But to infer from these facts any permanent and essential alliance between the dictatorship and that classic economic individualism which has led in the end to the modern capitalist system, would be as much a mistake in Germany as in Italy. German capitalists were to find in the Nazi Party, even more than the Italians in the Fascist, a hard task-master. If private ownership of capital was allowed to survive in Germany it was only on terms of absolute subjection to the will of the state, and to a state dominated not by the economic interests of the great capitalists but by the ideology of the National Socialist Party.

A parallel may be found in the support given at a later date to Hitler by some sections of the older landed aristocracy. The suggestion has been made that it was the pressure from the coterie of East Prussian junkers, alienated by a proposal to appropriate some of their lands for small-holdings, upon the younger Hindenburg, which induced that wooden colossus, the President, in the end to abandon Brüning. But the candidate of the junkers was not Hitler, but the ineffable von Papen; and the whole policy of the Nazis, since achieving power in Germany, as later in Austria, has been bitterly hostile to the old aristocracy and its claims. The three great dictators of present day Europe all arose from the masses: towards the *ci-devants*, contempt, mixed with a little fear, has been their natural attitude. The German and Italian dictators have been willing to use them, as Napoleon used the royalists, but only for their own ends.

A third body of supporters for the Nazi coup was found in the Army. More careful, with more political wisdom, possibly, than any other element in German politics possessed, the great German General Staff had preserved its traditions and survived during a period of socialism, pacifism and compulsory disarmament, by carefully cultivating a policy of apparent political neutrality. When a general with political ambitions, like von Schleicher, became Chancellor, after the fall of von Papen, and attempted to steal the Nazi thunder by wooing left and right at the same time, the General Staff as a whole remained discreetly aloof: hence it was uncompromised by the miserable collapse of the von Schleicher clique after only a two months' struggle. The neutrality of the Army allowed Hitler to come to power, but he was not their candidate, and on more than a few occasions since he became Chancellor the Army and the Party have been in conflict. On the whole, one may say that the German Army authorities have tended to confine themselves to professional interests and have only occasionally had an important influence over government policy. The downfall of its strongest man, the Commander-in-Chief, von Fritsch, himself, showed that the General Staff was not likely to regain under Hitler that commanding influence over high policy which it formerly exercised under Wilhelm II.

A further factor in the rise to power of the National Socialists can be dismissed very briefly. Anti-Semitism undoubtedly was one of the strongest cards in their hand; 'Down with the Jews' provided a more effective rallying cry than any other. It formed the really substantial element in the racial theory: it provided a scapegoat — such as was necessary if the national pride was to be restored — for the military defeats and the financial disasters that had befallen Germany, and it revived the very old German pastime of Jew-baiting. That Germany has only been partially affected by the great movements of thought which began with the Renaissance in Western Europe, is shown in nothing so clearly as in this survival of the more barbarous side of medievalism. Indeed, anti-Semitism is such a simple and crude relic of an earlier stage in European civilization that, cleverly as it has been used by the Nazi leaders, it hardly seems to demand any more detailed analysis, except in so far as the 'racialism' of which it is a manifestation represents a further development of nationalism: but this point will require special treatment later.

Thus nationalism and socialism, even though they made use of incongruous allies, remained the two essential forces in the formation of the German dictatorship. But one of these had to come first, one had to be the end and the other merely the means. Their conflict had begun in the early days of the Nazi movement: it was continued on the bloody night of June 30th, 1934, when the Führer became for a day 'the high court of the German people' in person. Did he scorn to add to his judicial functions the role of public executioner? In the miscellaneous killings of those twenty-four hours, the fate of the leaders of the left wing showed that the aims of the socialistic members of the party, if they were realized at all, would only be realized in the train of nationalism, and that the magnification of the power of the nation was to be the real end of the German revolution.

The law of March 1933, co-ordinating the states and the Reich and abolishing in effect the federal system in Germany, and the Civil Service law of April 1933, putting all judges and other legal officers, police, municipal officials, teachers in schools and universities, workers in public enterprises, and all public officials of any kind, under the same centralized control and unified discipline — these were merely the completion of a task left unfinished by Bismarck. More characteristic of the new form of government was the law making the Nazi Party the 'Bearer' of the government, a corollary of the process by which its leader had become the Head of the State. And since the Nation is the State, and the State is the Party, and the Party is the Leader, in German National Socialism the power of the modern dictator has reached its apogee.

§4 OTHER MODERN DICTATORSHIPS IN EUROPE AND AMERICA

To turn from a study of the three great dictatorships of our own time to that of their precursors in Central and South America, and of their imitators in Europe, is to revert from highly developed to primitive types, but it is necessary to do so if we are to realize how prevalent this form of government has become during the last century.

The part of the modern world in which dictatorship first became normal was Spanish America. Here once again we see the revolutionary sources of dictatorship, and its association with the ideas of the sovereignty of the people and nationality. To discover its origins we must go back beyond the revolts against Spain by which the Latin American states were established to the liberal thought of the eighteenth century, for despite all efforts of Church and State, the attempt to preserve Spanish America as a paradise of orthodoxy, untainted by post-Reformation thought, an Eden with no intellectual serpent, free from dangerous thoughts or deviations, had failed. Creoles who visited Europe could not be kept away from the infection. The regulations for the exclusion of contemporary European literature from Spanish America broke down in practice.[1] Its introduction is especially connected with the name of the adventurer Miranda, who had fought in the War of American Independence, and had intercourse subsequently with the advanced thinkers of Europe, from Tom Paine to the Empress Catherine, had been placed in command of a revolutionary army under Dumouriez, and inhabited a Paris prison under Robespierre.

Eighteenth-century ideas were bound to have the same disturbing effect upon the literate sections in the Spanish colonies that they had already had in Europe, because the colonists also had their reasons for discontent with the existing conditions of government and society. Again, as in Europe, enlightened despotism was digging its own grave. The attempt of the new Bourbon dynasty in Spain to increase the efficiency of the government of the colonies by extending central control had caused dissatisfaction

[1] B. Moses, *The Intellectual Background of the Revolution in Spanish America, 1810-1824*, 1926, p. 210, *n*. 7.

among the colonists; while by dissolving the Order of Jesus the Spanish government had sacrificed its most reliable allies.

The Napoleonic occupation of Spain gave the revolutionaries their chance. Under Bolivar and San Martin, Paez, O'Higgins, Sucre, and the other leaders of the heroic generation, the crusading armies of independence swept the Spanish forces into the sea. Some of these leaders had hoped, as they freed province after province from the hold of the Spanish bureaucracy, to set up a free federal state, embracing all the Spanish colonies, which for nearly three centuries had lived at peace with one another within the bounds of the Empire. But South America was not able to defeat the forces of separatism, from which Washington and Hamilton had only with great difficulty saved the revolting English colonies. The first effect of the revolution was that each centre of civilized population set up its own government and proclaimed itself an independent republic.

Given the general acceptance of eighteenth-century ideology by the revolutionaries, the establishment of republican government in the new states was practically a foregone conclusion. Moreover the colonists who settled in America in the sixteenth century had brought with them medieval traditions of local self-government, while geographical considerations, the necessity for organizing local defence against hostile Indian tribes, together with the decadence of the central bureaucracy, had preserved these traditions.[1] It was hardly likely that a revolution against a corrupt and inefficient monarchy would be prejudiced in favour of that form of government. Bolivar

[1] C. JANE, *Liberty and Despotism in Spanish America*, 1929, pp. 56-7.

summed up the general opinion when he wrote, 'I believe, for my part, that the time for monarchies is over, and that so long as corruption does not succeed in stifling the love of liberty, thrones will not again return to favour in the public opinion of the world. You say that the whole earth is covered with thrones and altars; but I will reply that these ancient monuments are undermined by the powder of modernism, and that fanatics, who care little for the damage they may do, hold in their hands the fuses already lighted'.[1]

But while republican government was perhaps inevitable, this did not necessarily imply a democratic, parliamentary constitution. The leaders in the War of Independence were fighting for social and political rights for the colonists as against Spanish officials; they aimed at the removal of the social barriers between the Europeans, the creoles — of pure European blood, but born in America — and even the mestizos, of mixed blood. This was the end, and liberal political ideas were the means. When Congresses were called during the Civil Wars, it was primarily for the purpose of rallying supporters. In so far as the new republics, copying the United States, established democratic constitutions, with the object of weakening the executive power, they were fighting against the needs of the day and making certain the failure of their own institutions; for to govern at all under such conditions a President had to override constitutional forms and set up what became known as a *pronunciamento* regime.[2] There was thus in practice from the beginning a bias in favour of

[1] BOLIVAR, *Choix de lettres, discours et proclamations*, trans. C. V. Aubrun, Paris, 1934, pp. 101-2; cf. pp. 111, 175-7.

[2] BRYCE, op. cit., vol. I, p. 228.

vesting all real power in the executive and not in the legislative.

A further point to be remembered in connection with the difficulties of the new states, is that their leaders were practically without political experience. There was no governing class. Spanish America had been ruled almost exclusively by Spaniards sent out from the Mother Country: among 750 viceroys, governors, presidents and so on, the names of less than 20 creoles appear.[1] The greatest of the revolting leaders was well aware of the deficiency of his countrymen. 'We were left', Bolivar says, 'in a sort of infancy, a permanent minority in all public affairs. If we had even been allowed to control our internal affairs, to administer the country, we should have had experience of the course of public affairs and their machinery, and we should enjoy at least a personal consideration, a certain automatic respect on the part of the people, sentiments very necessary in the case of revolution.'[2] Lacking such experience, it was very unlikely that the Spanish American states would be capable of working parliamentary constitutions successfully.

Many of the leaders of the War of Independence, among them Bolivar, San Martin and Montegeadu, realized this difficulty. San Martin, in personal opinion a monarchist of liberal tendencies, when he had to issue a *Reglamento Provisional* for Peru in 1821, established a dictatorial regime under a Captain General. Montegeadu, at first a strong democrat, found himself driven from the democratic principle of the sovereignty of the people to a

[1] JANE, op. cit., p. 7.
[2] BOLIVAR, op. cit., p. 168, cf. id., pp. 53, 167, 169.

dictatorial conclusion. 'I believe', he was writing as early as 1812, 'that one of the means best adapted to our condition would be to consecrate authority in a single citizen enjoying public confidence, to make him responsible for the conduct of the army and for the execution of all measures concerning public affairs; in a word, to place no other limit to his powers than the independence of the country, leaving to his will the appointment of the persons most perfectly qualified for office in each of the branches of the administration.'[1]

The greatest and the wisest of the founders of Spanish American independence was the Liberator himself, Simon Bolivar, whose analysis of the political situation and prospects of Spanish America combines idealism with realism in a remarkable degree. Bolivar was never an unqualified democrat in his political theory. Has there ever been, he asks, a democratic government in which power and prosperity were combined with stability?[2] Men are not equal; they do not know their own interests; liberty, to quote Rousseau, is a nourishing food, but it demands a strong digestion, and Spanish America has neither the experience nor the political morality for it.[3] Do not, he warns the new republics, strive after an impossible liberty, for you will only find yourselves thrust back into an extreme tyranny.[4] Above all, remember that the sovereignty of the people is not unlimited: it must not overstep the bounds of justice, nor must it go counter to its end, the interests of the people.[5] Sovereignty, rather, must be divided, and the legislative body must not be in a

[1] MOSES, op. cit., pp. 140-1.
[2] BOLIVAR, op. cit., p. 56.
[3] id., pp. 54, 58, 60.
[4] id., p. 74.
[5] id., p. 104.

position to monopolize it to the exclusion of the executive power.[1] Nothing is more dangerous to the interests of the people, he believes, than a weak executive.[2]

Thus in theory, as in practice, Bolivar is brought to recognize the necessity for some kind of government by one man. 'Only an absolute necessity, joined to the imperative will of the people, constrained me to accept the terrible and perilous charge of *supreme dictator of the Republic*,' he said;[3] nevertheless, he accepted it. The advice he gave Bolivia, when presenting it with a constitution, shows how far in the direction of strengthening the executive he was prepared to go. He proposes the institution of a Life Presidency, and adds to it the right of the President to appoint a Vice-President, who shall be his successor, so that the strife and anarchy resulting from constant elections to the executive power shall be averted.[4] But he advocates such a great strengthening of the executive power as a means of avoiding, not of instituting an arbitrary dictatorship. 'Proscribe for ever', he pleaded to the Congress at Lima, when he laid down his dictatorial authority in 1825, a year after he had been endowed with it, 'such a fearful authority, an authority which was the tomb of Rome . . . Now that the nation has obtained internal peace and political liberty, it should permit no other authority than that of the laws.'[5]

Such sentiments expressed rather what Bolivar hoped than what he expected. The conditions under which free governments were set up in Spanish America practically imposed military dictatorship. The rule of a general,

[1] Bolivar, p. 124.
[2] id., p. 70.
[3] id., p. 49.
[4] id., pp. 109-10, 112-13.
[5] id., p. 253.

dignified with the title of President, became almost at once their normal form of government. Later, politicians, generally lawyers, entered into competition and achieved a good deal of success, but the essentially dictatorial nature of the governments remained unchanged. Their regimes were for the most part tyrannical, bloody and short. Revolutions played the part of general elections, and the more changes they brought about the more it was the same thing. Among the host of petty dictators certain ones stand out, and while no detailed treatment is possible here, or indeed comes within the purpose of the book, we may pause to say a few words on one or two of these.

The inland state of Paraguay produced in Francia and the two Lopez the most remarkable succession of dictators that even South America has seen. The first of these, Don José Gaspar Rodriguez de Francia, who preferred to be called Dr. Francia, came to power in the first place as the dominating influence in the junta which set itself up as the government in Paraguay, as soon as the revolutionaries had succeeded in expelling the Spanish authorities. A liberal and an anti-clerical, he had been dismissed from his college post for his advanced views. As a lawyer he had become known for his ability and honesty, and for his interest in the welfare of the Guarani Indians of Paraguay. In 1813 he suppressed the junta and had himself made First Consul, in 1814 he became dictator for three years and in 1816 for life. A conspiracy of 1820 was suppressed ruthlessly, but apart from this his absolute authority was unchallenged until his death in 1840.

His policy for Paraguay was one of complete isolation. 'You know', he said very early in his rule, 'what my policy has been with respect to Paraguay; that I have kept it on a system of non-intercourse with the other provinces of South America, and from contamination by that foul and restless spirit of anarchy and revolution which has more or less desolated and disgraced them all.'[1] For nearly thirty years Paraguay under Francia remained a Forbidden Country. Governed by a personal despotism which covered every branch of national activity and almost every moment of individual life, so isolated was the state and so secret the government, that it is almost impossible to form any definite opinion on its merits or defects. Carlyle, who had, in the unkind but not inappropriate language of a brother Scot, 'the admiration of most men who have passed sheltered lives, for direct action and for strong government',[2] believed intensely in Francia. 'For some thirty years', he wrote, 'he was all the government his native Paraguay could be said to have. For some six-and-twenty years he was an express Sovereign of it; for some three or some two years, a Sovereign with bared sword, stern as Rhadamanthus: through all his years and through all his days, since the beginning of him, a Man or Sovereign of iron energy and industry, of great and severe labour.'[3] Cunninghame Graham, on the other hand says, 'Those who knew Francia best, hated him bitterly, and certainly have left a picture of him almost Satanic in its malignity'.[4]

The divergence of opinion is partly resolved by the fact that, while a ruthless tyrant to the creoles and Spaniards, whose lives and property he did not spare, and who were

[1] *South American Dictators*, ed. A. C. Wilgus, 1937, p. 67.

[2] R. B. Cunninghame Graham, *Portrait of a Dictator*, 1933, pp. 35-6.

[3] T. Carlyle, *Dr. Francia* (1843).

[4] Cunninghame Graham, op. cit., p. 36.

apparently even forbidden marriage except with a half-caste or an Indian, Francia was perhaps a benevolent despot to the oppressed Indians. His ability is undoubted, as is the success with which he promoted the economic welfare of the state on the lines of self-sufficiency. It is significant that he never thought it necessary to have an army of more than 5000 men. One has a feeling that Francia could have made out a good case in his own vindication if he had ever condescended to do so. Peace and prosperity, and the protection of the native population against oppression, are not inconsiderable benefits, and the history of *El Supremo*, one suspects, might have been different if the Guarani Indians had written it. The real judgment on his policy comes in the sequel.

Francia himself lived to the age of eighty years and died in full possession of his sovereignty. After a brief interval his place was peacefully taken by Carlos Antonio Lopez, who relaxed the isolation of Paraguay and governed successfully from 1844 to 1862. Francia and Lopez between them had done much for Paraguay. They had preserved order and peace, internally and externally, had promoted the economic prosperity and progress of their subjects, and had developed an intensely patriotic national spirit among them. The greatest achievement of Lopez, however, was the building up of the strongest army in South America, which in 1862 passed into the hands of his son, Francisco Solano Lopez. Now was seen what the rule of the two dictators had done in Paraguay. 'The rule of Francia and that of Carlos Antonio Lopez had reduced the Paraguayan to the state of a mere automaton. All individuality had been crushed out of him', says Cunninghame Graham. 'It left him helpless in the hands of the younger Lopez, mere cannon fodder for his ambitious schemes.'[1] For Francisco Solano had been to Europe, had read of Napoleon I and had seen the Second Empire. He dreamed of the establishment of a Napoleonic Empire in South America, and in the endeavour to realize it flung his little state recklessly into war with overwhelming forces.

This war has been represented as the gesture of an insane tyrant, defying the world, and followed by an ignorant and backward nation, which had been taught to obey its rulers blindly since the time of the Jesuit Missions, which had no means of discovering what was happening beyond its frontiers apart from the official news issued by the tyrant, and which believed that its enemies were intent on destroying the Paraguayan state, and rooting out every individual Paraguayan. So far as concerns the people of Paraguay this explanation is doubtless correct, but it hardly explains adequately the motives of their ruler, who was more of a villain than a madman. Francisco Solano Lopez had little real ability, but he was a man of immense will-power, he was industrious, and he was excessively ambitious. He had an exaggerated idea of the importance of his little state, but in the circumstances of South America, particularly granted the anarchic conditions in the Argentine Confederation, success would not have been impossible to an abler man. Lopez by his incapacity wasted the opportunity. Such is the opinion of the historian of the origins of the Paraguayan War: 'Paraguay has for too long been regarded as a small country fighting against terrible odds. The truth is that for a brief period a potential Prussia had appeared in South America; a

[1] Cunninghame Graham, op. cit., p. 74.

powerful war machine, despotically controlled, threatened the nascent liberties made possible by Caseros [the battle in which Rosas, dictator of the Argentine, was overthrown]. A candid examination of the facts suggests that Lopez had many chances in his favour when he gambled the future of his country. Had his political and military intelligence been in any way worthy of his iron will, unflagging energy and incomparable tenacity, he would probably have destroyed the liberal revolution in the Rio de la Plata, disrupted Argentine and organized in the great valley a new state deriving its vitality from the principles that had taken root in the Paraguay of the Jesuits and the old regime — principles that Dr. Francia had guarded from the contagion of the "anarchic demagogy" of Buenos Aires and her Unitarian apostles'.[1]

But this apparent rationality only applied to the beginning of the war. As it progressed the government of Lopez became such a frantic tyranny that it almost seemed as if he were competing with the hostile armies to discover which could be the more fatal to his unfortunate subjects. In four years nearly the whole adult male population of the country had perished; probably less than a quarter of the total population survived the war. Yet from defeat to defeat the infatuated Paraguayans fought for this insane sadist until they were approaching the point of extermination. If Francia could then have seen his country might he not have thought that he had taught his people too well the virtues of obedience and loyalty?

Compared with the younger Lopez every other South American dictator, even the famous Rosas, pales in hue, and seems a moderate man. Among the other dictators

[1] PELHAM BOX, *The Origins of the Paraguayan War*, 1927, p. 289.

the most remarkable is Porfirio Diaz, who ruled Mexico for thirty-five years. Nominally he was a President, governing under a republican constitution, and regular elections were held, when, in case no one else troubled to vote and the ballot boxes were found completely empty, a few soldiers would be dispatched with voting papers to deposit in them.[1] Porfirio Diaz was a very efficient and energetic tyrant, under whom Mexico made considerable economic progress. The great interest of his government is that it presents one of the few examples in the modern world of a dictatorship working itself out. After thirty-five years of absolute power, not unpunctuated by revolts, a final revolution broke out in 1911, which Diaz, who might have suppressed it in his younger days, was unable to quell. At the age of eighty he fled the country, leaving it a prey to the most ferocious civil strife, in which social was added to political revolution.

Out of a welter of bloodshed emerged in the end an authoritarian left-wing government, controlled by a National Revolutionary Party. The extent to which this is a genuine 'proletarian' government is still a matter of controversy: that it is authoritarian cannot be doubted. It has been alleged that behind the nominal government of the revolutionary party has been a series of barely concealed personal dictatorships, but this one is hardly in a position to prove or disprove. It cannot be questioned that the revolutionary authorities appear to have done more for the material well-being of the oppressed native Mexicans than their Spanish rulers did for them in four centuries. To the nationalism of most South American dictatorships the existing Mexican government adds a

[1] BRYCE, op. cit., vol. II, p. 561.

fairly advanced degree of socialism, if we may use the term here in a very general sense to imply social amelioration under strict governmental control, but it is as yet too early to say whether a similar socialistic element will appear in other Latin American republics — reproducing thus some features of the modern European development — or whether the co-existence of large semi-servile Indian classes with a Spanish or mestizo governing class will prevent elsewhere this development.

While Mexico presents certain interesting peculiarities, different but in their way equally interesting, individual characteristics are to be found in the evolution of the one Portuguese state in Latin America, Brazil, where until 1889 the self-effacing wisdom of Pedro II preserved monarchical institutions. When the monarch was eventually, with the expression of mutual regrets and regards, given his *congé* by the Brazilians, he was replaced by an oligarchy, the various permutations of which have since governed the country. In recent years the struggle of the other states against the monopoly of the Presidency by Saõ Paolo and Minas Geraes has led to the proclamation of the rule of President Vargas as a sort of dictatorship, but the situation in Brazil is still too obscure for any conclusions to be drawn from this development. The long absence of dictatorship from Brazil is the really significant fact.

It is not for us here to venture on any general summing-up. The most interesting feature of South American dictatorships is that they provide us with examples of a historic development practically unaffected by theorization, while they show the effect of political emancipation on nations lacking, as Bolivar and his colleagues in the work of liberation had realized, the experience and the other requisites necessary for the successful working of a parliamentary system.

Similar results were to be expected when political revolution faced many of the lesser, as well as some of the greater states of Europe, with the problem of self-government after 1918. Conditions in the different European states have varied so greatly, however, that it is hardly possible to make any general statement. A careful study of the earlier history, as well as of contemporary political conditions, would be necessary to explain why Valdemaras was for a time successful in establishing a dictatorship in Lithuania, whereas the Lapua movement in Finland failed, and Estonia contented itself with strengthening the position of the President. Ephemeral Balkan dictators like Pangalos in Greece and Tsankoff in Bulgaria would require explanation. The military dictatorship of Pilsudski in Poland, the mild *pronunciamento* regime, as it might almost be termed, of Primo de Rivera in Spain, the attempts to combine monarchy with dictatorship by Alexander in Yugo-Slavia and Carol in Rumania, the unsuccessful clerical dictatorship of Dollfuss and Schuschnigg in Austria, and that of Dr. Salazar in Portugal, the dazzling career of Kemal Ataturk — all these arise out of the special circumstances of the states concerned and each has its own peculiar features.

We have not the space for a detailed study of any of these, nor the extent of knowledge, for each would require its own separate explanation. But we may end this section with a provisional statement of two alternative conclusions. It must be admitted either that dictatorship as a form of government is extremely contagious, and that its development in one or two great countries is likely to draw their neighbours in the same direction, or else we must come to the conclusion that European civilization has now reached a stage in which the states included in it are peculiarly liable to adopt dictatorial political systems. These two conclusions, are, of course, not mutually exclusive, and both may well be true.

CHAPTER VI

THE DEVELOPMENT OF THE TOTALITARIAN STATE

§ I THE RISE OF THE THEORY OF NATIONALISM

UP to the present our attention has been concentrated on the history of dictatorship, without any attempt to draw general conclusions. We cannot pass directly to these because, functioning in different periods, and in states of very different types, a form of government cannot be expected to exhibit uniform traits. Hence it would be profitless to examine dictatorship in the void. Its operation is conditioned by its political environment, and if we wish to understand how it works in the modern world it will be necessary first to examine the nature of the modern state.

One of the most obvious features of the modern state is the principle of popular sovereignty, but this has already been discussed in an earlier chapter and is, moreover, not confined to the modern state, although it has doubtless received a great extension in more recent times. If one were seeking for the peculiarities of the state at the present day one would not think of this in the first place. Its new and yet fundamental characteristic is surely that it is thought of a *nation* state, based on the principle of nationalism, to which therefore we must primarily direct our attention.

Since a great danger in studying either political science or the history of political ideas lies in the use of terms without a clear understanding of what they mean, our initial problem is one of definition. The fact that the term nation, and its various derivatives, have become words of everyday use adds to the difficulty, because in consequence many different shades of significance have accreted to them, while they have at the same time acquired an emotional connotation which is likely to defy definition. Attempts to define a nation are innumerable, and in the nature of things none can be absolutely final; for the nations are not fixed units, but historical products, born out of the conflicting forces of the past, living their lives out amidst the political and spiritual turmoil of the present, and liable at any time in the future to be transmuted by the ebb and flow of circumstance into new forms. If we turn from the nation to the conception of nationality we find that as a psychological fact it is equally difficult of definition. Moreover it is a matter of degree and is not necessarily exclusive. Thus a French Canadian — a Canadian, as he would call himself — may have to a varying extent the consciousness that he belongs to three distinct nationalities. Fortunately it is not essential for us to attempt a definition of either nation or nationality: it is enough to remark that, whatever their precise meaning, they clearly imply something different from what is understood by the term state. The Austrian Empire before 1914 was a state: certainly we should not call it a nation.

Our particular concern here is with the nation state, with the particular association, that is, between the state and the nation which we call nationalism, and in this connection the problem is simpler: at least we can say what kind of thing nationalism is. It is a theory, or rather — since the basis of the theory, though many attempts have been made to rationalize it, is emotional — a belief. We may borrow the definition given by a distinguished historian in 1920. 'Nationalism', Dr. Gooch wrote, 'denotes the resolve of a group of human beings to share their fortunes, and to exercise exclusive control over their own actions. Where such a conscious determination exists, there should be a state, and there will be no abiding peace until there is a state.'[1] If we are considering nationalism as a political force in the contemporary world, it is in the corollary that the essence of the belief is to be found. Whatever a nation may be, it is the association of nation and state that has significance — the belief that, in the words of John Stuart Mill, 'One hardly knows what any division of the human race should be free to do, if not to determine, with which of the various collective bodies of human beings they choose to associate themselves'.[2] As another student of nationalism puts it, 'The nation is a state in process of growth, the state is a nation that has realized itself'.[3]

It is too often forgotten that these apparent truisms enshrine a principle that is the product of merely the last century and a half of human history. The words nationality and nationalism are hardly to be found in their modern sense before the nineteenth century, except in a few isolated examples.[4] There is no need to prove that such a belief

[1] G. P. Gooch, *Nationalism*, 1920, p. 8.

[2] J. S. Mill, *Considerations on Representative Government*, 3rd ed., 1865, p. 297.

[3] B. Lavergne, *Le principe des Nationalités et les guerres*, 1921, p. 16.

[4] cf. G. Weill, *L'Europe du XIXe siècle et l'idée de nationalité*, 1938, Introduction, § 1, pp. 2-6.

as nationalism did not exist in classical times. The fact was not so much that the Greeks and Romans were unacquainted with the idea of the nation, as that they *preferred*, it has been said, the city state; and from that they leapt to Empire without ever going through the intermediate stage of nationality. The organization of the barbarian invaders who disrupted the Roman Empire was tribal rather than national, and only towards the end of the Middle Ages do we detect the beginnings of nationality. Signs appear at this time that nations are crystallizing out of medieval society in Western Europe. The Hundred Years War produced after a long time a pretty clear differentiation of English and French; Machiavelli wished to see everywhere united under a single rule where the tongue of Dante was spoken; the Conciliar Movement had its nationalistic features. But two forces more powerful at the time prohibited the development of this new idea of nationality. Religious passions, rising out of the conflict of Reformation and Counter-Reformation, for a while submerged other loyalties; and when these were dying down men turned as to a saviour to the absolute prince, whose sovereignty left little room or need for any unifying force other than the classical idea of patriotism — loyalty to the state and its ruler, not to the nation.

Towards the end of the eighteenth century there appear signs that the European mind was awakening to the principle of nationality, which had lain dormant since the end of the Middle Ages. It is hardly necessary to go over this ground again; elsewhere we have tried to trace this movement in the years before the Revolution through its reflection in such contemporary thinkers as Burke and Rousseau. Herder, in Germany, was at the same time also developing the idea of the nation, though his conception of nationality was as an ethical and cultural principle, not necessarily related to the political state.[1] With the French Revolution we reach the age when nationality can turn into nationalism, which is soon to become the dominant political force, because, the monarch being now removed, the state can identify itself with the nation and patriotism swell into nationalism.

It is important to note, however, that at the end of the eighteenth century two rival conceptions of the nation stood face to face. The one, anticipated in some respects by Montesquieu, found its fullest development in Burke, for whom the nation became 'a moral essence', residing, not in the political authority of the central government, but rather in the various subordinate bodies and corporations. 'The body politic of France', Burke wrote in the *Letters on a Regicide Peace*, 'existed in the majesty of its throne, in the dignity of its nobility, in the honour of its gentry, in the sanctity of its clergy, in the reverence of its magistracy, in the weight and consideration due to its landed property in the several bailliages, in the respect due to its moveable substance represented by the corporations of the kingdom.'[2] A reactionary and undemocratic view, this; but we must allow, on the other hand, that, as Montesquieu saw, all these intermediate bodies in the state were so many barriers to despotism. 'In all these old countries', Burke goes on, 'the state has been made to the people, and not the people conformed to the state . . . This comprehensive scheme virtually produced a degree

[1] R. Aris, *A History of Political Thought in Germany from* 1789 *to* 1815, 1936, p. 243.

[2] Burke, *Works*, ed. of 1872, vol. v, pp. 219-20.

of personal liberty in forms the most adverse to it. That liberty was found, under monarchies styled absolute, in a degree unknown to the ancient commonwealths. From hence the powers of all our modern states meet, in all their movements, with some obstruction.'[1] This view of nationality, as implying and indeed founded upon a radical separation of powers, could never become a basis for dictatorial government.

The rival and more successful theory had its sources in the writings of the *philosophes* and the physiocrats, and reached triumphant expression in the work which inaugurated the Revolution — *Qu'est ce que le Tiers État?* by the abbé Sieyès. The basic idea of Sieyès, that the nation exists by natural right and is the master of its own destiny, we have already dealt with in an earlier chapter, where we endeavoured to show that he takes over intact the claim of the despots to absolute sovereignty and applies it to the nation. His importance lies not in the profundity of his ideas, but in the fact that he was merely putting into words what a large part of France was thinking.

A greater than Sieyès, J.-J. Rousseau, has sometimes been put forward as the real founder of this 'absolute' nationalism, and it cannot be denied that an interpretation — perhaps a misinterpretation — of the theory of the General Will played a certain part in the development of the idea. But the writings in which Rousseau's ideas of nationality are to be found are the *Corsica* and the *Poland*, and in these, although the claims of the nation are put very high, his affiliations are rather with Burke and Montesquieu than with the absolutist school of political thinkers. Sieyès, himself, denied that Rousseau had done anything

[1] BURKE, *Works*, ed. of 1872, vol. V, p. 254.

to establish the true 'principles of the social art'.[1] Certainly, Sieyès's view that the nation's will is expressed through representatives and determined by the vote of the majority is the exact opposite of the principle of Rousseau, who holds that the General Will cannot be represented and that it is in no sense to be identified with the will of the majority. Rousseau, for his part, makes it as plain as he can in the *Social Contract* that he is writing for the small city state of the ancient world, represented in his own day by Geneva, and that in his view the great nation state is incapable of having good institutions. Leaving Rousseau on one side, however, it is clear that from Sieyès and the revolutionaries a thorough-going theory of nationalism, associated with state absolutism, can be obtained. Indeed, one would have believed that the idea of national sovereignty could know no extremer expression than it found in the writings of Sieyès and the practice of the French Revolution, were it not for the developments of our own day, which have made all earlier nationalisms seem the modest essays of mere tyros.

Whatever its theoretical origins, the principle of national sovereignty was undoubtedly first put into practice by the French Revolution and bore its first fruit in the imperialist dictatorship of Napoleon. It did not appear at one bound, of course. The initial enthusiasm of the revolutionaries is more closely associated with the idea of citizenship than with the principle of nationality properly speaking. For Robespierre the *patrie* was the community where one was a citizen and a member of the sovereign: it was defined, that is, in terms of the state rather than of the nation and was still linked more closely with the classical ideal of

[1] G. G. van Deusen, *Sieyès: his life and his nationalism*, 1932, p. 27, *n.* 12.

patriotism than with the romantic principle of nationality. The latter found its immediate line of development rather in the opposition roused outside France by the progress of the Revolutionary and Napoleonic armies. The revival of the Prussian national spirit after Jena, the revolt of the Spanish against Napoleon, General Yorck at Warsaw disobeying the orders of the King of Prussia in the superior interests of the nation, Leipzig, battle of the nations — these are episodes in a well-known story. Although at the Congress of Vienna the claims of the nationalities to political independence went unrecognized, the full-blown modern theory of nationalism had already been achieved. Among the revolutionaries Sieyès had gone a long way towards it; the process was completed, in the ranks of reaction, by the German romantics.

A link between the two is provided by Fichte, who began as a disciple of the Jacobins and ended as a prophet of German nationalism. We are thus brought, by a somewhat different route, to the conclusion of Meinecke, that the appearance of an age of nationalist thought, immediately succeeding to the cosmopolitan idealism of the eighteenth century, was no mere coincidence, but that the one was a natural and logical development from the other.[1] Meinecke will not allow that eighteenth-century thought was decadent and exhausted and that nationalism rose to fill the gap it had left: on the contrary he claims that for long the two systems of thought were closely and inseparably associated.[2] Thus from the individualist teaching of the previous century Fichte derived his condemnation of the intermediate powers in the state; from its cosmopoli-

[1] F. Meinecke, *Weltbürgertum und Nationalstaat*, 6th ed., 1922, pp. 9-10, 19.
[2] id., pp. 125-6.

tanism, his idea that the task of each nation is to spread its own particular excellence as widely as possible until it has incorporated the whole human race in itself.[1] But it must be admitted that Fichte does not stop at this; though theoretically he may be integrating them in a higher synthesis, in practice he comes very near a simple negation of both the individualist and the cosmopolitan principles. 'Looking at the thing as it is, in truth', he writes, 'one finds that the individual does not exist; that he cannot count for anything but must disappear completely; and that the group alone exists and it alone must be considered as existent.'[2] As for cosmopolitanism, it can hardly survive the competition of the idea of the Germans as the *Urfolk*, the chosen race.[3]

The popularity of Fichte in post-war Germany, and his influence over modern German thought, is well known. There is hardly any element in the nationalist faith of present-day Germany which is not to be found in Fichte — the admiration for the Machiavelli of the *Prince*; the subjection, if necessary by force, of the individual to the state; politically, the subordination of legislative and judicial powers to the will of the executive; economically, the ideal of the self-sufficient state, with frontiers closed to trade; in religion, the scheme for a nationalist church; the ideal of education for the service of the nation. Only the present extreme doctrine of race is absent. In spite of all this we should be wrong if we took Fichte as the terminus of modern nationalist thinking, if only, as we shall see below, because of his failure to maintain the principle of the

[1] F. MEINECKE, *Weltbürgertum und Nationalstaat*, 6th ed., 1922, pp. 104-5.
[2] Quoted by ENGELBRECHT, op. cit., p. 85.
[3] id., p. 117.

autonomy of politics. Although in his later years he seems little more than a political propagandist, he never shook off completely his earlier philosophical bent. In theory, at least, ethics retains its primacy over politics for him: as he could not, Meinecke concludes, build up his ideal of the nation from the sad actuality of his own day, he had perforce to derive it from a universal ethical ideal.[1]

Similarly with the next great thinker in the history of nationalist thought, Mazzini, for whom the nation is above all a spiritual unity. Whereas in Fichte and other thinkers of the German romantic age nationalism had already come to be associated with authoritarian government inside the state, for Mazzini it is linked with the idea of freedom. Mazzini, in fact, is a nationalist with a difference. In the name of nationality he denounces 'the narrow spirit of *Nationalism*', and 'the stupid presumption on the part of each people that they are capable of solving the political, social, and economic problems alone; their forgetfulness of the great truth that the cause of the peoples is one; that the cause of the Fatherland must lean upon Humanity . . . and that the aim of our warfare . . . is the holy Alliance of Nations'.[2] It is ironic to think that in the face of such sayings modern Italians can yet appeal to Mazzini as the prophet of the fascist state.

It was not Mazzini, however, who triumphed in Italy, but Cavour, while in Germany the idea of nationalism was captured by Bismarck. Treitschke, for whom the principle of national sovereignty was as strong as it had been for the French revolutionaries, but who at the same time carried on and completed the dissociation of the idea

[1] MEINECKE, op. cit., p. 127.
[2] MAZZINI, *Faith and the Future*, preface to ed. of 1850.

of the unity of the nation from the idea of political liberty, is the prophet of the new dispensation. His views involved a partial withdrawal from the revolutionary identification of the state with the nation and a return to the eighteenth-century emphasis on the political unit. 'The natural tendency', Treitschke admits, 'is that the conceptions "Nation" and "State" should coincide with one another. That is the instinct of all great nations, but history shows us how remote this has been from actuality.' In this respect he was a realist: 'Almighty God did not put the various nationalities into separate glass cases, like a collection of biological specimens; and we can see for ourselves what transformations have been effected among them in the course of history. Nationality is not a settled and permanent thing.' As H. W. C. Davis observed, for Treitschke a real community of interests and the unifying force of the central government are more important bonds than the 'sentimental ties of common descent and a common mother-tongue'.[1]

The *realpolitik* of the Prussian state, put to the task of unifying the German nation, marked a reaction from the idealistic nationalism of a Mazzini or even a Fichte, and a step towards a more frankly Machiavellian view of politics. But the national idea was too strong to be side-tracked in this way. It returned minus its idealism and shorn of its non-aggressive implications, in the imperialism of the later nineteenth century; and as it merged with the idea of the state more completely,[2] it took over the

[1] H. W. C. DAVIS, *The Political Thought of Heinrich von Treitschke*, 1914, pp. 185-6.

[2] cf. BLUNTSCHLI, 'The Nation came into being with the creation of the State . . . we may say, "no State, no Nation".' (J. K. BLUNTSCHLI, *The Theory of the State*, trans. from the 6th ed., Oxford, 1885, II, 2, p. 86.)

principles of blood and iron with which the latter had lately reasserted itself. Acton truly said that the nationalist movement in Germany and Italy had opened a new age for Machiavelli.[1] No longer could the Mazzinian ideal of the nations of the world working in harmonious partnership for the common good of humanity be upheld. As we shall see later, a misconceived Darwinism having taken the place of the Newtonian thought of the eighteenth century, from the celestial harmony of the spheres mankind descended to the bellowings of the jungle. The law of nature came back, but not the nature of Wordsworth or the *Elegy in a Country Churchyard*. 'The State is not a violet blooming in the shade',[2] remarked Treitschke, somewhat superfluously. In the 'eternal conflict of separate states' lay for him 'the beauty of history'.[3]

Nationalism, thus interpreted, implies a kind of moral indifference, which replaces the ideas of right and wrong by the simple conception of power. It supplies a force, greater probably, and certainly more irresponsible and uncontrollable, than any other in the contemporary world of politics. During the nineteenth century it was taken for granted that the emancipation of the subject nationalities automatically implied the extension of liberty. More recently, nationalism has proved the handmaid of tyrants. In fact no assumption that it is necessarily bound up with any political system is justified by the evidence of history.

To our description of nationalism it is necessary to make an important addition, however, for a further

[1] ACTON, *History of Freedom and other essays*, 1907, p. 225.
[2] DAVIS, op. cit., p. 177. [3] id., pp. 153, 155.

element which has appeared in the nationalist faith has modified seriously this political impartiality. Historians of nationalism have pointed out that while in Western Europe the nation is in a sense the creation of the state, in Central and Eastern Europe the state has been created by the nation.[1] This is particularly true of the nations which have emerged from the former Austro-Hungarian Empire. Modern nationalism was here cultural in its origins; the nations looked back to their medieval sources, revived their historical traditions and ancient customs, and brought again into repute their national languages and literature. History was truly, in the words of Seeley, 'the school of patriotism'.[2] By such forces were built up many of the new nation states of Europe, and the cultural ideal of nationality rapidly spread to other Central and Eastern European countries, though it did not stop there.

Modern nationalism is thus seen to be the meeting-point of a number of historical movements. The idea of patriotic loyalty to the state became transformed during the revolutionary era into the political principle of nationalism, and to this was added later the association of a nation with a *Kultur*. This new idea of the nation took the place of the revolutionary idea of the people, the essential difference between them being the presence of certain individualistic and utilitarian elements in the idea of the people, which were absent from that of the nation. The bond uniting the people was the common welfare, whereas the nation was held together by history, descent, language, culture, in any case by non-utilitarian

[1] cf. C. A. McCartney, *National States and National Minorities*, 1934.

[2] Seeley, *Lectures and Essays*, 1870, X, *The Teaching of Politics*, p. 298.

ties. When the theory of sovereignty, associated with the idea of the people by the French revolutionaries, as we saw in the second chapter, was transferred to the nation, it lost its last limitation, because it ceased to have any implied connection with the principle of the common good. Thus the ideas of state, people, nation and sovereignty finally meet: to the state, now based on the great emotional force of nationalism, is attributed the sovereignty of the people, while its interests are conceived in terms of power and prestige borrowed from the despotic pre-revolutionary state; and of both these, and not merely of the idea of absolute sovereignty, is dicatorship in modern times the heir.

§ 2 THE TOTALITARIAN CONCEPTION OF THE STATE

Nationalism is usually conceived under its external aspects. From its beginning, when it took the form of a reaction against foreign aggression, to its ultimate transformation into imperialism, its history has been written in terms of its relations with foreign powers; it would almost seem as though nations have only been able to define themselves through their enmities. But the association of nationalism with the idea of popular sovereignty, which is evident in the origins of both during the revolutionary period in France and Europe, brought with it internal as well as external implications. The significance of the cleavage between the nationalism of Burke and that of Sieyès or Fichte becomes apparent in this connection. It was the latter — through which the nations of the nineteenth century became the heirs of the benevolent despots of the eighteenth — which prevailed, and it proved that absolutism is not a monopoly of kings. This internal development of nationalism is primarily responsible for the appearance of the kind of state which is now called totalitarian, and which is particularly associated with dictatorship. It might be termed the absolute state.

'When I speak of the absolute state', writes Walter Lippmann, 'I do not refer to the constitutional arrangement of powers within the state. It is of no importance in this connection whether the absolute power of the state is exercised by a king, a landed aristocracy, bankers and manufacturers, professional politicians, soldiers or a modern majority of voters . . . A state is absolute in the sense which I have in mind when it claims the right to a monopoly of all forces within the community, to make war, to make peace, to conscript life, to tax, to establish and disestablish property, to define crime, to punish disobedience, to control education, to supervise the family, to regulate personal habits, and to censor opinions.'[1]

When, however, Lippmann goes on to say that, 'The modern state claims all these powers, and in the matter of theory there is no real difference in the size of the claim between communists, fascists, and democrats',[2] one is compelled to protest that this is an undue simplification of the problem, unless he wishes to identify what he calls democratic theory exclusively with an extreme brand of Jacobinism. Most modern theories of the state, it is true, assert the autonomy of the community, but to

[1] W. Lippmann, *A Preface to Morals*, 1929, p. 80. [2] id.

maintain that in practice, from the point of view of absolutism, all states are on a level, would be to disregard obvious facts. One may believe that there is an historical connection between democracy and dictatorship, while at the same time holding that if we base ourselves rather on the ground of practice than on that of theory, the differentiation between the liberal parliamentary state and the dictatorial state is patent. Both are nationalistic in their external relations, but in the latter the spirit of nationalism, being turned in upon itself, makes the theoretical absolutism a practical reality.

It might be said, of course, that the liberal state has never been democratic, but this raises a question which we do not wish to pursue, as we have up to the present been able to find no clear definition of democracy, apart from Aristotle's, which is inapplicable to modern political conditions. Modern democracy is recognizable as a theory, or rather as a number of theories, not very satisfactorily co-ordinated; it might be described as an attitude of mind, for it implies a whole nexus of mental dispositions; but as a practical political fact, a form of government, we are by no means certain what it involves. Therefore, in studying the characteristics of the totalitarian dictatorship of to-day we do not propose to compare it with a hypothetical democratic state, but with a kind of state which we know and understand — the liberal parliamentary state of the nineteenth century.

From this comparison we can see what is the essential distinction between the two: the liberal state is individualistic in its political principle, while the totalitarian state proclaims itself as organic. Until recently the organic idea of the state was no more than a theory, but the progress of what we have called the internal aspect of nationalism has produced a vigorous attempt to transfer this theory into practice, and of this attempt totalitarianism is the result. Here, however, we are making a bald assertion, for which we must in the following pages attempt to provide both elaboration and proof.

Although the organic conception of the state developed, during the last century, in close connection with the idea of national sovereignty, it must be clearly distinguished from the pure theory of sovereignty, which in itself does not necessarily imply either the national or the organic principle. The example of Hobbes is sufficient to show that the extremest assertion of political sovereignty might be erected upon an uncompromisingly individualistic basis; but this merely proves that Hobbes's *Leviathan* is in this respect hardly relevant to present-day conditions, and that it is not the mere fact of state absolutism which is the essential characteristic of the modern state, but the nature of that absolutism. For Hobbes the commands of Leviathan are the dictates of a ruler above and external to the individual. The triumph of the theory of the sovereignty of the people brought with it the conception of government as the embodiment of an authority not merely accepted by, but in some sense identifiable with the will of the people itself, and this was the first step towards the organic theory.

This first stage was the work of the Contract school. Already in Locke the state, instead of being something forced on individuals by an authority external to themselves, has become the result of their own free choice. In Rousseau, with whom contractual thought culminates, the state is much closer to the individual, for, once created, it becomes an intrinsic element in the individual's own psychological make-up. He goes a long way towards emancipating it from any limitations other than those implied in the terms of the contract itself, but the conception of the self-determining individual still remains a basic element in his thought. For Rousseau the state is prior to political man, but not to the individual, the natural man, with whom he starts, and to transfer man from the state of nature to the state of society he still requires a social contract, the terms of which provide a limitation on the power of the state.

The alternative development in eighteenth-century thought is represented by Burke, who abandons the contractual theory altogether, and accepts the state as a natural fact, but for whom it remains by its very nature subject to natural or divine law. Thus at the end of the eighteenth century the two most significant political thinkers take opposing paths. Rousseau sacrifices to a considerable extent the control of Natural Law but keeps the Contract, while Burke abandons the Contract, but upholds the authority of Natural Law. Such a summary is inevitably an undue simplification, but it conveys fairly adequately their general position. Neither can be said to put forward an organic theory of the state, though in different ways each is moving towards it.[1]

For a further advance we have to look not to England or France but to Germany, and it is significant that the thinker in whom we can see most clearly the trend towards the organic theory is also one of the founders of nationalist

[1] I have dealt with this point in greater detail elsewhere, and therefore I feel able to dismiss it rather summarily here. cf. COBBAN, *Edmund Burke and the Revolt against the Eighteenth Century*, 1929, pp. 89-91; *Rousseau and the Modern State*, 1934, pp. 136-9.

thought. Fichte appears in the *Principles of Natural Right* (1796-7) as a wholehearted disciple of the contractual school; but in his later writings, concurrently with his advance towards nationalism, he moves, as Gierke points out,[1] in the direction of an organic theory of society, though he never achieves a complete expression of this.

Fichte's 'Absolute Form of the State' echoes Rousseau's General Will — 'Where all the powers of all men are called into activity for the necessary purpose of the whole community, each individual binds all others just in so far as he is bound by them; and each individual is thus at once a complete Citizen and a complete Subject.'[2] He breaks away from Rousseau, however, in seeing this idea of the state in process of realization in his own day;[3] and in recognizing the sovereignty of the state without the rigorous conditions imposed by Rousseau. If all of Fichte's rather scattered observations on the state could be taken together, we should have something like an approximation to an organic conception of the state. But, on the one hand, his individualism never completely disappears, and on the other hand, he does not recognize the complete autonomy of politics. On the whole, though exceptions may be found, he tends to exclude the spheres of religion, philosophy and virtue from the area of state authority, and, for him, as a disciple of eighteenth-century thought, the nation, if it is to triumph, must express the rule of reason and a supra-national system of ethics. The emancipation of the nation state from every

[1] GIERKE, op. cit., ed. Barker, vol. I, pp. 133-4.
[2] *Works of J. G. Fichte*, trans. W. Smith, 1889, vol. II, p. 170.
[3] id., vol. II, p. 169.

form of spiritual or material limitation is thus still far from complete.

On the purely philosophical ground this process does not, and perhaps never can, reach finality. Hegel, the high priest of idealism, attributes all that he possibly can to the philosophical idea of the state. 'The state is the divine idea as it exists on earth.' 'All the worth which the human being possesses — all spiritual reality, he possesses only through the state.'[1] Such citations could be multiplied many times. But even so, Hegel's state, however closely it approaches to the Kingdom of Prussia, always remains sufficiently the Kingdom of God on earth not to be completely identifiable with any earthly kingdom. His philosophical theory of the state cannot in the full, scientific sense of the word, be described as an organic theory. A modern Hegelian, the Cambridge philosopher McTaggart, has emphasized the absence from Hegel of the description of society as an organism, and the association in his philosophy of the idea of a closer unity of the whole with that of an intenser individuality in the members.[2] The true lesson of the philosophy of Hegel, says McTaggart, is that earthly society can never be an adequate end for man. 'Each of us is more than the society which unites us, because there is in each of us the longing for a perfection which that society can never realize.'[3]

References to the state as an organism, although in somewhat vague terms, are to be found in most of the German thinkers of the Romantic period. The conception

[1] ENGELBRECHT, op. cit., p. 89.

[2] J. E. McTAGGART, *Studies in Hegelian Cosmology*, 2nd ed., 1918, ch. vii, § 190, pp. 178-9.

[3] id., ch. vii, § 202, p. 193.

is particularly evident in Schliermacher, who is interesting because he consciously associates the idea of organism with the national idea.[1] It is carried into absurd detail by Bluntschli later, who writes that nations are 'organic beings, and as such are subject to the natural laws of organic life. In the history of their development the same stages may be distinguished as in the life of individuals'.[2] Bluntschli's political theory might be described as anthropomorphic: he is particularly insistent on the masculine character of the state, the church, on the other hand, being feminine. Here, and even more in the school of social psychologists that believed in the group mind, the abandonment of a philosophical basis and the dominance of ideas derived from other sources becomes patent.

One can see that though political philosophy approaches nearer and nearer to a fully organic theory of society, yet in the nature of things the process can never reach completion in the realm of philosophy, because the philosophical theory of the state is never able to emancipate itself completely from the theory of ethics, and ethics can never cut itself adrift at the same time from the conception of a universal law and from the claims of the individual conscience. But during the course of the last century philosophy has sunk into the background and with it the attempt to give an ethical basis to the theory of the state has been abandoned. The most significant characteristic of nineteenth-century thought is the disappearance of the autonomy of ethics, and in the place of ethics has been put natural science: the new religion of science, it was thought, could provide its own ethical

[1] ARIS, op. cit., p. 301.
[2] BLUNTSCHLI, op. cit., II, 2, p. 81.

principles. Leibnitz, with his 'whatever is, is right', was at last justified. The application of a misinterpretation of the scientific hypothesis of the survival of the fittest, in a field in which it is really irrelevant, produces the true organic theory of the state. By being translated out of the language of philosophy into terms of science the idea of the nation state is at last able to become organic in the fullest sense. The nature of the biologist, red in tooth and claw, usurps the place of ethics, and in this background the nation state finds its true explanation.

Here, too, is a partial explanation of the more recent development of nationalism into racialism. A nation is an historic or ideal unit, and therefore quite different from the organic entities with which biological science deals. A more materialistic conception was needed as a basis for a new pseudo-Darwinism, and it was found in the race, conceived as a biological species. In practice, however, this became in Germany a kind of biological Manichæism. The so called Aryan race, reaching its highest point in the Germans, embodied the principle of good, and the Jews that of evil. It might be said that if the Jews had not existed, Hitler would have had to invent them. The population of Europe, and particularly of Germany, is of so mixed an ancestry that the difficulties in the way of establishing general racial characteristics have proved almost insuperable. Lacking positive features, therefore, race has had to be defined by negative ones. The presence in Europe of a Semitic people, possessing for the most part certain clearly marked physical characteristics of its own, made racialism a political possibility, because it provided an alien element by contrast with which non-Jewish peoples could be made nation- and race-conscious.

The scientific absurdity of racialism is easy to demonstrate but quite irrelevant to the issue. Not the truth, but what is believed to be true, is the political force. Racialism, which has come to be of practical importance as a result of being expounded in Germany by demagogues of genius, represents the final stage in the development of the organic theory of the state. Since it is still mainly a German phenomenon, however, we will continue to speak of nationalism rather than racialism; and, to bring this part of our inquiry to its conclusion, ask finally what are the ultimate political implications of nationalism, in the fuller, organic sense that we have been discussing in this section.

In one sense we may define the modern theory of the nation state as the political expression of Nihilism — the belief that there is no true, no absolute state of affairs, no law but the law of force, no 'thing in itself'.[1] Nietzsche is its noblest prophet, and it will not do to condemn his doctrine as a merely negative one. It might be called the most positive of all, for it is the assertion of human will against all other claims. 'Let anyone think', writes Nietzsche, 'of the *loss* which human institutions suffer, when a divine and transcendental *higher sphere* is postulated which must first sanction these institutions! By recognizing their worth in this sanction alone . . . *their natural dignity is reduced*, and under certain circumstances *denied*.'[2]

In Italy a conception similar in this respect to that of Nietzsche is to be found in the philosophy of Giovanni Gentile, whose *Actual Idealism* has been described as

[1] F. Nietzsche, *The Will to Power*, trans. A. M. Ludovici, 1909, p. 13.
[2] id., p. 245.

'the apotheosis of immediacy, of passing impulse, of uncriticized, uncriticizable self-assertion considered as synonymous with unlimited freedom'.[1] The realization of the self in action thus becomes the only ethical aim, though for Gentile, as for Nietzsche, the emphasis is still primarily on the individual will.

No political theory can really be drawn from Nietzsche, it is true. His dream, says Barker, is not of the tyrant, but of the super-species; the modern state was ever a slave-society to him; at bottom he was hostile to all political organizations.[2] The politician, however, cannot accept this. Nietzsche's apotheosis of the individual will was transferred by those who mis-read him to the state, which now could stand or fall in and by itself: it was its own justification. In this way, at last, the idea of an independent, supra-national ethical principle is demolished. The standards required for any attempt to understand society must henceforth emerge from the social organism itself.

The eighteenth-century idea of progress here joins forces with the nineteenth-century theory of organic evolution to provide a substitute for the ethical criterion in the laws of historical development. There is, in fact, in modern thought, a general tendency for history and science to take the place of philosophy and ethics. But the only criterion that history can provide is success, while science, or to be honest pseudo-science, if it attempts the illegitimate task of judging moral values is flung back upon such delightful ideas as 'the creative urge of superior germ-

[1] A. Crespi, *Contemporary Thought in Italy*, 1926, p. 200.

[2] E. Barker, *The Romantic Factor in Modern Politics*, in *Philosophy*, vol. XI, 1936, pp. 388-9.

plasm'. The survival of the fittest — that is, the survival of those who are most able to survive — is the only law that natural organisms know. The nation state, already emancipated in practice from any ethical control, having no end other than its own interests, or *raison d'état*, finds in this conception of itself as a natural organism, existing in the realm of natural science and not of ethical philosophy, its appropriate theoretical explanation. The nation state takes its place in the world of the lion and the tiger, the wolf pack or the ant hill, not in the ethical and philosophical dream world of Plato or Aristotle, Burke or Rousseau.

When we say that nationalism regards the nation state as an organic unity, then, it must be remembered that the term is used in a scientific sense, and not with any philosophical meaning. Philosophically, as we have suggested above, the so-called organic theory of the state was never able to escape from the idea of the intrinsic ethical importance of the individual; whereas modern nationalism, in those states in which the national idea has come to dominate not merely the external relations, but also the whole internal life of the state, reduces the individual to a simple cell in an animal organism, and erects a state absolutism more all-inclusive and more total in its claims over the life of the individual than any other political government the world has seen. This is what we understand by the internal development of nationalism, and this too is the real nature of the absolute state of which Lippmann speaks.

Practically all modern states, of course, as Lippmann points out in the passage quoted at the beginning of this section, claim a right of final decision in any matter affecting their members, but there is a world of difference between a claim to a right of control exercised in a limited number of cases and for the sake of the general utility of the sum of individuals in society, and a regular control asserted day by day, over every aspect of individual and social life, as a good thing in itself and regardless of any ends that can be conceived in terms of individual welfare. The idea of absolute sovereignty, applied to a national state which is conceived as an organic unity, has developed into something so different in degree as to be almost different in kind from the absolutism of the *ancien régime*, and from the nationalism of the nineteenth century. Nationalism has become, to employ a useful new term, totalitarianism. Let us go to the Mahomet of totalitarianism for a definition of this. 'The Fascist conception of the state', writes Mussolini, 'is all-embracing; outside it no human or spiritual values can exist, much less have value. Thus understood, Fascism is totalitarian, and the Fascist state — a synthesis and a unit inclusive of all values — interprets, develops, and potentiates the whole life of a people.'[1]

The modern state has progressed from divine right of kings to the idea of popular sovereignty, from that to nationalism, and from nationalism to totalitarianism. Its association with dictatorship can be detected in embryo in the first stages of the historic process. It becomes clearer when the assertion of popular sovereignty is seen to lead up to Bonapartism. We have yet to examine the association in its latest stages, and this involves making a closer study of the totalitarian state than we have hitherto ventured upon.

[1] B. Mussolini, *Fascism, doctrine and institutions*, 1935, p. 11.

The meaning of totalitarianism, and its connection with dictatorship, will become clearer if we return to our comparison with those states which are evidently not totalitarian, and ask why we believe that they are not so, even although they accept the principle of the autonomy of the state and acknowledge in theory its universal competence. In the first place, in these states the power of government is less unified, authority is divided, both in source and functioning; in fact, to put it in brief, there is a real, if not a theoretical separation of powers. In two further aspects of social life we find that the non-totalitarian state voluntarily abstains from more than a limited assertion of its theoretic claim to power — in the economic activity of the community, and in its spiritual life, including under this head both religion and culture and the field of individual morality. The characteristics of the totalitarian dictatorship of to-day, and wherein it differs in practice from the non-totalitarian state, can be apprehended by a study of its activity under each of these headings in turn.

NOTE

The belief that in modern German thought the traditional idea of the state has been abandoned is borne out by a study of *Mein Kampf*. Its author insists on the distinction between the 'patriotism' of the old Austrian Empire and the 'racial nationalism' which he is never tired of preaching (ed. of 1935, vol. I, ch. i, p. 11). He proclaims that the principal task of the state is the preservation of the race, because racial purity is the first aim of nature (id. I, iii, p. 104; I, xi, p. 324; I, xii, p. 327; II, ii, pp. 430-I, 443). 'The fox is always a fox, the goose a goose, the tiger a tiger ...' (I, xi, p. 312), and of course the German a German. 'All that, in this world, is not of pure race is as chaff' (I, xi, p. 324).

The source of these ideas is clearly as we have suggested above. 'The racial conception of the world', writes Hitler, 'corresponds to the innermost will of nature, because it re-establishes that free play of forces which leads to progress by natural selection' (II, i, p. 422). 'The struggle for daily bread brings the defeat of every being who is sickly or feeble or less resolute, while the struggle of the male to conquer the female gives the right of procreation only to the healthiest-conditioned individual ... Strife is always the means of developing the health and power of resistance of the species, and is consequently a primary condition of its progress' (I, xi, pp. 312-3).

Many more quotations might be given, but these should be enough to show that the twin formulae of popular Darwinism — struggle for existence and survival of the fittest — are the bases of National Socialist thought. Whereas the eighteenth century, building on the foundations laid by the philosophers and mathematicians of the seventeenth, identified Nature with Reason, and believed in natural equality and the brotherhood of man, the twentieth century, seeing nature with the eye of the nineteenth-century biologist, puts the emphasis on natural inequality and the struggle for existence. The real strength of National Socialist ideology lies in the fact that it merely systematizes an interpretation of human life and history which a civilization fed on popular biology as well as nationalistic history, was ready to receive.

CHAPTER VII

THE NATURE OF THE TOTALITARIAN STATE

§ I THE POLITICAL BASIS OF TOTALITARIAN DICTATORSHIP

LIBERTY, it has been said, is ancient, and it is despotism that is new.[1] Certainly, in the history of political societies, separation of powers and the belief in a fixed law independent of human volition are early characteristics, whereas the idea of sovereignty appears late. It is not necessary to outline again the process by which in modern times European political thought passed from the dominance of the former set of ideas to that of the latter. The end of the eighteenth century and the beginning of the nineteenth formed the critical period. In the eighteenth century proper, if Pufendorf in Germany and the physiocrats in France had already denounced the idea of a separation of powers, the stronger influence of Locke in England and Montesquieu in France had upheld the older ideas so successfully that when Rousseau transferred sovereignty to the people, he still insisted that the principle of a separation of powers was essential to the organization of any legitimate government.

When in 1789 France attempted to put the sovereignty of the people into practice, the revolutionaries failed to realize how inconsistent with the principle of separation

[1] ACTON, *History of Freedom*, p. 5.

was their fundamental idea of popular sovereignty. The political writer whose influence was probably greater during the French Revolution than that of any other, the abbé Mably, was partly responsible for the strength of this theory of separation. Sieyès, who asserts the absolute sovereignty of the nation, embodied in the legislative assembly, also proclaims the necessity for a rigid separation of powers. The more moderate views of Montesquieu and Rousseau being neglected, the theory was turned in practice against the king and his ministers, the executive, which according to Mably was to be regarded as 'eternally the enemy of the legislative power',[1] and it was maintained with such a profound faith that Duguit can say it was treated as if it were 'a metaphysical concept analogous to the Christian Mystery of the Trinity'.[2]

Under the pressure of circumstances the government of the great Committee of Public Safety reversed this tendency for a year, but after the fall of Robespierre the revolutionaries went back to the theory of separation, though in practice their government amounted to the dominance of the oligarchy controlling the Convention. So little had political theorists learned after ten years of unsuccessful experimenting, that Sieyès in 1799 was still under the impression that the trouble with the constitutional arrangements of the French Republic was that there was not a sufficiently radical separation of powers. In 1789 he had feared the tyranny of the executive in the person of Louis XVI; now, under the shadow of Bonaparte, he transferred his fear to the legislative. Sieyès played such an important, perhaps a decisive part,

[1] MABLY, *Gouvernement de Pologne*, I, iv., *Œuvres*, 1792, vol. VIII, p. 45.
[2] L. DUGUIT, *Manuel de droit constitutionnel*, 3rd ed., 1918, p. 163.

at the beginning and at the end of the revolutionary decade, his opinion was so influential, and he led his contemporaries so systematically astray, that he has some claim to be regarded as the evil genius of the Revolution.

But now for the second time practical politics took charge. If the theorists would not see the inconsistency of their attempt to combine absolute sovereignty with separation, they were to have it forced on their attention by facts. The creation of a real unified sovereignty, and the dissolution of the separate powers in the state, was to be the work of no theorist, but of a man of action, General Bonaparte, with the aid of Sieyès First Consul, soon to be Emperor. The union of executive and legislative was at last achieved by the suppression of the latter. The Napoleonic dictatorship retained, like later dictatorships, a certain parliamentary façade, but the Legislative Body and the Senate now set up were a mere piece of perfunctory lip service to democratic principles. Their only significance lies in showing how difficult it is for a modern dictatorship to separate itself completely from democratic ideas.

The experience of the French Revolution shows, then, that it is not necessary to look for a theoretical justification for the abandonment of the principle of separation of powers; indeed, one would not be very easy to find, once we have left the rule of the absolute, hereditary prince behind. The subjection of the legislative to the executive power, which is a universal characteristic of dictatorship, is a practical and not a theoretical development. Further, one is compelled to ask whether it is altogether peculiar to the dictatorial as opposed to the parliamentary state, or whether it does not represent a more general trend in the modern state. Can one not observe during the nineteenth century, even in parliamentary countries, a similar movement towards a closer connection between legislative and executive and an increasing control of the latter over the former? The key to this tendency seems to be provided by the great development everywhere of an extra-constitutional political organ, through the influence of which the activity of both legislative and executive is unified — the political party. In what way, one might reasonably ask, does the rule of a political party in a parliamentary state, dominating legislative and executive alike, and appealing to the public through the personality of its leader, a Baldwin, say, or a Roosevelt, differ from the similar rule of a party in a dictatorial state? Only, it might be answered, through the existence in the former of alternative parties. A vital difference, admittedly, but one not particularly relevant to the principle of separation of powers. One is forced to the conclusion that the control of the legislative by the executive power represents a general trend in modern politics and therefore is not by itself a safe criterion of the totalitarian state or of dictatorial government.

Under modern conditions a more effective test is the subordination of the judicial power to the executive — appropriately enough, for it was with the proclamation of the independence of the judiciary that the theory of separation really became historically significant, in the writings of Locke and the achievements of the Glorious Revolution of 1688. The separation of executive and legislative powers is important in the history of political technique: the independence of the judiciary has something more fundamental behind it. Separation of powers in this connection has been described by the great jurist, Roscoe Pound, as the formula which the eighteenth century found for the attempt to avoid the over-personal administration of justice.[1] It is more than this, it is essential to what Dicey called the Rule of Law. It is the modern version of the theory of natural law, of the belief, in the words of Gierke, that, 'Law is not a common will that a thing shall be, but a common conviction that it is'.[2] The importance of this principle is so well put by the same great thinker that we cannot do better than quote him again. 'I still live to-day in the conviction that our legal theory and our legal life can only thrive on one condition — that "positivism" should somehow learn to preserve for the idea of law that original and independent title to existence which was vindicated for it by the School of Natural Law.'[3]

While the separation of legislative and executive yielded to practical political developments, the independence of the judicial power, based on the principle of natural law, was attacked by theorists. The history of the idea of natural law, from the time of the Stoics, through the *jus naturale* of the Roman lawyers and the medieval canonists, to its association with the great triumphs of the Western mind in the seventeenth and eighteenth centuries, was brought to a sudden halt by the rise of German romanticism in the early years of the nineteenth century. The romantic revolt against the rationalism of the eighteenth century swept out, along with much that was new, the law of nature, which was also the law of reason, and which was very old. The time spirit took charge of European

[1] ROSCOE POUND, *An Introduction to the Philosophy of Law*, 1922, p. 102.
[2] GIERKE, op. cit., ed. Barker, p. 225. [3] id., p. 226.

thought with the birth of the historical age. Law was henceforth to be deemed the product of the unconscious reason of the past. Germany, and indeed all Europe more or less, was beginning to 'think with its blood'. Law was now conceived as the juristic formulation of history; but this still had to be the history of something. The principle of the law of nature still had a chance: it might have reasserted itself if law could have been conceived as the reflection of a civilization or of humanity. But such Voltairian ideals were not for the age of romanticism and nationalism. The future lay with the nations, not with civilization, and law, according to the new romantic ideas, was an expression of the history of a nation. The new attitude towards law was expanded and systematized by Savigny and the historical school. Later theorists even went behind the nation and tried to find the basis of law in race consciousness, while psychologists like Fouillée and McDougall interpreted law in terms of communal psychology.

What was the practical result of these revolutionary changes in the conception of law? It is worth while pausing here to examine an interpretation of this development which was offered by Krabbe in his *Modern Theory of the State*, because, although very different from our own view, it will assist us to our conclusion. According to Krabbe, the effective cause of the nineteenth-century change in the conception of law was the fact that during the eighteenth century the idea of sovereignty — which had co-existed with the idea of law since the end of the medieval world — began to encroach on the control which the old common law had hitherto exercised over most fields of social life. As a result of a great increase in the legislative activity of the sovereign, it became possible, and indeed natural, to attribute the binding force of all law to the exercise of the sovereign's will. Finally, when sovereignty, as a result of the French Revolution and subsequent changes, was transferred to the people, a new basis for law appeared in the legal convictions of the nation. The result of this development is, according to Krabbe, that a spiritual power has taken the place of a personal authority.[1] 'We do not in the least deny', he concludes, 'that the notion of sovereignty has been justified; we hold merely that among civilized people it is now no longer recognized and that accordingly it must be expunged from political theory.'[2]

These two conclusions we wish to stress, because, while the statement of the development up to this point seems admirable, here the writer produces an interpretation of it which is exactly the reverse of our own. We are quite willing to agree with him that sovereignty and law have come closer together, but our suggestion is that where the process has reached completion sovereignty has swallowed law, and not the contrary. One must admit that it is more easy to see this now than when Krabbe wrote. Secondly, instead of a spiritual power having replaced a personal authority, it seems to us that the conception of the law of nature — which might be considered a spiritual authority — as the sanction behind positive law, has been abandoned, and the state has taken its place. In the end the result has been that a much more and not a much less arbitrary and personal conception of law has appeared.

[1] H. KRABBE, *The Modern Idea of the State*, trans. G. H. Sabine and W. J. Shepard, 1922, ch. i. [2] id., p. 35.

Our argument will be made clearer if we take certain specific examples of the changed attitude towards law, and consequently towards the separation of powers, in the totalitarian state. The new conception of law is to be observed first in the French Revolution, with the development of the idea of revolutionary justice, and the setting up in 1793 of a Revolutionary Tribunal to deal with counter-revolutionary charges. Six months earlier, in the September Massacres of 1792, Marat had attempted to assert popular justice in his own way. The Committee of Public Safety was more systematic, but when it declared Terror the order of the day, it meant just what Marat meant. The idea of justice as a weapon in the class struggle was beginning to emerge. Robespierre's early contributions to judicial reform show that one of his objects was the transference of judicial power from the privileged classes to the masses.[1] That in practice the rules of law and the administration of justice in the eighteenth century, as in most or all other times, took for granted and upheld the existing class structure of society, can hardly be questioned. A revolution which attempted to alter these class relationships, it might be argued, was therefore bound to alter the judicial system, to take its administration out of the hands of the ruling classes and give it to the people.

In the French Revolution, then, is to be found a foreshadowing of the new ideas about law. A century later, the Russian Revolution brings us into the new world, juridically speaking. The belief that law and justice are merely a weapon in the hands of the ruling class is now triumphantly vindicated. The law, in the U.S.S.R.,

[1] J. M. Thompson, *Robespierre*, vol. I, p. 98.

according to the official definition, is 'a system of social relationships, which corresponds to the interests of the governing class and which is placed under the guarantee of the organized force of that class'.[1] Thus it is defined in terms of interests: the idealistic conception of the law of nature disappears, and law becomes no more than a scientific statement of the social and political utilities of the ruling class. But in theory this conception of law still has one foot in the past. When the classless society has at last been reached, an equal justice for all will be proclaimed, and that justice will presumably be based on universal principles, valid in any and every such society.

The conception of justice as a revolutionary instrument is also to be met in Fascist Italy, but here again the theory does not break absolutely finally with traditional ideas. An Italian jurist can make out a plausible case for Fascist 'illegalities'. 'Devotion to justice', writes del Vecchio, 'does not consist in mere devotion to legality . . . Over and above the legality of to-day we are required to prepare that of to-morrow . . . If ever the struggle for justice requires us in any case to pass beyond the established order, this must never occur . . . out of mere individual interest or judgment, but (for such is the nature of justice) only in obedience to another law, higher and more severe; which we recognize as already operative and whose morally serious and onerous duties we accept and undertake.'[2] This can only be interpreted as upholding some form of the theory of natural law. Where the Russian

[1] B. MIRKINE-GUETZEVITCH, *La Théorie Générale de l'Etat soviétique*, 1928, p. 125.

[2] G. DEL VECCHIO, 1926, quoted by SCHNEIDER, op. cit., p. 108.

and Italian dictatorships break away from accepted principles is not so much in their theoretical aberrations as in the important practical change by which they take large classes of offences out of the scope of the ordinary law and the ordinary tribunals and submit them to special political courts, which, like the Revolutionary Tribunal of Paris, are concerned not with the administration of justice but with the maintenance of the revolutionary dictatorship. So long as such courts exist one is bound to say that in essence a revolutionary condition survives; and as there is no apparent likelihood of their ever coming to an end while these dictatorial regimes last, one is compelled to conclude that fundamentally revolutionary conditions will be perpetuated.

This also holds true of Germany, where People's Courts sit in secret session on political offenders and sentence them without any right of appeal. The abandonment of the independence of the judiciary, and the triumph of sovereignty over law, should be clear enough from these examples. Where Germany represents an advance on Italy and Russia is in the final substitution of the law of the nation for the law of nature. The principles of romantic political thinking in Germany have at last been put into practice by the new dictatorial government. When the Nazi Party came into power not only were many new laws rapidly decreed, but all existing legislation required to be re-interpreted. 'All those statutes and rules of law', states an authoritative legal periodical, 'which in their wording have been carried over into the new state, undergo by that transition a fundamental change. They are no longer to be interpreted according to the meaning of the legislator who first gave them form, but according to the spirit and content of the national socialist *Weltanschauung*.'[1] What is this *Weltanschauung*? According to Dr. Goebbels, 'It has nothing whatever to do with learning'. It is the thought of the German people, 'reduced to its primitive and original formulae'.[2] Perhaps this does not clarify the idea very much; but clarity is hardly necessary to an idea that is itself a revolt against rationalism and the expression of a mystical belief in the nation as the fount of juridical virtue.

The hostility of the modern totalitarian state, both in political theory and in practice, to the separation of powers, to the rule of law in the community and to the idea of natural law, should need no further elaboration. Here certainly we have in the field of government one fundamental characteristic, or group of characteristics, by which to distinguish it. But this is a negative feature; we are compelled to go on to seek a more positive political basis. Totalitarianism is frankly opposed to the principles of the liberal, parliamentary state; in the nature of things it cannot exercise the political methods of divine right monarchy. What then, we must ask, is its own political technique? With the answer to this question we come at last to the necessary association, in the political sphere, between totalitarianism and dictatorship. Evidently the particular form of government of the totalitarian state, as the examples we have given show, is the concentration of all possible authority in the hands of a single man, who is regarded not as king or despot, and not quite as dictator or tyrant, as the ancient world or the Middle

[1] Quoted by C. H. Wilson, *The Separation of Powers under Democracy and Fascism*, in *Political Science Quarterly*, vol. LII, no. 4, Dec. 1937, pp. 481-504, p. 493.

[2] id., p. 495.

Ages knew that kind of government. Totalitarianism, in fact, has evolved a form of dictatorship which has peculiarities of its own. This is a development which calls for further examination.

The question before us is, in its simplest form — what is the function of the dictator in the totalitarian state? He may, like Napoleon, or Kemal Ataturk, or Mussolini, have great executive ability, but a brief examination of modern dictatorship suggests that the actual task of government is not his primary political function. What this is can be understood best by a brief examination of the conditions under which dictatorship appears. As we can see from many examples, it arises when society is dissolving, or believes itself to be in danger of dissolution. In such circumstances the simple emotional forces in human nature re-assert themselves; men governed by panic look not to an institution but to an individual for salvation and leadership. In essence, then, the dictator must be a leader: the very terms used to describe him — Führer, Duce — say as much.

Psychologists during the last fifty years have come to realize the immense importance of the element of leadership in social relations. Not that practical politicians have ever been ignorant of the fact. Psychologists have observed, as again politicians have always instinctively known, that the appeal of the leader must be to the emotions as well as, perhaps even rather than, to the intelligence; they have pointed out that men are less ruled by ideas than has been generally supposed, but respond more readily to the appeal of the symbol, especially if it is incarnated in an individual.[1]

[1] W. H. R. Rivers, *Psychology and Politics*, 1923, p. 51.

W. H. Rivers went so far as to say that the emotional appeal of a leader was essential to the success of any great movement at the present day,[1] and the study of more recent history does not induce one to treat this as an exaggeration. One would even admit that Freud's association of leadership with the psychological technique of suggestion and hypnosis does not seem far-fetched to-day.[2] Equally illuminating is his belief that there exists a libidinal tie between the members of the group and the leader; the relaxation of such a tie, leaving the individual with a feeling of isolation and insecurity is, he observes, a natural cause of panic.[3] And conversely, we may suggest, a group which is conscious of its incoherence and insecurity will seek out a leader to restore its self-confidence. The history of post-war Germany supplies a striking illustration of this process. Without necessarily accepting the details of the Freudian psychological analysis, it must be said that the political evolution of Germany in recent years seems more easily explicable in terms of psycho-pathology than in any other way.

Before modern psychological theories were thought of, the gospel of leadership had been preached by one who wholeheartedly believed in it — Thomas Carlyle. His political formula was simple. 'Find in any country', he wrote, 'the Ablest Man that exists there; raise *him* to supreme place, and loyally reverence him: you have a perfect government for that country; no ballot-box, parliamentary eloquence, voting, constitution-building, or other machinery whatsoever can improve it a whit.

[1] W. H. R. RIVERS, *Psychology and Politics*, 1923, p. 53.

[2] S. FREUD, *Group Psychology and the Analysis of the Ego*, 1922, p. 100.

[3] id., pp. 45-7.

It is in the perfect state; an ideal country. The Ablest Man; he means also the truest-hearted, justest, the Noblest Man: what he *tells us to do* must be precisely the wisest, fittest, that we could anywhere or anyhow learn — the thing which it will in all ways behove us with right loyal thankfulness, and nothing doubting, to do!'[1] There is much more to the same effect, but this is enough. Carlyle, in the England of Peel and Cobden and John Stuart Mill, was right to find the times out of joint for him. He was born — or at least lived — in the wrong country, and a century too soon. Passages like that quoted above read more like translations from a contemporary German National Socialist speech then like a product of nineteenth-century England, and indeed the feeling of a German original is not mistaken, for the inspiration is to be found in Fichte, and 'Carlyle's acknowledgement', it has been said, 'was hardly as great as his borrowing'.[2] Once again, thus, we are forced back on German romantic thought as an essential source of the new political principles.

There is no aspect of modern dictatorship for which it is more difficult to find a comprehensible explanation in rational terms than this theory of leadership. Even in Italy, when we approach this question, the severely realistic Machiavellian attitude gives way to an overflow of neo-Idealist mysticism. Let us take two attempts to explain the principle of leadership, the first from the official Statute of the Fascist Party, issued in October 1926. This states, 'The order and hierarchies without

[1] T. Carlyle, *On Heroes, Hero-Worship*, VI, in *Collected Works*, 1870-87, p. 234.

[2] C. F. Harrold, *Carlyle and German Thought*, 1819-1834, 1934, p. 192.

which there can be no discipline of force nor education of the people, must receive their light and rules from the head, where a complete view of the powers and tasks, of function and merits is centred'.[1] The second explanation comes from an individual apologist: 'Our champions, and first and greatest the *Duce*, have been urged and inspired from on high — from those heights which are in every man and from which springs the creative flood of will. There is no need of dogma; discipline suffices. This is Fascism's only dogma.'[2] We might be forgiven if we did not find these definitions precisely lucid: but in fact the fault would be ours, for desiring a rational explanation for something that is essentially emotional and non-rational.

Although leadership, in varying forms, is a universal feature of communal life, different peoples apparently experience the need for individual leadership to differing degrees, whilst the type of leader desired obviously depends on what for want of a better term we must call national character. It is not an accident that a Hitler should be a kind of twentieth-century Luther, a Mussolini a Cæsar Borgia on whom the gods have smiled, and a Stalin a Bolshevik Peter the Great. The leader, moreover, is not merely a reflection of the national character, for his followers will, consciously or unconsciously, model themselves upon him.[3]

The totalitarian dictator is, in the first place, the leader of a party, and his ambition is that the relation of his subjects towards him shall be that of the members of the

[1] Fascist Party Statute, 1926, quoted by SCHNEIDER, op. cit., p. 318.

[2] SCHNEIDER, op. cit., p. 357.

[3] cf. W. BAGEHOT, *Physics and Politics*, 1872, p. 37.

party to their leader. A Nazi felt no more under compulsion in following Adolf Hitler than an English conservative did in accepting the leadership of Mr. Baldwin, and the key-note of dictatorial propaganda has been the struggle to extend this attitude from the party members to the whole nation: that is the meaning of the attempt to identify the nation with the party. The particular virtue of this process, from the point of view of political technique, is that it enables the dictator to satisfy the psychological requirement that the people shall not feel unfree, whereas the plebiscitary methods of dictatorship merely provide a formal satisfaction of the principle of popular sovereignty.

The combination of the principle of leadership with the technique of party government has temporarily achieved remarkable success. Whether it can provide a permanent basis for government is another matter. Oswald Spengler, in the midst of masses of cloudy verbiage, has some pertinent observations on this problem. The ideal of a single national party, which comes to every dictatorship, and which is not absent elsewhere, is, he says, absurd. 'It is the infantile disease of all revolutions, this belief in a triumphant unity when in fact the problem of the age from which they themselves spring *demands discord*.'[1] His fundamental criticism of dictatorship is precisely that it is too much like democracy and not sufficiently dictatorial, that the dictator — like the leader of the mob of Paris in 1848 — is merely running at the heels of his followers. 'Mussolini's creative idea', again to quote Spengler, 'was grand, and it has had an international effect: it revealed a possible

[1] O. Spengler, *The Hour of Decision*, trans. C. F. Atkinson, 1934, p. 183.

form of combating Bolshevism. But this form arose out of imitating the enemy and is therefore full of dangers: revolution from below, organized and participated in for the greater part by men from below; an armed party militia, paralleled in Caesar's Rome by the bands of Clodius and Milo; the tendency to subordinate intellectual and economic leadership to executive working-out because of inability to understand it; to disregard others' property, to confuse the conceptions of nation and mass — in a word, the socialistic ideology of the last century.'[1] One cannot help suspecting that, for Spengler, Fascism and National Socialism are in the end phenomena not very different from Bolshevism.

This criticism may be true, but the fact that all modern dictatorships arise out of party, and even mass movements, makes the personality of the leader not less but more necessary. The belief that civilized man has evolved away from the primitive craving for personal leadership and is now capable of giving his loyalty to an idea, embodied in an institution, has been shown by recent historical developments to require considerable modification. The conceptions of law and order, and security, have become bound up with the idea of the unity of the state, and in most communities it appears that in time of crisis this has to be translated into terms the people can appreciate if panic is to be averted — in other words, the abstract idea of the state has to be embodied in a person. For this reason a well-constituted and firmly established monarchy is less likely to become a dictatorship than any other form of government: because the emotional craving for an individual, not necessarily to

[1] O. Spengler, *The Hour of Decision*, trans. C. F. Atkinson, 1934, p. 187.

govern, but to symbolize the unity of the state, is already satisfied. A constitutional monarchy, in the language of Bagehot, puts instinctive personal loyalty behind a government which is in fact parliamentary and impersonal. The monarch is better placed than any dictator can ever be for obtaining the permanent loyalty of the people. Because he takes little or no part in the actual government, he is above responsibility. By his descent he is a visible link with the past of the nation, an embodiment of historical continuity. The pageantry that surrounds him on formal occasions supplies an element of colour and ceremony which, because it is the genuine thing, invented by medieval men, who were masters of the art of pageantry, and hallowed by centuries of usage, can only with difficulty be replaced by the synthetic stage-craft of dictatorship. Only where the monarchy was too saddled with responsibility for national disasters, as in Russia and Spain, or where it had little historical connection with the greater part of the country, practically no pageantry, and a singularly insignificant personal appeal, as in Italy, did a dictatorial movement have its chance.

Thus, to sum up, in politics the triumph of dictatorship in the totalitarian state implies the complete subjection of the legislative power to the executive, the abolition of the independence of the judiciary, the rejection of the rule of law, and of the idea of natural law, the absence of any king capable of effectively personifying the unity of the state, and the substitution for these of the principle of leadership, based on the support of a political party, which is identified, as far as possible, with the nation.

§2 THE ECONOMIC BASIS OF TOTALITARIAN DICTATORSHIP

It is not possible to isolate the study of political institutions from that of other factors in the life of the community. The sovereignty of the people, transmuted into nationalism, may have been the initial motive force behind the modern totalitarian dictatorship; the concentration of authority, the rise of party government, and the principle of leadership may have provided its political technique; but these do not by themselves fully explain its origin or nature. Nationalism had become intransigent enough, had developed in many countries into imperialism, but it cannot have been by itself alone productive of the totalitarian state, otherwise the great nationalist movements in nineteenth-century Italy, in the succession states of the Austro-Hungarian Empire, and in Ireland, to mention no more, would have presented the characteristics we call totalitarian. At the same time dictatorship by itself does not necessarily imply totalitarianism, for in the past there have been plenty of dictatorships which can hardly be described as totalitarian. To discover the further element or elements that are needed to explain why the combination of the modern movement termed nationalism with the old method of government called dictatorship, or tyranny, has led to totalitarianism, it is necessary to look beyond ordinary nationalism, and outside the field of political technique, to the economic and spiritual foundations of the state. We will make no profession of determining which, if either, of these has priority, but will begin with a consideration of the economic factors, purely as a matter of convenience.

A certain historic connection between dictatorship and economic conflict is apparent at first sight, but the nature of that connection requires further examination, for evidently the economic policies of a Robespierre or a Napoleon, a Stalin or a Mussolini, are not at first sight explicable on identical grounds, while in the economic attitude of dictators such as Louis Napoleon and Hitler a certain dualism can be observed. Our first conclusion is that if we take the alternatives in modern economic policies to be socialism and capitalism, using these terms in a loose general sense, without any pretence at precise definition, then it is not self-evident that dictatorship as a political instrument is exclusively attached to either system or creed.

The totalitarian state of to-day, it must be admitted, involves an authoritarian control of the economic life of the community which is the antithesis of the *laissez-faire* individualism of nineteenth-century capitalism, but since the same tendency is to be observed in all industrial or semi-industrial states to some degree, it cannot be claimed that dictatorship must itself have been responsible for the loss of this Eden of economic purity, and equally it does not follow that its loss necessarily involves what is commonly called socialism. But before we can attempt to understand how dictatorship comes into the story and the effects of its intervention, it will be necessary to discuss very briefly the change that has come over the economic outlook of European civilization during the last half century.

There is no novelty in suggesting that capitalist society was built up in its early days on the Calvinistic virtues of the middle class. How far Calvinism was a cause, and how far a result, we need not stay to argue here. Among these virtues the greatest was thrift, which was the highest economic virtue in the nineteenth century. The men who were creating a vast accumulation of capital resources and conquering the world for industrialism were not for the most past extravagant, though they could not personally have consumed more than a small proportion of the wealth that was being created even if they had wished to do so. With the masses, toiling in field and factory, economy was a compulsory virtue, for their income was kept as near to starvation level as was possible. At the same time government was cheap, for there was little of it, and wars were on a comparatively small scale.

The end of the nineteenth century saw a change in the situation. The austerity of the captains of industry began to break down, especially when the ownership of great business undertakings passed to the second or third generation, and the real work of industrial control fell into the hands of salaried technical officers. A psychology of spending was taking the place of a psychology of saving in all classes, for at the same time the masses became aware how much wealth they were creating and how little share they had in it themselves. Their grievances were given voice and form by the various schools of socialism, latest child of the rationalist and utilitarian eighteenth century, which may be described in general terms as the conviction that economic evils — the poverty of the masses, the catastrophe that a slump is for those who cannot go much lower in their scale of existence without going under altogether — are not inevitable, and that it is the duty of the community to remedy these conditions. Just as the principle of the sovereignty of the people, or in a general sense democracy, was the conquest of the eighteenth century, so the ideal of socialism, which extended the idea of equality from the political into the economic field, was the achievement of the nineteenth century.

The first actual effort at improvement, that led by the Utopian Socialists of the early nineteenth century, achieved little success. The next development, which took the form of militant but untheoretical trade unionism, coinciding with a great increase in the productivity of industry, produced a considerable advance in conditions of life for the masses in Western Europe and North America. In periods of prosperity gains were made, but in times of slump the reaction was still felt severely. The connection between politics and economics now began to be realized. It was discovered that the political machinery of the state formed a weight that could be thrown into the balance against the struggling industrial workers with certain effect. The conflict between the classes on the economic ground therefore tended to develop into a struggle to obtain control of the state; but in a society organized on a land-owning and capitalist basis it was found that the ordinary processes of parliamentary democracy did not easily allow real political power to be obtained by socialist parties. Hence there was a split between the section of the socialist movement that continued despite discouragement to put its faith in the ballot box, and the section that, as we have seen earlier, was prepared to sacrifice parliamentary methods and turned to the idea of physical force.[1]

[1] cf. above, p. 113.

Though in theory the principles of political liberty and economic equality may necessitate one another, in practice it has not proved easy to progress towards both objects at the same time. To this difficulty can be traced the association between socialism and dictatorship, which is so evident in modern times. Wherever the school of revolutionary socialism prevailed one may say that arbitrary government was inevitable; for if the revolutionary party triumphed, then it would be necessary for it to institute a party dictatorship to crush the opposing class, and this, as the history of revolutionary France and Russia shows, turns only too easily into a personal dictatorship. If, on the other hand, it did not achieve a victory, the struggle would produce in the community that fear of the dissolution of society and of the impending collapse of law and order, from which dictatorship is most likely to result.

In this sense it is true that dictatorship is the child of the class war, and the increasing violence of social conflict in the twentieth century is the explanation of the increasing prevalence of dictatorship. If modern dictatorship generally originates in this way, the extension of the totalitarian control of the state from the political to the economic sphere follows naturally from it, whether the dictatorship actually comes from the right or the left. Where the revolutionary socialist party gains the day, it is obvious that, whatever its subsequent history, it cannot altogether deny its origin: it is bound to attempt to introduce some form or other of socialism. Since this is certain to be opposed by the possessing classes, and since revolutionary socialism believes in force anyhow, it is not likely to rely simply on persuasion to introduce the new social system, but will violently take control of the whole economic life of the state.

Suppose, however, that the struggle against the forces of revolutionary socialism is successful. What is curious is that the more common type of dictatorship, which results from this victory, itself has similar consequences, and this fact demands a fuller explanation. John Stuart Mill remarked on the association between individualist economic principles and free politics: in proportion as people were accustomed to managing their own affairs, instead of leaving them to government, he believed, their desires would turn to repelling tyranny rather than tyrannizing.[1] Without necessarily agreeing with this as an interpretation of nineteenth-century politics, it is not difficult to see how, on the other hand, the connection between totalitarian economic principles and political dictatorship has arisen.

In the first place, if a large proportion of the people has been influenced by vague socialistic ideas, as it has in every Western country, the dictatorship will inevitably have to incorporate some socialist elements in its appeal, in order to gain support among the masses of the population. Secondly, as it is inevitably the heir to the economic problems of its predecessors, these will bring it down, unless it solves them, as surely as they brought down the previous regime. By the simple fact of being a dictatorship it has taken on itself the responsibility for the economic welfare of the state.

Now for earlier dictatorships, in a simpler agricultural economy, a reasonable degree of prosperity was not such

[1] J. S. MILL, *Principles of Political Economy*, ed. Ashley, 1909, Bk. V, ch. xi, § 6.

a difficult matter to secure. The maintenance of law and order, internal peace, and the re-establishment of confidence, were the chief requisites. When Napoleon was able to add to these the skilful regulation of state finances, the state promotion of industry, and the careful supervision of the economic interests of the departments by his prefects, he had done all he could do, and all that it was needful to do. France being mainly agricultural and self-supporting, given confidence and competent administration, there was no serious economic problem, since social equality in the economic sense was not yet a demand of the people. If it had been, the problem would at once have become more difficult, as Robespierre and Saint-Just, attempting by the law of the *maximum* to prevent the exploitation of the people by speculators, and by laws redistributing the property of enemies of the Revolution to introduce a mild degree of equality, had already discovered.

As a result of the demand for a higher standard of living, the claim to economic equality, and the menace of the cyclic system of boom and slump, the economic problems of modern dictatorship are infinitely more complex. Already in the career of Louis Napoleon, the Saint-Simonian Emperor, we can see the preoccupation with the economic problem beginning. His appeal to the poorer classes by his pamphlet on pauperism, his successful attempt to win the support of the industrial workers, of whom he represented himself as the friend, in opposition to the selfish class policy of the Assembly, his not always unsuccessful overtures to the socialist leaders, the stimulation he gave to public works, his encouragement of social reform, of working-class organizations, even of trade unions — all are evidence of his awareness of the importance for his government of the economic problem. Aided by the fact that he rose to power at a time of economic distress and thus obtained the credit for the subsequent recovery, and by the adoption of an economic policy which was more enlightened than that of Louis Philippe and the conservative Assemblies of the Second Republic, Louis Napoleon achieved considerable success in his early years. Later he found himself caught between the rising tide of socialism and the unwillingness of the employing classes to grant economic concessions. The war between the Commune and the Versailles Assembly was the fitting and tragic epilogue to his reign.

Louis Napoleon's dictatorship represents a transitional stage. While the economic problem had assumed considerable importance by the middle of the nineteenth century, it had not obtained the dominating influence it exercises to-day. The socialistic demand for economic progress and the principle of social equality were not as yet leading features in the political landscape. Post-war dictatorships have had to reckon with both these developments. Even though they represented a victory of the propertied classes over revolutionary socialism, they have still had to pay for their suppression of liberty by performing obeisance to the idea of equality, and by attempting to meet the demand for economic improvement. Given the change in the economic wind since the nineteenth century, to which we referred earlier in this chapter, it was inevitable that they should try to inaugurate prosperity by a policy of spending. Hence they have had recourse to vast expansions of credit, backed by the state and used for grandiose projects, some of economic value, some dictated by considerations of prestige, but all determined primarily by the need to provide employment for the industrial masses. To these sources of expense should be added the cost of huge armaments and of actual wars, such as the Abyssinian and the Spanish campaigns. The necessary consequence under a system of *laissez-faire* economics would be inflation, an internal rise in prices, the collapse of the exchange value of the currency, ruin for millions and revolution. Republican Germany saw the process from beginning to end.

Dictatorial regimes, threatened with the same menace, have defended themselves more vigorously. Prices have been kept below a fixed level, internal credit maintained, and exchanges stabilized. But how has it been done? Only by the government seizing control of the whole economic life of the nation. Thus the Marxian dictatorship from the left finds itself rejoined by what was perhaps in the minds of many of its supporters intended to be a capitalist government of the right, in a common policy of economic totalitarianism, compared with which the economic interventions of earlier dictatorships are almost negligible.

We may describe this process in another way by saying that nationalism has spread from the political into the economic sphere. It is, in fact, at the same time a source of the problem and of its temporary solution. The effect of the introduction of nationalist emotions into the sphere of economics is explained by a wholehearted admirer of Italian fascism as follows: 'Only by appealing to their nationalistic sentiments', he writes, 'could the Italian masses be induced to submit in the long run to the inevitable curtailment of their economic freedom, and to co-operate wholeheartedly by means of the Corporations. A supreme patriotism had to be aroused in order to suppress or moderate the selfishness ingrained in the mind of a generation brought up on the gospel of nineteenth-century liberalism.'[1] The same writer recognizes that in their fundamental economic structure fascism and communism present many similarities.[2] The ideals behind the two systems were doubtless in the beginning very different, but here we are not pretending to analyse ideals or to deliver judgments concerning value, but merely to discover historical facts.

Economic totalitarianism is nowhere yet complete, but the economic activities of dictatorial governments are gradually becoming more and more far-reaching. Whether any permanent success will be attained by the new tactic of economic totalitarianism it is still too early to say. Its achievements in Russia and Germany have obviously been remarkable: it is probably true that they have prevented economic collapse and revolution. But the materials for a sound judgment on the economic merits and defects of totalitarianism hardly exist as yet. We are not concerned in this chapter, however, with the consequences, but only with the nature of totalitarianism, and the bases of its authority; and on this point a doubt may be expressed in conclusion whether a government can ever obtain more than a passive adherence by its economic merits, though its economic deficiencies can easily bring about its fall.

[1] P. Einzig, *The Economic Foundations of Fascism*, 2nd ed., 1934, p. 100.
[2] id., pp. 7, 109-10.

§ 3 RELIGION IN THE TOTALITARIAN STATE

Neither political nor economic policies are a final explanation in themselves of totalitarian dictatorship. They are part of its machinery of government, but if we wish to know the real foundations of the regime, we have to seek for something which is less easy to apprehend but more fundamental in the life of society. All government rests on public opinion; a weak government is at the mercy of the vague, floating, transient opinions of the day, but a strong, well-based government obtains its support from deeper layers of opinion, that can be relied upon in fair or foul weather. Such opinion must be immune from petty personal calculations of self-interest, safe from the questionings of the sceptical, individual intellect, perhaps generally below the level of the conscious political mind altogether, for society must be protected from day to day aberrations. In other words, it must be held together by faith.

Divine right of kings was such a faith, and with its decline has come the rise of a new political creed — nationalism, which to-day plays very much the same part, and on which dictatorship has to rely as the uniting motive in society. How powerful a political force it is we have already seen. But with what we have called the internal development of nationalism it has now become something much more than an ordinary political movement, something very like a religion, indeed; for in the service of totalitarian dictatorship it puts forward as absolute a claim to exclusive moral and spiritual allegiance as the most intolerant religion that ever existed. With this aspect we reach the ultimate stage of totalitarianism, though every dictatorship does not necessarily go as far as this in practice.

The first implication of this new development is obviously that there could not have been room for the new religion of the state unless existing forms of organized religion had already been sufficiently weakened in advance. This process has been going on for a long time in Western Europe, though where the power of the Church over the masses of the population had not decayed sufficiently, as in Russia, the new dictatorial regime itself undertook the task of hastening the end. The war of the communists against the Orthodox Church in Russia, as of the French Revolutionaries against the Catholic Church in France, is primarily to be attributed to the intimate association of each Church with the social order which they were fighting to overthrow. In addition, however, there was the conscious desire to extirpate the existing religion in the mind of the country, because they had a new and a better creed to preach. As early as 1920 one very shrewd observer had remarked that communism was not a mere political party, but a faith, and had realized that herein lay its great strength. 'If all communists', wrote Bertrand Russell, 'become religious fanatics, while supporters of capitalism retain a sceptical temper, it may be assumed that the communists will win.'[1] Twelve years later Count Sforza commented, 'When in Russia — especially the Russia of the Five Years' Plan — I was constantly struck with the impression that I was watching the flowering of a new religion'.[2] The implication, that

[1] B. RUSSELL, *The Practice and Theory of Bolshevism*, 1920, preface, pp. 8-9.
[2] COUNT CARLO SFORZA, *European Dictatorships*, 1932, p. 162.

where the conditions existed which made communism possible, if it was to be defeated, it was only to be by another political religion, akin to itself, was but too true.

The economic structure of capitalist society was, of course, itself hardly capable of being turned into a religion, at least as long as it was a reality. In retrospect the Jacobites of political economy may have had the vision of its ghost clad in the mantle of divine right, and have burnt incense to its memory, but the true counter-religion to communism, which was found and applied by the dictators, was the force of nationalism. The religious spirit had not been lacking in such nationalists as Mazzini. Dictatorship institutionalized and turned to its own ends the new religion of the nation state. Thus fascism in Italy became what a historian of the movement calls a 'pseudo-religion', with its party saints and mythology, ceremonials and liturgy and holy days.[1] The signing of a Concordat between the Church and the Fascist state in Italy in 1929 should not mislead one into believing that there has been any abandonment of the claim by the Fascist Party to spiritual as well as material leadership. Napoleon, too, signed a Concordat with the Pope. Church and state in Italy found it to their temporary advantage to come to terms, but unless either party was willing to abandon the essentials of its own creed, it was an armistice and not a permanent alliance: the Church of Hildebrand, though it might reluctantly abandon the temporal sword, could not give up the spiritual as well.

In Italy the fact that the Catholic Church is also a national church, combined with the possession of a shrewd

[1] SCHNEIDER, op. cit., p. 228.

sense of the possible by the leader of the fascists, has prevented the outbreak of a frank struggle between Church and state. In Germany the conflict of allegiances between the Roman Church and the German state is open and acknowledged. Universality is, after all, a fundamental principle of Catholicism: a Church which claims to be Catholic, despite temporary political advantages, cannot sink into being a mere religious department of the fascist or National Socialist state. For a time the Vatican, possibly putting its immediate above its permanent interests, may have been willing to march side by side with the dictators against a common enemy, but the decline of the communist threat should allow the true alignment of forces to reveal itself more clearly. Rome knows, naturally, how to bow its head to a storm: an open war with the new nationalist religions is not necessarily to be looked for. But on one battlefield hostilities have already begun. The control of education is a key point in the struggle. The Church fought bitterly for this in France against the Republic; but the negative anti-clericalism of the lay schools in France was always less of a menace than ecclesiastics had feared. The positive teachings of the totalitarian state are a far greater danger.

The erection of nationalism into a new kind of political religion is evident enough in those dictatorships which have arisen out of the struggle against Marxian socialism. But the general tendency of the totalitarian state in this direction also finds confirmation in the evolution of the dictatorship in the U.S.S.R. While the former type of dictatorship learned from the devotion which communism inspired in its followers the power of faith in politics, communists in turn learned from their opponents that nationalism is the greatest of political faiths in the modern world. The communism of Marx and Lenin will have left something behind in Russia, just as the Jacobinism of Robespierre did in France; but in each case the revolutionary religion was doomed to decline in intensity. In the U.S.S.R. its place shows signs of being taken, not by a revival of the old orthodox religion, but rather by a Muscovite version of the new dictatorial nationalism. Such, at least, is one possible explanation of the mysterious changes that have been taking place since the rise of Stalin to supreme power. Dogmatism, where nearly all the facts are disputed, would be absurd; but it is not unreasonable to suggest that Russian communism will soon have little left in common with the bolshevism of Lenin and Trotsky, Zinoviev and Kamenev, Tomsky, Radek, Rakovsky, and the other men, great or small, noble or base, who made the 1917 Revolution, but its name and the figure of Josef Stalin. There are more than a few signs that in Russia nationalism is taking the place of internationalism, and since Russian religion has been under the control of a department of state since the time of Peter the Great, it would not be an unreasonable surmise to suppose that the new nationalist religion is likely to prove not uncongenial to a new Holy Russia.

As the communist and the anti-communist dictatorship draw closer together, the antithesis between nationalism and the older religions will stand revealed in its nakedness, nor will the fight be only with Catholicism. While Catholicism comes into conflict with totalitarianism from one angle, Calvinism opposes it from another. It is worth noting that no country in the history of which Calvinism has played a considerable part has up to the present produced a totalitarian dictatorship. One might associate this with the fact that the Calvinist Church is at bottom a collection of independent congregations. Whereas Catholicism conflicts with totalitarianism because it is above the nations, Calvinism is below. The basic source of opposition is the same, however: the Church universal, whether finding its visible expression in the one Catholic Church recognizing the authority of the Pope at Rome, or in a host of autonomous congregations, is the only spiritual authority either religion recognizes. The nation cannot be more than a political unit for them.

Lutheranism provided a better foundation on which totalitarian dictatorship could build. 'One can understand', writes a Swiss pastor, 'why Luther is so popular in the state of Adolf Hitler. The great reformer has invested the ruler with so much religious authority that he can really claim to be fulfilling a divine mission among his people — as millions of Christians in Germany actually believe he does. The German Church has always been accustomed to live in close relationship with the state, and has seen no difficulty in recognizing the Prince as supreme bishop, *summus episcopus*, of the territoral church ... It is easy to understand why contemporary German theology, trying to find an ethical and religious basis for the state, has fallen back on the theory of Luther'.[1] Important sections, even of the Lutheran Church, however, have revolted against the spiritual discipline imposed on them by the state. The truth is perhaps that any kind of Christianity is a little difficult to reconcile with the worship of the state. So the Roman state found when it was a very young religion, and the Empire asked for no more

[1] A. KELLER, *Religion and Revolution*, 1933, pp. 160-1.

than a very trivial, formal acknowledgment of its spiritual claims.

The view has been put forward that what totalitarianism is really doing is re-creating the ancient state, taking us back to the classic world, before Christianity came to build a City of God in rivalry with the City of Rome. Greek thought, one must admit, drew no hard and fast line between the religious and the political sphere; in fact it was hardly aware that there was such a cleavage. In a sense the state was sufficient religion for most Greeks, and the city of Rome was the chief object of Roman religion. But to conclude from this that an analogy can be drawn in this matter between the Greek and Roman state and the totalitarian state of to-day would be a mistake. Totalitarian nationalism has come into a civilization saturated for nearly two millennia with religious thought. Its leaders have been bred in the school of Luther and Loyola, Augustine and Athenasius. They are soaked in Hebraic ideas of theocracy and are carrying over into politics a religious attitude of mind with which the classical world was unacquainted. The new nationalist religion of National Socialism is not an echo of the Athens of Pericles: it is a political version of the jealous tribal religion of the Old Testament Jews.

A further respect in which the totalitarian differs from the classical state lies in its use of the modern idea of sovereignty. The Greek city was never sovereign in the modern sense, because above the state there was always the law, and under the state there were always the citizens, who were active participants in what the Romans called the *imperium*. The conception of citizenship, in Aristotle's definition the capacity among free men for both taking the lead and following another's initiative, is fundamental in Greek political thought.[1] Poetry and philosophy in Greece and Rome, even when they glorified the state, were the work of free men. They represented in the state that element of spiritual independence which is necessarily incompatible with modern dictatorship. Even the tyrannies in the classical world are a long way removed from totalitarianism. Sparta might possibly provide a parallel, but it is surprising how little we really know concerning Sparta. Such a state has no history. Moreover, Sparta was an aristocracy or oligarchy, not a dictatorship.

One final consideration remains to be mentioned. It is necessary to point out that the religious, like the economic and political development of modern totalitarian dictatorship, represents no radical breakaway from the general trend of European history in the last two centuries. The dominance of the state over the Church, together with the laicization of all forms of social life, were basic principles of eighteenth-century thought. The whole school of *philosophes*, led by Voltaire, was in agreement on this point, and on this, too, Montesquieu and Rousseau were with them. The last chapter of the *Social Contract* is as uncompromising an assertion of the authority of the state over religious as well as temporal matters as could be found anywhere. Hobbes alone, asserts Rousseau, has clearly seen the evil and the remedy. 'He alone has dared to propose the reunion of the two heads of the eagle, and the restoration of political unity to the whole state, lacking which a state or government will never be well constituted.'[2]

[1] cf. J. L. MYRES, *The Political Ideas of the Greeks*, 1927, especially chs. iii and vi.

[2] *Contrat social*, Bk. IV, ch. viii.

But Hobbes should have realized, in Rousseau's opinion, that such a system is incompatible with Christianity; Hobbes, it is hardly necessary to add, did realize it but thought it better not to say so.

The revolutionaries of 1789 were the first to attempt to put these principles into practice. The Civil Constitution of the Clergy, the cult of reason, the cult of the Supreme Being, the *culte décadaire*, were so many attempts at a state religion. Napoleon, with greater realism, saw that these movements were premature, and concluded an armistice with the Church. It is interesting to find, about the same time, an echo of the revolutionary religions in the German nationalist, Fichte, who produced a curious sketch of a German national church[1] such as was only to be attempted in practice a century or more later.

With what may be called the religious aspect, totalitarian dictatorship reaches its highest point. Here its sway ends, for it has become co-extensive with human life. Totalitarianism takes the spiritual discipline of a religious order and imposes it on forty or sixty or a hundred million people. Its aim is a nation of Jesuits, serving not the Vicar of Christ, but the *Führer*. 'The German people', to quote Keller, a very moderate witness, again, 'are not simply indulging in hero worship: they have clad their leader in the religious glory of a Messiah sent by God Himself to deliver His people from dishonour, slavery and misery.'[2]

[1] v. ENGELBRACHT, op. cit., pp. 103-6.
[2] KELLER, op. cit., p. 163.

§4 THE ROLE OF EDUCATION IN THE TOTALITARIAN STATE

In the previous section we have described the development of totalitarian dictatorship from a practical political expedient into a national faith, but how this was possible has still not been made clear. The decay of institutional religion is insufficient by itself to account for such a vast revolution, especially for one which appears to run counter to what, until recently, had been supposed to be the inevitable trend of modern history.

For better or for worse it is evident that many of the principles, which have hitherto been believed to be fundamental in the development of the modern state, have lost their validity. Among these, one basic assumption, which underlies the general political conceptions of the last two centuries, may be explained as follows. The idea of progress, slowly developed during the eighteenth century, had reached its climax by the time of Condorcet, and during the nineteenth century it had ceased to be a matter for argument, it was taken for granted. It was measured, perhaps, by somewhat arbitrary standards, but among the various criteria of progress invariable ingredients were, in the first place, the degree of political liberty existing in a community, and secondly the extent of the development of the intellectual and moral faculties of the individual: it was assumed, in brief, that 'enlightenment' was the true progress of the human race. Such was the eighteenth-century gospel, and education, added the nineteenth-century gloss, spells enlightenment.

Now no one can deny that education has made amazing

advances in the last fifty years all over the world. Yet it has not been accompanied by similar strides towards political and intellectual liberty, but by an increasing trend towards dictatorship and authoritarianism. We are therefore surely called upon to examine more closely the assumption that education and liberty, in the accepted sense of the words, go hand in hand. It should be observed here that we do not propose to enter into any discussion of the real nature of liberty, but merely to ask why the progress of education has been accompanied by an increase of nationalist, dictatorial, totalitarian tendencies, rather than of what the nineteenth century, rightly or wrongly, called liberty.

The belief not merely that the general spread of education was necessary for political liberty but that it would itself bring it about, was widely held in the last century. A closer examination of the origins of the idea of universal education might have aroused doubts, however. Its desirability was proclaimed during the last half of the eighteenth century by the Physiocrats, who were writing in defence of the idea of benevolent despotism. Their ultimate aim was the establishment of the 'natural and essential order of society', a despotism of natural law; but they were well aware also that public opinion, 'whatever it may be, is the true *Regina d'el mundo;* even when it is only a prejudice, an error, there is in the moral order no force comparable to it'.[1] When men are ignorant of the evidence from which the necessary order of society may be deduced, government is left at the mercy of mere opinion.[2] It follows that the first and principal task of

[1] LE MERCIER DE LA RIVIERE, op. cit., ch. ix, p. 63.
[2] id., ch. xliii, pp. 457-8.

government must be to remedy this situation, and the only method of doing so is by 'the establishment, the maintenance and the progressive improvement of universal education'.[1] Given this approach to the problem of education, it was natural that even the most liberal among the physiocrats, Turgot, should be able to write that the function of the Ministry of Education is to inculcate 'a uniform patriotism'.[2]

At the beginning of the nineteenth century the principle of universal education found a second wave of supporters in the German romantics and especially in Fichte, who after Jena saw in a new educational system the only hope of maintaining the German nation in existence. The kind of education he desired, and the arguments with which he supported his demand, would not have been without significance for any who could have foreseen the future. One feature on which Fichte particularly insisted was the complete removal of the child from the dangerous influence of his family, at least until a new outlook had been given to the whole nation. 'Not until a generation has passed through the new education can the question be considered as to what part of the national education shall be entrusted to the home.'[3] The aim of this education was to create a nation that could reverse the defeat of 1806, just as a century later a new education was called into being to redress the humiliation of 1918, for Fichte saw truly that education meant discipline, and discipline military power. 'The state which introduced universally

[1] BAUDEAU, *Première introduction à la philosophie économique* (1771); Daire, op. cit., p. 781.

[2] TURGOT, *Mémoir au Roi sur les municipalités*, 1775; *Œuvres*, 1884, ed. E. Daire, vol. II, p. 507.

[3] *Reden an die deutsche nation*, IX, § 138.

the national education proposed by us', he wrote, 'from the moment that a new generation of youths had passed through it, would need no special army at all, but would have in them an army such as no age has yet seen.'[1]

The association of the idea of universal education with the principles of authoritarian government and of nationalism was not fortuitous or mistaken. Lacking a certain degree of education the individual was capable neither of intelligent obedience to the law, nor of sharing in any degree in the political life of the nation. Now without some such active participation of the individual, the nation in the modern sense of the term, as a conscious entity, could hardly come into existence, and nationalism would be impossible. It was believed by nineteenth-century liberals that education was necessary to the protection of the individual against the state: the idea that lack of education might be the more effective protection would have seemed to them preposterous. Yet we can see to-day that the increase in the powers of the state has gone step by step with the progress of education. Governments have discovered that a limited measure of education is necessary to make the individual a profitable object of national propaganda and an efficient servant of the state. Experience has proved that the advocates of benevolent despotism were right when they looked to universal education to increase the authority of the government, and that the prophets of German nationalism were right when they put forward a national system of education as one of the chief springs of nationalist sentiment. Except in so far as he was anticipated in this, as in other respects, by Frederick the Great, Napoleon, the first of modern

[1] *Reden an die deutsche nation*, XI, § 167.

dictators, was also the first to put these ideas into practice; he may to a certain extent be regarded as the founder of the modern system of state education.

But though the degree of literacy which is all that the masses have been able to obtain, even in the Western countries where education has been most widespread, may merely have been enough to make more efficient servants of the totalitarian state, it will naturally be said that the alternative is of course not less education, but more. What, then, of those whose education has been carried to a much higher level? The part that higher education has played in the past cannot be misconceived. So long as there has been an educated few, a 'clerisy', as opposed to an illiterate mass, civilization has been cared for and the state has been mainly controlled by that minority. In the Middle Ages the Church provided the small group of men who, because of their inevitability as lesser or greater ministers of state, either directly or indirectly guided society; and the medieval ideal ensured that they should have an education covering all the fundamental fields of thought of their day, and informed with purpose and unity through the crowning study of theology. The later Middle Ages may have seen some falling away from the traditional ideals: the universities may have passed temporarily under the control of the hair-splitting schoolmen, who were to suffer, not altogether fairly, the derision of the Renaissance. But a new educational ideal was rising to take the place of a decadent one, and the control of the state was passing into the hands of men of the new training, whose education was clearly conceived as a preparation for their duties as a ruling class.

The literature, history and philosophy of the ancient

world were its basis, along with the arts, including that of a cultured life, the laws of their country, practical administration and war. Such were the studies, to take England as an example, of More and Cecil, Cromwell, Clarendon and Marlborough, Stanhope, Fox and the two Pitts; even in the days of Peel and Gladstone the same tradition was not dead. Men trained in this way governed England from the sixteenth to the nineteenth century, and men with a more or less similar training provided the effective governing class for the great European monarchies. The implication which will be noticed here, though we have not the space to discuss it, is that the art of government is something that needs learning, either by theory or practice, and that it normally requires some special training and education to make an efficient statesman or even politician, just as much as to make an engineer or chemist, lawyer or doctor.

The political significance of the older education, then, was that it helped to produce a governing class, an aristocracy which was not merely one of birth. The question we are asking in this section is whether education still does this, or whether the great advance in education which is characteristic of the last few generations in most countries has been achieved at the price of a decline in political wisdom.

In answering this question we may put on one side the progress of primary education: a knowledge of reading, writing and arithmetic, although desirable, does not by itself make a statesman, even when an unnatural capacity for communicating emotion and confusing issues is added to it. As for the higher branches of education, it is evident that, as a result mainly of the great development of science during the last half-century, they have undergone a revolution, which can be observed in every civilized or semi-civilized country. An inevitable consequence of the growth of scientific education has been a concentration on the training of specialists. The scientific expert reaches his high standard by confining his attention to a specific branch of knowledge, and the accumulation of material is forcing him to concentrate on an ever narrower field. Whereas in the past knowledge was incompletely fragmented, and even the specialist had to be a person of general education, to-day every subject, or branch of a subject, demands a special training for itself, and it is becoming increasingly difficult to be anything but a mere expert.

It might be thought that the intensive study, even of some very restricted branch of knowledge, would at least teach an appreciation of scientific method, and provide a mental training which would enable the scientist to deal with problems in fields other than his own. But it seems to be generally agreed now that while training may develop specific abilities these are not necessarily transferable from one sphere to another. There is little evidence that scientists are more scientific in their thought outside their own particular fields than the rest of the community, nor indeed is it to be expected. The scientist is dependent on the possession of a large body of scientifically ascertained evidence: where he has not this he must either take refuge in agnosticism, or base his opinions on prejudice and guess-work. Now the mere labour that the acquiring and maintenance of his expertness in his own subject demands, by itself prohibits the specialist from devoting the time necessary to the study, either in theory or practice, of the problems of government. In the world of politics he is in fact likely to be not more but less educated than the normal educated man of past centuries.

Superficially this argument may remind one of the hackneyed criticism of the scientist as an uncultured barbarian. But this attack, if it ever had any force, is certainly worthless now, for the student of non-scientific subjects is in just the same boat. His education, too, has been becoming increasingly that of a specialist. Even in literature, history and philosophy the cult of the expert has conquered. Thus philosophy is becoming more and more technical, is separating itself from general interests and rejoicing in its isolation. True, the philosopher lives and breathes in a region of pure thought far removed from our everyday businesses. One is not suggesting that the role of the speculative thinker is to reduce himself to the level of an advocate of party programmes. Yet one cannot but remember that Plato and Aristotle, Aquinas and Locke, Hume, Kant and many more, did not cherish a cloistered virtue. They did not sedulously separate philosophy from morals and politics, religion and history. Our pure philosophers may achieve results undreamed of by the less pure thinkers of the past; but whether they do or not, they will certainly succeed in assimilating philosophy as a subject of education to all the other disciplines for the training of experts.

The historian, again, is nowadays too often disposed to spurn that reflective element which used to be considered the chief educational merit of history. Literature, similarly, has tried to cut itself off from the life of the community, to write in a language understood only by the initiated, so full of allusions and echoes as to be appreciable only by a small coterie. If even our philosophers and our poets have become experts, where shall the common man look for guidance?

The same tendency is marked in the study of languages. It is only necessary to consider what the older education in the classical languages could be at its best — the study of letters, but also of history and politics, philosophy and the arts, an attempt to obtain direct from the originals the great intellectual heritage of classical civilization — and compare this with the present study of modern languages, to appreciate the change in aim. Even classics itself has been infected. How much of its time now, one must ask, does it spend in producing a linguistic expert, and how much in producing an educated man? It is a reversion from the age of Erasmus and Montaigne to the age of the Grammarians. How far higher education has moved, even from the ideas of the last century, is evident if one recalls the phrase of Newman, 'If then a practical end must be assigned to a University course, I say it is that of training good members of society'.[1] The juxtaposition of this with the contemporary educational ideal speaks for itself.

To find an important cause of the trend towards dictatorship in the existing concentration on specialization in higher education may at first sight seem an exaggeration.[2] Yet is there anything far-fetched in attributing to an educational system a leading, even a decisive influence,

[1] J. H. NEWMAN, *The Idea of a University*, 1852, VII, 10.

[2] The cult of the expert has nowhere progressed so far as in Germany and it is interesting to observe that Count Sforza anticipated from it precisely this result—'In Germany, confidence, admiration, go to the specialist, to the *Fachmann* (expert) . . . Stresemann was a practically unique exception; but Stresemann – I have it from himself – took good care to avoid indulging in lengthy parleys with any *Fachmann* of his department . . . So long as the *Fachmann* remains on his pedestal there is no hope of any rapid ripening of the

on the progress of a civilization? Again, in England, at least, it might be asked whether we are not over-estimating the importance of formal education and exaggerating its place in the national life. In the past this would have been a valid criticism; but at present in all countries social custom among the wealthier classes, together with a system of scholarships for the poorer, is directing a large proportion of the intelligent youth of the country into the universities. There, educational convention or economic interest concentrate their attention on a single field of learning, in which they receive a specialist training. As this tendency progresses, it is not unreasonable to assume that in future the ablest minds from all ranks will be drawn into the service of society as scientists, or technicians, or specialists in some form or other. In many ways this is an admirable development; but it has the result that education can no longer be regarded as a preparation for government. And if it be argued — though to my mind the argument is false — that it never was this, it still remains true that the older educational system at least did not call for the whole-hearted devotion that modern specialization demands, and often obtains. The absence in most countries of the most highly trained sections of the population from political life is a necessary consequence, and in itself a sign of their inability to contribute, except as experts, to the commonweal.

When the tradition of a class brought up to the task of government has died out, can the experts take its place? In so far as the expert is a scientist it is not to be expected

political atmosphere of Germany. *Fachmann*-idolatory is one of the first germs of the disease from which Dictatorships come.' SFORZA, *European Dictatorships*, pp. 154-5.

that he should. The statesman must have a scale of values: the scientist must know no such thing. One scientific fact may be more significant than another, it cannot be better. The scientist must be, like Adam and Eve, innocent of the knowledge of good and evil, philosophically naked and unashamed. What of the economist, the psychologist, the sociologist, the administrative expert? All these can give essential advice and information; they can provide studies of technique and show how to obtain one objective or another: they cannot explain why one is to be preferred to another. On the ends of the state, in so far as they are pure experts, they can say nothing. As for the methods of ruling the state — the technique of politics is a technique they do not learn. In that field, compared with the authors of *Mein Kampf* or of *Leninism*, who have devoted their lives to learning it in the hard school of experience, they are babes in arms. On the whole, is it not true to say that we have created an educated class, to which we are giving a monopoly of future education, which has little philosophy, lacks any profound social or political principles, and has small knowledge of or perhaps even interest in the ends of the state? Science has bestowed unprecedented power upon society at the very time when it is taking away from education its value as a preparation for exercising control over that power. One of our experts can do more to control the material universe than the tens of thousands of slaves who toiled at the building of the Pyramids; but he may have as little understanding of ultimate social purposes, and as little control over social ends, as they.

Is it false, then, to say that the type of education which was a preparation for government is disappearing? Is it paradoxical to suggest that it is the very progress of education which is threatening to rob this country, as it is already robbing others, of a politically educated class of rulers? The strength of aristocracy in a country like England in the past was that it gave to a selected class a training in the art of government and an education appropriate thereto. The class was chosen, of course, by heredity, and therefore naturally a large proportion of it would be quite unfitted to profit by the opportunities it received; but there remained a sufficiently large residue capable of learning its lesson and taking over the government of the country. True, even without adequate training a genius in politics may appear. But if a nation is to rely only on the chance appearance of a political genius then it will have no choice but between anarchy and dictatorship.

There is the further consideration, too, that government is not merely a technique: it is also a psychological attitude. The latter is not easily taught; it is more likely to be transmitted by birth, though there is no doubt that it can be acquired. The aristocracies of the past were selfish, of course, but it was only where they were excluded from government, as in the France of the Bourbons, that they lost their governing capacity. At the worst they continued to believe in themselves and the social order for which they stood. The new aristocracy of experts has no such easy self confidence or acceptance of things as they are. Its ideals are far higher: it demands progress, social improvement. Yet what criterion has it for knowing these when it sees them, or what capacity for securing them?

Since this chapter was written I have found what seems to me a confirmation of the view adopted; and because, among all the ideas expressed in this book, those on which this section is based are the most likely to meet with a natural resistance on the part of its readers, I feel called on to quote it at length. José Ortega y Gasset in *The Revolt of the Masses* arrives by an entirely different route at a very similar conclusion to the above. He points out rightly that our age is still at heart under the domination of the idea of progress, still cherishes, in his own words, 'the strange presumption that it is superior to all past time'. 'If it felt that it was decadent', he continues, 'it would then look on other ages as superior to itself, which would be equivalent to esteeming and admiring them and venerating the principles by which they were inspired. Our age would then have clear and firmly held ideals, even if incapable of realizing them. But the truth is exactly the contrary; we live at a time when man believes himself fabulously capable of creation, but he does not know what to create. Lord of all things, he is not lord of himself. He feels lost amid his own abundance. With more means at his disposal, more knowledge, more technique than ever, it turns out that the world to-day goes the same way as the worst of worlds that have been; it simply drifts.' In his judgment of his contemporaries Gasset is more ruthless than we should venture to be, 'Anyone who wishes can observe the stupidity of thought, judgment, and action shown to-day in politics, art, religion, and the general problems of life and the world by the "men of science", and of course, behind them, the doctors, engineers, financiers, teachers, and so on'.[1]

The educated man of to-day — doctor or lawyer, architect, engineer, teacher, administrator or business man — whatever his race and state, is in the same position.

[1] J. Ortega y Gasset, *The Revolt of the Masses*, trans. 1932, pp. 47, 124.

Unlike the aristocrat of the past he no longer has handed down to him the tradition of government, nor does he inherit the traditional standards. In so far as the modern educated world, regardless of race and religion, had any principles, they were those worked out by the eighteenth century in theory, applied by the Revolution, turned into shibbolcths by the nineteenth century, tested and found inadequate by the twentieth. For these ideas were created before the great nation state had appeared or the progress of science had produced the possibilities and problems of the present day. The political ideas of the Enlightenment are no longer relevant in the terms in which they were stated, and a disinherited generation is conscious of the intellectual void their collapse has left.

Not merely Western Europe and its offshoots in the other continents, but the whole of the more or less civilized world is suffering from the same disease — older civilizations, where a remarkable development in technical control has been accompanied by the destruction of old faiths and traditional ways of life, even more acutely than the newer. It has been discovered that a country can acquire all the material wealth and power of civilized states merely by educating a sufficiently large class of experts: but at the same time either the traditional beliefs will be undermined and leave only an unhappy scepticism, or if they are retained, they will prove quite inappropriate to the new conditions created by modern technique.

The result is that in Western and Eastern countries alike the educated classes have been, consciously or unconsciously, throwing off their allegiance to their former intellectual and moral ideals. If we were all of us, all our time, porkers not even from the sty of Epicurus, if we could ignore ends other than that of material welfare, the loss of old principles and the absence of new ones would be of little consequence, and we might be happy, for material comfort would be all that we should need. But a spiritual void insists on being filled: a nation lacking good ends will find bad ones for itself. Prophets and teachers will not be wanting to play on the passions and exploit the ignorance of an educated class that is spiritually bankrupt, *déraciné*: such is what Julien Benda has called *la Trahison des Clercs*. Unguarded either by belief in an ancient creed, or by a rational study of the problems of social life, the expert is ready to fall a victim to any new heresy. He will seize on any gospel that has the appearance of providing a safe orthodoxy on which to base the crumbling state, so long as it is presented by demagogues sufficiently clever or by tyrants sufficiently powerful. If it can be given a pseudo-scientific veneer so much the better.

In these conditions it is not difficult to understand why the general acceptance of the principle of universal education, and the great advance of specialist studies, should have been accompanied by the rise of dictatorship and the development of the totalitarian state. Here is an explanation, that at least deserves consideration, for the otherwise inexplicable fact that the return to government by naked force and faiths unhallowed by tradition has gone on concurrently with a great increase in the size of the educated classes. For what requires explanation is not the fact that it has been found possible in many countries to work up the masses into a state of fanaticism. There is nothing new in that: indeed, the not inconsiderable amount of passive and active hostility manifested by peasants and industrial workers in such countries as

Germany, Russia and Italy, towards the authoritarian regimes under which they at present live, is, all things considered, the more remarkable fact. The really surprising development is the extent to which the new doctrines, however wild and irrational they may seem, have won the sincere adherence, not of the illiterate, poverty-stricken masses, but of the professional classes, the technicians, the lawyers, doctors, scientists, engineers, administrators — in short of the experts who tend the complicated machinery of modern civilization. It is the educated, not the uneducated masses, who form the real problem in the modern state.

The Ages of Faith may be returning, but will it be a faith built up on the inherited culture of a great civilization, developed by the efforts of a long series of saints and philosophers, holding up a high standard of behaviour and belief to a barbarous world, and guarded by a Church which, whatever its faults or merits, at least believed that Reason was divine, or will it be the fetishism of a new Dark Age? Whatever it is, it will be imposed by force, for the expert has armed authority with almost irresistible power. Like the slaves who dug their graves in preparation for their sacrifice at the death of some mighty despot of the old world, the scientist has invented the instruments of his own immolation as a free scientist. He has invested authority with the weapons which will be used, and which indeed are being used, for the destruction of that freedom of thought from which in the beginning science sprang, for the abandonment of the social and political principles with which its progress has been accompanied, and — who knows? — for the slow but irresistible barbarization of the Western world.

CHAPTER VIII

SUMMARY AND CONCLUSIONS

§ 1

THE HISTORICAL EVOLUTION OF DICTATORSHIP AND OF THE TOTALITARIAN STATE

In the previous chapters we have attempted, so far as space allowed, to give a brief history and analysis of dictatorship and of the totalitarian state. It remains to be seen what conclusions can be drawn from this inquiry. Our aim here is not to erect a juristic theory, nor to attempt an ethical and philosophical treatment. The final task must be not to justify or condemn, and certainly not to try to comprehend *sub specie aeternitatis* such a terrestrial phenomenon as dictatorship, but to draw together the material obtained in the course of our inquiry and on that basis to examine its operations in general terms and state any conclusions which the facts appear to justify.

Before venturing on this it will be desirable to spend a few pages in recalling the stages through which our argument has proceeded. The history of modern dictatorship begins with the birth of the theory of sovereignty, along with the modern state, in the time of the New Monarchy. From the example of Bodin, by general acceptance the first real theorist of the state in modern times, we saw how far sovereignty was in the sixteenth century from possessing the vast extension of attributes it has been given in later centuries.

The New Monarchy developed into benevolent despotism, but sovereignty remained for long unemancipated from the theoretical restrictions of natural law, and the practical limitations implied in the nature of divine right monarchy and in the claims of the aristocracy and the Church. Although in the seventeenth century Hobbes and Spinoza evolved the idea of a really absolute sovereignty, their work had no practical consequences at the time. In the eighteenth century, however, the Contract school of thinkers succeeded in transferring the idea of sovereignty to the people; and in this connection the Hobbesian conception of a sovereignty as absolute and unlimited as could be imagined, found its true destiny, while its application in practice was encouraged by the precedents recently established by the benevolent despots. The advocates of the political rights of the people seized on the idea of sovereignty with ardour and applied it with a ruthlessness that put the efforts of divine right monarchy to shame. Sieyès summed up the political ambitions of the sovereign people when he asked, 'What is the Third Estate?' — 'Nothing.' 'What ought it to be?' — 'Everything!'

The French Revolution was thus the first effort to put the idea of absolute sovereignty into practice. The resistance of the privileged orders and the Church, and the political inexperience of the revolutionaries, together with the threat of foreign invasion and the breakdown of the French economic structure, brought panic and with it terrorism. As a consequence the claims of sovereignty were intensified, and political liberty was sacrificed to the necessity of revolutionary dictatorship. For a year the Jacobin party, headed by Robespierre, ruled France in the name of the People, but after the fall of the Jacobins the idea of the People gradually merged into that of the *patrie*, and nationalism became the strongest motive force in French politics. This, combined with the general demand for stable government, gave his opportunity to the first dictator of modern Europe, the heir of the sovereign people and the real beneficiary of the revolutionary transference of sovereignty, Napoleon Bonaparte.

His own ambitions, which roused and maintained against him the hostility of Europe, brought about Napoleon's downfall, but the attempt after 1815 to restore the government of divine right monarchy was doomed to failure. The second revolutionary assertion of the sovereignty of the people, in 1848, was the first truly modern revolution, because in it socialistic aims were mixed with the demand by the disenfranchised classes for political power. The fear aroused in the minds of the French peasantry and bourgeoise by the agitation of the small group of socialists and the undisciplined clamour of the starving working classes of Paris flung the country into the arms of its second dictator.

Again a Bonaparte came to bring peace, domestic and foreign, to France, and again constant wars brought him down. The miserable failure of Louis Napoleon's foreign policy led to the setting up of the Third Republic in France, but this differed from its predecessors in that the Republic itself crushed, at the very beginning and in the most cruel and ruthless fashion, the parties demanding a drastic social change. Freed from the association with social revolution, it was possible for a conservative parliamentary and republican regime to be set up successfully in France.

Parliamentary institutions spread widely during the later years of the nineteenth century, but the last blow was only dealt to divine right monarchy by the war of 1914-18. The collapse of the Russian autocracy and the defeat of the Central Empires apparently set the seal on the triumph of parliamentarism, and the third great revolution of modern times, which broke out in Russia in 1917, began in the form of a democratic demand for a wider franchise and Parliamentary government. The dispersal of the Russian Assembly by the bolsheviks, and the establishment of a government based frankly on force, which developed later into something very like the personal dictatorship of a single man, was the first sign that the triumph of parliamentarism was an illusion.

The political evolution of modern Italy was on very different lines from that of Russia, but here also a dictatorship, based this time on a combination of syndicalist with nationalist ideas, emerged from the defeats and disillusionment of the war, and drove home the lesson. The rival forces of dictatorship, which had thus staked out their claims in Italy and Russia, continued their struggle with peculiar fierceness and characteristic dogmatic ardour in Germany, but whether the Communist or the National Socialist Party won, dictatorship was the inevitable outcome. Meanwhile many other European and Asiatic countries were experimenting in dictatorial or quasi-dictatorial governments; while in Latin America dictatorship had been the normal type of government ever since the collapse of the Spanish Empire.

Thus there is every appearance now that we have entered on an epoch not of parliamentarism but of dictatorship. This is in itself not particularly remarkable. The Greek world saw two distinct waves of dictatorship; Rome had its essays in Cæsarism, before Augustus finally set up the Empire; and in the medieval Italian city states dictatorship became endemic. We should not lightly conclude, however, that the present wave of dictatorship will merely reproduce the characteristics of similar epochs in the past. The peculiarity of the contemporary movement, as we have seen, is that it has applied the dictatorial method of government to the nation state and out of the combination has arisen the new totalitarian idea.

Again, however, it must not be taken for granted that totalitarianism is merely the child of dictatorship. Just as dictatorship can be traced back in practice for nearly a century and a half, and in theory for much longer, so the origins of totalitarianism are to be found embedded equally deeply in modern history.

The elements which have gone to the building up of the totalitarian view of the state have been analysed briefly in the two previous chapters. Again we have to start with the idea of sovereignty. In their conception, as in their consummation, dictatorship and totalitarianism are united. Again, as with dictatorship, despite the achievements of a Louis XIV or a Frederick the Great, totalitarianism proper is not born out the idea of sovereignty until the sovereign and the subject are united in the idea of popular sovereignty. When the French Revolution brought this idea into practical politics it gave political unity to the sovereign state, and took a long step towards totalitarianism. The first element to be added to sovereignty in the process leading up to totalitarianism was thus the democratic idea of the sovereignty of the people.

At the time when this idea of popular sovereignty

was approaching its first triumphs in France, the idea of the nation was also emerging into political consciousness in the reaction against the aggressions of the benevolent despots. Corsica and Poland present two instances of this, but it was a ruler who has been called the greatest of the benevolent despots, and the first dictatorial heir of the sovereignty of the people, Napoleon Bonaparte himself, who called to his support in France, and aroused against him in the other countries of Europe, the new force of nationalism on a large scale. Now whereas the 'People' is an intellectual conception, incorporating an ideal, but corresponding to no easily apprehended concrete reality, the idea of the nation was able to contribute to the growth of the totalitarian state a very real emotional force, and one which put the cohesion and self-consciousness of the primitive tribe behind the great state of modern times.

The new national ideal of the state, which gave it a unity far surpassing the former political unity derived from common subjection to a single sovereign, became the dominant political force of the nineteenth century. Idealist philosophy lent its support to the new idea of the state, and in the attempt to provide a rational basis for the new scheme of things even the aid of natural science was enlisted. As mathematics and astronomy had provided the scientific analogies upon which seventeenth- and eighteenth-century political thinking had been built, so in the nineteenth century biology exercised the leading influence, and the state, instead of being, as it had been to Locke or Hobbes, a sum in addition, came to be conceived on the analogy of a biological organism. The intensification of political unity, which had been produced by the fusion of sovereign and subject in the revolutionary state, and had been given an emotional connotation by the ideal of nationalism, was now brought under the influence of the biological idea of organic unity, which completely merged the individual in the community. Where this development was pushed to its conclusion the state passed out of the sphere of Western political ideas, and came under the sway of so-called racial ideas that revived in a new form the blood-tie of the primitive tribe.

To make this idea a reality in the great modern state, however, political, economic and cultural developments were necessary. The arguments we have adduced for believing that the modern system of education played an important part in the development of the totalitarian state need not be repeated. Similarly we need not do more than mention the contribution of the political methods evolved in the development of parliamentary party politics to the technique of the single-party state, and the growing concentration of political power that has been characteristic of all modern states.

Finally, we must not forget the part played by socialism, both in the theoretical preparation for totalitarian dictatorship and in the causation of the actual historical situation from which it emerges. Our reference here is not, of course, to the vague, humanitarian, undenominational socialism, as one might call it, which was no more than an indignant protest against the conditions of life under which the new industrial masses lived, but to certain systematized forms of socialism, which contributed to the development of the totalitarian age in three ways. With the school of Saint-Simon, socialist theory broke away from orthodox individualist economics and attributed to the state extensive positive duties in the economic sphere. This has swollen into the claim on the part of the totalitarian state to a monopoly of economic control in society. Secondly, seeing that Parliaments were merely the tools of the wealthier classes, and accepted even the most patently necessary social reforms only very slowly, if at all, socialists began to abandon the democratic theory and to nourish the idea of an *élite*, that should enforce in an authoritarian manner the changes which democracy had failed to achieve by persuasion. This was the easier because the theory of historical materialism, which became the fundamental dogma of the most influential school of socialist thought, led, as Ruggiero has pointed out, to a neglect of political values by socialists.[1] Socialism, he adds, through its worship of the technical expert, tends to convert politics into bureaucracy,[2] though we cannot agree with him that the change is entirely one for the worse. Thirdly, with Karl Marx rose also the theory of the class war, and where this has won general acceptance a dictatorship of the right or the left is, as we have argued in an earlier chapter, a fore-ordained conclusion.

Thus, to sum up, out of sovereignty, democracy, nationalism, the organic theory of modern political philosophy, the biological idea of organism, the progress of education, the system of party government, and socialism in some of its various forms, especially Marxism and syndicalism, was born the totalitarian state.

For the state which is conceived in theory and works in practice in the totalitarian fashion, dictatorship has proved the appropriate form of government. The con-

[1] G. DE RUGGIERO, *The History of European Liberalism*, 1927, p. 387.
[2] id.

sequences of the association of the political method of dictatorship with the totalitarian idea of the state are momentous, but before we can discuss these it is necessary to examine first the general characteristics of dictatorship.

§2 THE ORIGIN AND END OF DICTATORSHIP

It would be natural to begin our task of analysis at the beginning, with the origin of dictatorship, and ask when and why it originates. But there is a preliminary question. Is it, we must ask, a form of government which every state has to experience? This question can be answered without delay: it is clear that dictatorship is not a stage through which every state, at some time or other, has to pass. Sparta, and some of the cities of Bœotia and Arcadia in the Greek world, Venice among medieval Italian cities, and a number of modern states, including up to the present Great Britain, have failed to enjoy the advantages of a true dictatorship. It is assumed here, incidentally, that dictatorship is a stage in the history of a political community and not a final consummation, but the problem of what, if anything, comes after dictatorship may be postponed till later in our discussion.

If we ask, secondly, whether, when dictatorships have developed, it has been at any specific stage in the growth of political society, it will be difficult to give a simple answer. Obviously they do not appear in primitive communities, if we may permit ourselves the use of that very questionable term. This is only what one would expect; in fact it follows from the definition of dictatorship; for, whatever we mean by primitive, at least we may say that in such societies the religious and customary sanctions of government would be strong enough to prohibit the appearance of a ruler whose authority was based on other foundations, unless he were a military conqueror. The only apparent exceptions to this rule are the dictatorships of Latin America, and there, although many sections of the community may be extremely backward, the politically conscious class is far more advanced in its ideas; the same explanation would apply to such post-war dictatorships as those of Portugal and Poland.

However, the use of such terms as 'primitive' or 'advanced' is fraught with danger. It is difficult to disentangle them from the assumptions of the idea of progress. Moreover, they imply that there is a normal course of evolution, or of life history, through which states, like other living organisms, have to pass, and that various forms of government correspond to the various stages in this evolution. As we do not propose to examine in this place whether there is such a norm of development or not, and as we certainly cannot take it for granted, we are left with the alternative of setting the question in different terms, and instead of asking at what stage, examining rather under what conditions dictatorship appears.

Let us take, first, economic conditions, because these provide the most fashionable explanation. It is often suggested that dictatorship is the final recourse of a decadent capitalist system, driven to defend itself by turning its hidden tyranny into an overt one, and substituting naked force for the veiled oppression of the bourgeois parliament. This argument, and the concomitant moral indignation aroused in the Marxist breast by the discovery that the capitalist animal, when it is attacked, actually defends itself, are too familiar to require elaboration.

But the real subject of this explanation is not dictatorship but Fascism; and Fascism cannot be studied in the manner in which we wish to study dictatorship, because, as the term is used by Marxists, it is not an historical fact but a theory about history. This is no quibble, nor an attempt to evade the issue by changing the field of discussion and using the term 'fact' in a philosophical sense; but, accepting the normal recording of an event in history as an historical fact, clearly the rise of a party calling itself the Fascist Party is this, but equally clearly the Marxist theory of fascism is not. It is what we have just called it, a theory, like capitalism or feudalism, put forward to explain a complex social development, involving a mass of historical detail; the Marxist explanation of the function of dictatorship is one feature of this historical theory, and is therefore dependent on its general validity. This, however, it is not necessary for us to examine, since obviously the Marxist theory cannot be generalized as an explanation of the origin of all kinds of dictatorship. Dictators have appeared in Greek states and South American republics that can hardly be said to have reached the capitalist stage of development; while a left-wing dictatorship such as the Mexican or the Russian has been used as a weapon against and not in support of capitalism.

Again, the stage of economic development reached in a society can hardly be considered the decisive factor in the appearance of dictatorship. For example, the Spanish colonies in the early nineteenth century, which turned to dictatorship as soon as they had achieved their independence, were clearly not farther advanced in economic organization than the English colonies which revolted in the eighteenth century, nor did Russia in 1917 represent a more highly developed stage of capitalism than France or Great Britain. Further, we cannot even say that dictatorship results, if not specifically from capitalism, then when any possessing class is trying to defend itself. This explanation would cover many examples, but it would still leave the revolutionary dictator unaccounted for, and is of doubtful relevance to many of the Greek and medieval Italian dictatorships.

In fact it is impossible to define in economic terms the conditions out of which dictatorship arises. The one common factor is acute internal conflict in society. One may allow that this seems generally to be what one can describe as class conflict, that it is therefore generally economic in basis. But it is a kind of conflict that may or may not arise during any phase of transition in the economic history of society, and that if it arises may not become acute, for in many states such transitions have been undergone without recourse to dictatorship.

The causes of conflict may vary so greatly that to examine them all would involve writing an economic history of Western civilization. One feature which is associated with several epochs of dictatorship is worthy of notice, however. A period of economic disequilibrium may be initiated, or at least characterized and intensified, by the more or less sudden cessation of an age of colonization. In Greece one finds the first period of tyranny appearing immediately after the great age of colonization has drawn to its close.[1] An exception to this statement is apparently provided by the continued sending out

[1] *Camb. Anc. Hist.*, vol. III, pp. 514-15.

of colonies from the state of Corinth, but here the enlightened commercial tyranny of Periander deliberately prolonged the wave of colonization in the interests of its nascent commercial imperialism. Again, Rome had just ceased to send out colonies in the age of the Gracchi. Similiarly, it is not perhaps fantastic to establish a connection between the development of dictatorship in modern Europe and the sudden termination of the great nineteenth-century wave of migration.

The explanation of this apparent connection is not hard to find. When a society has been accustomed to send out a continual stream of emigrants, the consequence of a damming up of this stream is likely to be serious to economic equilibrium, by producing over-population relative to the economic structure of the country, and therefore unemployment and distress. A further consequence of a different nature, but one with almost equally dangerous possibilities, is to be found in the fact that the adventurous youth of a nation is thus robbed of its customary outlet. In both ways, economic difficulties and psychological tension may be produced in the community, leading eventually to a class struggle, revolution and finally dictatorship.

This, of course, is only one of many possible causes of that violent conflict in the state out of which dictatorship emerges. These causes are not necessarily economic in nature; the point to be stressed is that dictatorship always and everywhere is the child of a domestic struggle so acute that it amounts practically to civil war. It is in times of governmental weakness or anarchy that there arises in the cause of authority and order a Cæsar or a Napoleon, a Francia or a Mussolini.

It is for this reason that dictatorship is most likely to appear in those states where there is no room in the constitution for the temporary emergence in a crisis of strong, personal government. The English Cabinet and the American Presidential systems possess this safety valve, which was conspicuously lacking in the French Constitutions of 1791 and 1848. On the other hand Article 48 of the Weimar Constitution did not serve to save Germany from dictatorship.

Writers on history and politics have been apt to regard with trepidation the menace of a total collapse of the social fabric, but judging from experience this fear is singularly misplaced. Political systems may be overthrown, empires may fall, but social life and political government goes on, unless the community is physically destroyed by dispersion or massacre. When, as in a revolutionary epoch, the traditional authorities have lost their hold on men's obedience, and society seems threatened with the onset of chaos, then is precisely the moment when human nature demands, and creates for itself, a ruler who, by persuasion or by force, will guide it back into the path of obedience and social discipline. The success of any ruler is measured by his ability to capture what Lippmann calls the symbols by which public opinion is moved,[1] and of these the dictator has at his command the greatest of all in the idea of law and order. For a leader who can restore these, society will sacrifice any claim to individual independence or political freedom.

It might be thought that we should add to the feeling of internal weakness as a cause of dictatorship the fear

[1] W. LIPPMANN, *Public Opinion*, 1922, pp. 206-7.

of foreign conquest. Thus Syracuse looked to her tyrant for protection from the Cartaginian peril, and during the French Revolution the demand for authoritative government emerged when foreign enemies were menacing France by land and sea. On the other hand, the many times when Rome, England, Venice, the Netherlands, to mention only a few, were assailed by apparently overwhelming force, without having recourse to tyranny, are evidence that the foreign peril is not more than a contributory factor in its rise. Strong government is the natural response to any crisis. During the first World War a Lloyd George, a Clemenceau, a Wilson, temporarily concentrated in their hands a colossal authority; but if these played the part of the old Roman dictators, their position was quite different from that of the dictator in our definition. Although dictatorship relies mainly on the motive of fear, then, the fear of foreign enemies is not a primary cause. The essential element is always the consciousness of internal weakness and the existence of civil strife, and this is our first conclusion.

Behind the class and the party struggle which is the immediate occasion of dictatorship, we can, in the second place, observe one necessary preliminary condition, not so much of the strife itself as of the panic aroused by it. Dictatorship, as we have already had occasion to remark more than once, appears only on the grave of traditional authorities. Whilst a government exists that has the sanction of custom or divine right, indeed, so long as the traditional authorities have any viability at all, the reaction against disorder and the general fear of anarchy will inevitably turn to its advantage. The monarchy seemed weak enough in the England of the Roses or in the France of the Religious Wars; but excess of evil brought about a concentration of power on the throne as soon as there was an occupier who was capable of wielding it When a regime has lost its prestige for good, when there is no longer any possibility of believing that it can have the will or the power to govern effectively, then is the time when the passions let loose in society complete the process, and dictatorial rule emerges. This collapse of traditional authorities is at least as notable a feature of pre-dictatorial conditions in the ancient and the medieval as in the modern world

It may be asked how these statements are reconcilable with the so-called monarchical dictatorships of rulers such as Alexander in Yugoslavia or King Carol in Rumania or with the clerical dictatorship of Dollfuss and Schuschnigg in Austria. The answer is that none of these were true dictatorships. The Balkan kings were merely attempting to return to a more absolute form of monarchy, borrowing some points, it is true, from the technique of dictatorship, but maintaining essentially monarchial regimes for all that, and relying for their chief support on the traditional loyalty to the crown. The Christian Socialist rule in Vienna was more like a true dictatorship: but here the limits set to the authority of the state by the claims of the Church, recognized not, as in Fascist Italy, for the sake of political convenience, but on the basis of right, prevented the government from having the autonomy, the complete theoretical absolutism, the freedom from any law but its own will, that a true dictatorship should have. Both these systems might, of course, be transformed by comparatively simple changes in government technique into true dictatorships, but this could only be done by a sacrifice, in the one case of the monarchy, and in the other of the claims of the Church, that is, of the essential principles on which they were based.

This connection between the development of a situation in which dictatorship is possible and the collapse of the traditional sanctions of authority, indicates one reason for the association, which is discovered in history, between dictatorship and democracy, if we may for the moment use the latter term in a loose sense for any attempt, real or illusory, at what is called government by the people. It might be argued that dictatorship only becomes possible when social, political and intellectual developments have made democracy apparently inevitable.

In modern Europe we can see this process at work in the eighteenth century, in what has been called the Age of Reason; for there is no stronger solvent of traditional authority than the rational, utilitarian intellect, which, at the same time as it produces a sceptical attitude towards claims to political authority based on custom or religion, promotes a belief in self-government as the most obviously rational form of government for rational beings.

Democracy, in Revolutionary France, was a development of the theory of sovereignty; but it has another connection which helps us to understand why in modern times it has proved peculiarly vulnerable. Although theoretically based on the principle of the absolute sovereignty of the people, the democratic idea in fact inherited many of the liberal presuppositions of the eighteenth century. These, though a strong safeguard against old-fashioned despotism, have proved a source of weakness in so far as they have left the door wide open for the assaults of dictatorship. Liberal political systems have to fight dictatorship with their hands tied behind their backs. Freedom of meeting and organization, toleration of hostile opinion, liberal press laws, ineffective laws of libel, and so on, have all contributed to give dictatorial movements their opportunity to overthrow the liberal state. The theoretically absolute sovereignty of parliamentary democracy has received so little positive application, since its destruction of the divine right of kings and the privileges of the *noblesse*, that one cannot but wonder whether the people is indeed capable of exercising sovereignty. The historic task of many parliamentary systems appears to have been to prepare the way for the sovereignty of a dictator. The first of contemporary dictators frankly recognized the affiliation between democracy and dictatorship, when he wrote that Fascism might almost be described as 'organized, centralized, authoritarian democracy'.[1]

Dictatorship in modern times has arisen so often out of so-called democratic institutions that it seems almost as though it could not appear where there had been no previous attempt at self-government; but whereas the decline of traditional authorities is an invariable pre-requisite of dictatorship, the establishment of what might be called a democratic government is not always to be found among the events preceding its rise. In the Greek cities, for example, we often seem to pass directly from the overthrow of an aristocracy to the rule of a tyrant. In the modern world, however, a positive attempt at government by the people, however false or fleeting, has

[1] *Enciclopedia Italiana*, vol. 14, 1932, art. *Fascismo*, by B. Mussolini.

nearly always intervened between the fall of an hereditary monarchy and the establishment of dictatorial rule.

Since the French Revolution, the principle of popular sovereignty has spread to every more or less civilized country in the world. Any dictatorship which is set up to-day has therefore inevitably to exist in an atmosphere created by democratic ideology. Although in fact the dictator may be relying on the support of a small organized minority, in theory he has to claim to rule as the agent of the popular will. It might conceivably — though in our opinion incorrectly — be argued that the Greek tyrant was the representative of a class, Cæsar the embodiment of an army's power, the medieval Italian tyrant the leader of a faction, but it remains a characteristic of modern dictatorship, in any country which has fallen under the influence of Western political ideas, and few have not, that, however he has acquired his power, the dictator finds it necessary both to appeal to the will of the people as its source, and to proclaim the interests, spiritual and material, of the people as his guiding principle. Attempts to resuscitate aristocratic or monarchical principles, such as that of the *Action Française*, or the Fascist theory of an *élite*, have up to the present been doomed to failure, and there are no signs that they will succeed better in future. All epochs of dictatorship have appeared only after the decay of monarchical or aristocratic authority; the peculiarity of the modern dictator is that he might almost be called a creation of democracy, and from that origin he can never emancipate himself.

If we pass now from the origins of dictatorship to its mode of operation, the same association continues to be apparent. Here, indeed, it is not confined to modern

Europe but is to be found in all states and ages. Aristotle, time and again, calls attention to the similarity between tyranny and extreme democracy, and his opinion is not to be neglected, for one cannot but remark on the extent to which subsequent experience confirms the description of dictatorship he gives; nor need this surprise us, since he was able to base his views on more ample historical evidence of its working than any subsequent student of politics. The only other political writer who approaches him in the scope and realism of his observations is Machiavelli, who also had the advantage of coming at the end of a long period of experiments in dictatorship.

By democracy, it is hardly necessary to say, Aristotle does not mean the kind of parliamentary government which is usually given that title at the present day. He means by democracy, as every political writer up to the end of the eighteenth century meant, the direct government of the people by the people. Its usual accompaniment is demagogy, and as most modern dictators are primarily demagogues, dictatorship is much nearer to democracy in the classical sense than is parliamentary government. But demagogy is not the whole art of the dictator. The paradox of dictatorship is that it is based at the same time on popular support and on the forceful suppression of opposition. Government, political scientists sometimes say, must be by force or by consent. Dictatorship essays to combine the two and govern by both at once. The methods by which it does this can in essence be reduced to two — demagogy and terrorism, and the degree of success achieved by the dictatorship is largely a matter of the balance between them. Neither force can be entirely neglected, but the less the dependence on terrorism the greater can be adjudged its success.

Modern science has contributed largely to the progress of demagogy. The press, the cinema, and broadcasting have re-created the demagogic possibilities of the ancient city state in the modern nation state, and the ministry of propaganda has become a key post in dictatorial governments. The technique of the demagogue, however, is too familiar to require elaboration.

Government by terror, though better known now than a generation ago, calls for a little more discussion, because whereas demagogy can hardly be over-done, terrorism has to be used with care, and applied in practice only to a restricted section of the people, if it is to be an effective basis of government. When too large a portion of the community feels itself constantly under the menace of governmental terrorism, a revolutionary situation may easily develop. Above all, a government that has to call at all largely upon terrorist methods to retain the loyalty of its own servants is in a parlous condition. Suppose, however, that the terror is successful — and persecution, if sufficiently ruthless, often succeeds in its immediate aim — its intensity will then diminish, as in France under the Bonapartes or in Italy under Mussolini. The Nazi dictatorship in Germany and the Stalinite dictatorship in Russia being still in their early days, the terror in these countries still rages with some of its first fierceness. But when the older generation, less amenable to discipline, has, in the natural course of time and persecution, died, a better trained generation will appear.

That the combination of demagogy and terrorism may achieve an overwhelming temporary success is apparent.

But can they maintain a government permanently? To answer this question we must ask what is the normal effect of dictatorship on the political spirit of a nation. After the initial enthusiasm has waned, the usual sequel is a widespread lack of interest in politics and a spirit of cynicism and disillusionment. This is to be observed for example, in France before 1814, under the Second Empire before 1870, and in Italy after the conclusion of the Abyssinian war. One would naturally expect this phase to arrive some fifteen or twenty years after the establishment of a dictatorship, since in this period those with a pre-dictatorial ideology will have passed away, the young enthusiasts who followed the leader to victory will have grown into sedate, middle-aged men, anxious mainly to keep the good jobs that were the reward of their early services; while a new generation of young men will be pressing on their heels, but finding all the avenues of advancement open only by party favouritism, and most of the highly placed posts likely to be occupied for some time to come by those who were put into them as young men when the leader came into power.

When the dictatorship has entered this phase its survival becomes largely a matter of chance. All history bears witness that a permanent government cannot be founded upon the arts of the demagogue and the terrorist. Their very nature is a guarantee that the government which relies on them will be ephemeral. Dictatorships in the past have generally not lasted beyond the lifetime, sometimes abbreviated, of the dictator. Defeat in war has been the cause most often productive of disaster. An aggressive foreign policy in the end drives other states to take action to suppress a government that has become an international menace, as the neighbouring South American powers destroyed Carlos Antonio Lopez, and practically the whole of Europe united against the first Napoleon and made his abdication a condition of peace. History does not lead one to suppose that a purely internal movement can normally bring down a dictatorship. Even when a dictatorship has been overthrown by a mainly domestic movement, as were those of the successors of Peisistratus in Athens and of Dionysius in Syracuse, the leverage has had to be obtained by an external point of support, in the one case Sparta, in the other Corinth.

Whatever factor brings about its fall, all the evidence affirms that dictatorship is, as Aristotle stated, the most short-lived of all forms of government. The reason for this is that its permanence depends upon success. In the Bonapartist state, to use the words of Treitschke, in the last resort the ruler depends on good luck; loyalty and law count for nothing.[1] A legitimate government can survive many mistakes: a dictatorship is always in the nature of things insecure.

One final problem remains — what will follow its collapse? But this we can say as little as precisely when or how it will end. The experience of medieval Italy, classical Greece and modern South America, suggests that so long as the conditions which evoked the dictatorship continue, revolution and dictatorship will follow one another in a vicious alternation. Only where the forces making for political stability in the community are sufficiently strong to break the succession, as in nineteenth-century France, is another regime able to emerge.

[1] H. W. C. Davis, *The Political Thought of Treitschke*, p. 208.

§ 3

POLITICAL AND ECONOMIC CONSEQUENCES OF TOTALITARIAN DICTATORSHIP

The conclusions which are derived from a study of dictatorship in the past should apply equally to dictatorship at the present day, but the fact that it operates in the new totalitarian state introduces an element which vitally affects its working. The consequences of totalitarian dictatorship therefore call for special examination. They may be considered, as in Chapter VII, under four heads, namely, political machinery, economic consequences, international consequences, and the influence on the intellectual and moral or spiritual life of society. In the first three at least of these fields, moreover, we can legitimately come to some conclusions, without entering the field of ethical philosophy. Thus, to take the political aspect first, we can ask, without denying the existence of other criteria, whether totalitarian dictatorship produces, or can produce, an efficient and stable government and a politically contented people.

The peculiar characteristics of totalitarian dictatorship as a political form are the great extension it gives to the scope of government, the union of all powers in the hands of the executive, and the principle of leadership. Obviously, these factors in themselves greatly increase the power of the state, and it is necessary to bear in mind in this connection the observation of Treitschke that, 'the existence of a government is the less secure in proportion as its activity is extended more widely'.[1] The greater the

[1] H. W. C. DAVIS, *The Political Thought of Treitschke*, p. 91.

scope and power of government, the greater its responsibility, provided, of course, that it is responsible at all. The despotism of the priest-kings of the ancient world was not endangered by their omni-competence, because the sanction of religious awe bestowed on them the mantle of irresponsibility. In inheriting and exaggerating the powers claimed on behalf of the community by the extremest democrats and socialists, modern dictatorship has inherited not only their problems but also their responsibility. The penalty of failure is loss of power, and not by the peaceful process of a general election. If every failure opens the door wider to revolution, the mighty power of the dictator is only bought at a very heavy price, and this is the first criticism we must make on political grounds.

Secondly, we must ask whether the great concentration of power in the hands of the dictator necessarily promotes efficiency of government. Undoubtedly it provides the most effective, perhaps the only means of rapidly carrying through extensive changes in the structure of the state, and the importance of this in a crisis, or when society is so rotten that only revolutionary changes can save it from decay or destruction, must not be under-estimated. A Napoleon or a Cæsar may achieve a work of the greatest importance in surmounting a crisis or reorganizing the state. On the other hand, the inability of parliamentary governments to cope with severe internal crises, and their inaptness for effecting great changes in society, however necessary they may be, are notorious.

When we turn to consider the normal government of a country, however, the conclusion is different. In the long run there seems no reason for supposing that the despotism of the chosen of the People will be any more efficient than that of the chosen of God, or a *Führer* more capable of controlling the affairs of a great state with permanent success than a *Roi soleil* — rather the contrary, since the problems of government have become infinitely more complex and less susceptible of solution by arbitrary decree. The defects of despotic government have not changed, and they are too well known to require description.

The revolutionary regime admittedly gives an impetus to the state in its beginnings, and its mastery of the arts of propaganda, along with the absence of criticism, may maintain appearances for a while. But even a degree of efficiency can only be preserved in any state by the establishment of an administrative system based on sound institutions. This it is difficult, if not impossible, for a dictatorship to provide, since in the first place it implies a degree of political stability that dictatorships rarely achieve, and, secondly, dictatorship cannot escape from the fact that by its essential nature it is a government of one man and not an administrative regime. It will have the advantages and disadvantages that personal government necessarily has. Subsequent regimes may inherit the accomplishments of the dictatorship, as later governments in France inherited the Code Napoleon and the prefectoral system, but the dictatorship itself does not find the real sources of its power in such achievements; to estimate what one might call its survival-value, so far as its political basis goes, we must look not to the merit of its institutions, but to the personal loyalty that the dictator is able to evoke. The key to the political success or failure of dictatorship lies not in its laws or institutions but in the psychology of leadership.

As we have suggested in an earlier chapter, the fundamental condition which the dictator has to fulfil in the modern state is that he shall obtain recognition as the leader not merely of a party or a class, but of the nation. The degree in which the dictator is able to identify loyalty to himself as the chosen leader with patriotism to the state, is the measure of his success. This identification is only possible in the presence of a new conception of the state, for the nineteenth-century liberal view was too closely bound up with utilitarian and individualistic ideas to permit the development of strong nationalist emotion and of that organic conception of the unity of the state, which is necessary if totalitarianism and the Leader-principle are to be possible. The modern dictator must be thought of as an incarnation of the unity of the nation, a reconciler of all conflicts, an inspired leader through whom the power and prestige of the state is placed above all the personal interests of its individual members. The political potentialities and limitations of the dictatorial regime depend primarily upon the possibility of satisfying this condition, and this therefore demands detailed examination.

It must be premised that the dictator cannot at first be a truly national leader, because he has to look for support in the beginning to one or other of the warring classes in society, sometimes to a possessing class and sometimes to a revolutionary one. Successful attempts to establish a dictatorship on the latter basis are, however, rare, since the ideology of left-wing movements in modern times has usually been a barrier to the rule of a single man. They have normally been under the influence of liberal and parliamentary principles. Even communism found it difficult to emancipate itself entirely from these ideas; at least in theory it accepted dictatorship only as a temporary phase and at first attributed arbitrary authority not to an individual but to a party, though the principle of dictatorship proved more difficult to tame than the Marxists had expected, and the evolution of the Soviet government showed — as had the development of the revolutionary government in France a century earlier — that a party dictatorship easily becomes a government of one man.

Whether he comes from right or left, however, there is an inevitable dualism in the position of the successful dictator. He must appeal to those possessing power or wealth, those, that is, with something to lose, and at the same time to those still in revolt and dissatisfied. To the former he is a restorer of law and order and social security; to the latter he offers the fulfilment of at least some of their desires. Revolution and reaction meet in his policy: he is the synthesis to their thesis and antithesis. For the dictator, from whichever side he starts, has to grow from a party into a national leader, if he is to complete his ambition and fulfil his national destiny in society. Although he may have achieved power as the agent of a party or a class, he must emancipate himself from its control as soon as he can. He must appear, like the two Napoleons, as a 'saviour of society', governing in the interests not of a small fanatical clique or of a revolutionary class, but of the nation as a whole, if personal dictatorship is to become possible.

The support which the dictator may in this way obtain from general public opinion is not, by itself, however, an adequate basis for his government. Something more concrete is needed, round which support may crystallize.

This indispensable nucleus is provided in the beginning by the party or faction organized in support of the potential dictator. Here, incidentally, is a valid reason why a general whose authority is purely military cannot become a true dictator. Even a Cæsar, a Pilsudski or a Kemal Ataturk has to make himself a politician, at least to the extent of building up a political faction, if he wishes to become the ruler of the state.

But this association between dictatorship and the rule of a faction raises a further point. The leader of a faction is bound to that faction; if he wishes to emancipate himself from it, he can only do so at the cost of an internal crisis that will shake the whole state. The 'blood purge' of Hitler and the massacre of the so-called Trotskyites in Russia, illustrate what happens when a dictator finds it necessary to remove the faction, or any part of the faction, that brought him to power. But purges are notably lowering to the system, and even such drastic operations as these can rarely be complete. Moreover, although he may destroy those of his own faction who are obdurate, buy over those who are venal, and present himself to the people as a true national leader, the dictator still needs the support that only an organized party can give. However great a wave of popular enthusiasm may have carried him to power, enthusiasm will not provide a permanent basis for government without organized support.

Again, whereas in the small city state the tyrant could be the effective ruler, in a great nation state, even if he is not a mere figurehead he can only be the chief of a body of personal supporters, who in effect govern the country. The dictatorship, although it may attempt to disguise itself under the appearance of being a genuinely national government, is in fact a hidden oligarchy, which according to Spinoza is the worst of all. Government by party seems inescapable in the modern world; but the party will now be not the enthusiasts, the revolutionaries, but the time-servers, the useful hypocrites, the Vicars of Bray, and their loyalty will be bought and will have to be paid for by material advantages.

Here we approach a contradiction: for this reliance on party, however necessary it may be, prevents the dictator from retaining permanently his position as reconciler, above the strife of factions. His party must have been drawn in the main originally from one of the warring sections of society. Even apart from this, its mere existence is sufficient to create a new cleavage, because it forms a new privileged class in the state; and against it and its leader will be concentrated all the jealousies and hostilities of those who are excluded, or who exclude themselves, from its ranks.

If the dictatorship is not to merge into an ever narrower party tyranny and rapidly collapse, the dictator must be able to keep the loyalty of a sufficiently large section of the population outside the immediate ranks of the party. Useless to talk of identifying the party with the nation, for the peculiar characteristic of the party is the possession of an extraordinary loyalty to the dictator, such as the mass of non-political citizens can only experience sporadically. The party must comprise those whose loyalty is preserved by the ties of self-interest and by the possession of particular privileges, which would become meaningless if extended to the whole nation.

Even in the party itself loyalty will be endangered,

as the possibility of distributing rewards becomes limited, after the halcyon days of revocations and dismissals, executions and suicides, and a new generation of youth grows up, as we have already said, to find all the posts of advantage in the state occupied by those who were the young heroes of the revolution, and who will not vacate them in the course of nature for another twenty or thirty or forty years. As the prospects of promotion narrow, the circle of discontent widens.

The nation, however grateful it may have been to the dictator in the beginning for having saved the state from anarchy, will not, if it has known the idea of political liberty, continue to accept his government, without a continuance either of the menace that drove it in the first place into the embrace of dictatorship, or of the benefits which were expected to accrue from it. Modern dictatorship, emerging from democracy, must continue to serve, in one way or another, the people, and public opinion is the most insatiable of masters. The dictator must continually re-create the conditions that called him into existence. In so far as dictatorship is the result of a psychological condition of the people, that condition must be perpetuated. If it arose partly as a reaction against some real or supposed menace, such as Bolshevism, Judaism, Capitalist Imperialism, or Trotskyism, then that enemy has to assume a thousand forms and die a thousand deaths that the dictatorship may live.

The modern dictator is thus essentially in the position analysed by Aristotle. Politically his government has all the traditional weaknesses, and it is the fate of every dictatorship to find itself isolated with increasingly few genuine supporters in a rising tide of disillusionment and discontent. If these are our conclusions, where, it must be asked, is to be found political stability, or even the assurance of effective government? Certainly it is not to purely political forces that totalitarian dictatorship can look for a permanent basis.

But politics, we are often told, are subordinate to economics. Next, then, we must examine the economic consequences of totalitarian dictatorship. We have already agreed that dictatorship arises out of an internal conflict which is generally economic in its motivation. It would therefore be natural to expect that it should have to take decisive steps in the way of economic reform.

All dictatorships intensify the activity of the state in the economic field, at the present day more than in any previous age, because in all of its various manifestations modern dictatorship represents a reaction against the more liberal and individualistic economy of the nineteenth century. But it also signifies the end, along with divine right of kings, of the claims of the privileged classes, who had survived in the shelter of monarchy, and above all of what used to be called the sacred right of property. In this respect dictatorship might be said to be continuing the work of the French Revolution and of nineteenth-century liberalism. Thus at the same time it marks the culmination and the contradiction of the European liberal movement of the eighteenth and nineteenth centuries. Against the medieval 'liberties' of the privileged classes, which Burke and Montesquieu had associated with political liberty, democracy and socialism have asserted, also in the name of liberty, the rights of the people. Dictatorship has completed the work of destruction, but instead of substituting for aristocratic 'liberties' the liberty of the people, it has set up the power of the state.

The fundamental difficulty is that the problem of liberty is not only a political, but also an economic one. Nineteenth-century liberalism failed because political liberty did not bring with it the necessary economic advantages. Indeed, coinciding with the great industrial revolution, it was accompanied instead by the growth of a huge industrial population, living under appalling conditions. Hence the various schools of socialism were able to erect a damning indictment of liberalism, the essential point in their criticism being in effect that the cart had been put before the horse. They found themselves forced to the conclusion, which Proudhon had already proclaimed in 1848, that social reform did not in fact result from political reform.[1]

The dictatorships of to-day have come into being largely because they have promised, in return for the loss of political liberties, to give the people the economic improvements that earlier regimes failed to bring about. The principle of social equality, although not strictly speaking an economic good, is the first of these.

Hence the appeal of the dictatorships to the proletarian elements in society. On the other hand, it is one of the ironies of history that the middle classes, from the wealthy rentier to the small shop-keeper or office-worker, who by their panic contributed so greatly to the rise of dictatorship in Italy and Germany, are the classes which have probably suffered most and gained least from its economic policy. The poor have at least gained employment and entertainment of a kind; the big pikes in the capitalist

[1] P.-J. PROUDHON, *Solution du problème social*, 1848, ch. ii, § 3.

fish-pond can always look after themselves; but the middle classes have been the greatest losers by the revolution they themselves made. It is an interesting speculation whether they will resume in consequence their historic role as the truly revolutionary class in European history, or whether the dictatorships, led by Russia, will succeed in squeezing them out of existence. If they do succeed, when middle-class mentality is no more, when the bourgeois — someone who, in the French definition, has '*reserves*', spiritual and material, and is willing to fight to the end in their defence — has disappeared, certain things that have been reckoned not least among the achievements of Western civilization may be found to have disappeared with him.

The principle of equality has been carried a long way in Russia and Germany, not very far in Italy, and up to the present has hardly appeared at all in the other European dictatorships. It is not to be dismissed for this reason as an exceptional phenomenon. The same tendency, though the degree of levelling aimed at may vary, is to be seen in most dictatorships of the past. The reduction of subjects as far as possible to a single level is a classical feature of the technique of tyranny. We need hardly recall Dionysius and the tall poppies or Signor Mussolini and his ministers. Aristotle's observations on this point, Cæsar's treatment of the Senate, the tendency in the medieval Italian cities to esteem personal qualities above inherited rank, *la carrière ouverte aux talents* of Napoleon, and the action of South American dictators, such as Francia, against caste divisions in the state, provide further illustrations.

It might be asked whether liberalism could not do as

much, whether indeed in a country such as the United States of America it has not achieved at least as genuine an abolition of social caste as any dictatorship can show. But even if there is some truth in this, in the older countries of Europe the same progress has not been possible. Further, there are more concrete causes of economic discontent, and therefore of the tendency towards dictatorship, which still remain, in the form of widespread poverty and unemployment. A peasantry, living in a system of self-sufficient agriculture, can suffer only the blows of the climate, and for these the government can not very easily be held responsible. The aberrations of the modern industrial and financial machine, periodically producing violent depressions, are less easy to accept as purely natural phenomena, and for these governments are called to account. But this responsibility is precisely what the liberal state rejected in the past.

Whether the failure of parliamentary liberalism is due to its lack of authority in general, or to its particular inability to control and direct to social ends the activities of the great capitalist and financial interests in the state, we need not inquire. The point in either case is that a drastic increase in these powers is necessary to alter the situation. But in the presence of such an increase the state ceases to be liberal in the accepted sense. The question, to which no answer has yet been provided, is: can the liberal state reform itself economically, can it even defend its economic interests as conditions to-day require, and remain liberal?

The urgency of the economic problem and the need for a remedy must be admitted. It does not follow that totalitarianism provides this, but we should not under-estimate its achievements in this field. The early years of a dictatorship are often accompanied by economic improvement, resulting from more energetic government, unity of control, increased national confidence, and the appearance of political stability. At the present day it is the proud boast of Soviet Russia and Nazi Germany, the two countries in which totalitarianism has been pushed to its farthest point, that they have abolished unemployment. The whole man power of these countries has been put into operation and great achievements in industry and transport have resulted. Exchange control has prevented the currency fluctuations that are so menacing to contemporary parliamentary governments. Finally, the great emphasis laid in the dictatorial states on physical culture and the constant endeavour to supplement bread with circuses deserve to be remembered.

It is too early to give any final verdict on the economic advantages of totalitarianism. Moreover, since the relevant statistics are mostly provided by dictatorships themselves it would be dangerous to attempt to draw any very definite conclusions from these. One can venture on a tentative opinion, however, that the tightening of the belt which seems to have become an habitual exercise in some dictatorial states does not suggest that the cup of economic well-being is filled to overflowing. Moreover, experience in the U.S.S.R. suggests that dictatorships are not immune from human fallibility and that when they make an economic blunder they make it on a large scale. Russia, however, with its vast, unexploited resources, and its mainly agricultural population, is in an unusually fortunate position, and one which may allow the dictatorship there a fairly long run;

but the modern industrial states farther to the West have already begun to show signs of grave economic difficulties.

It would not be very rash to suggest that even in times of comparative plenty elsewhere the totalitarian states have shown that they have not yet solved the economic problem. Whether they will be able to face a world slump successfully we shall doubtless see in due course. Unless totalitarianism succeeds in breaking the economic cycle, the dictatorship, which may have come in with, or even inaugurated, a boom, will, if economic precedents hold, inevitably have to face what is now euphemistically called a recession: and while a government cannot obtain permanent support because of temporary economic advantages, it may have to face revolution because of its economic sins or misfortunes.

All this is in the realm of speculation. Considerations of a different order can be presented, however, bearing on the fundamental nature of the economic activity of the totalitarian state. Its peculiar feature, in the economic as in the political sphere, is that it is a world to itself. It is envisaged as an economic unit. The principle of economic self-sufficiency or autarky, to adopt the Aristotelian term, which has been particularly emphasized in Germany, is sometimes presented as a conclusion drawn from the experiences of the World War; but though doubtless the blockade, and the part the economic weapon played during the last war, has had its effect in intensifying this tendency, it can be found much earlier in German thought. Fichte, at the beginning of the nineteenth century, had already sketched out a whole plan for a closed economic state, and Lassalle represents the same idea in the latter half of the century.

Practical developments have reinforced these theoretical tendencies. A state such as the Soviet Union, which broke away from the existing economic structure, found autarky thrust upon it by the effort of the capitalist states to isolate and if possible stifle a rival economic system. The vast expenditure which the political aims of the dictatorships in Italy and Germany have demanded would have ruined the currency of these countries if it had not been sterilized against exchange variation; but this was only possible by an increasing limitation, as well as by a rigid state control, of economic connections with the external world.

Earlier dictatorships, for example that of the first Napoleon, made slight attempts at economic self-sufficiency, the most obvious example being the Continental System, used by Napoleon as a means of striking at England, but they are hardly to be compared with modern essays in autarky. Whereas in former periods the only serious consequence might be the deprivation of certain sea-borne luxuries, to-day the state which tries to isolate itself economically evidently suffers a severe loss of raw materials and of articles manufactured abroad, as well as of markets for its own products; the economic sacrifice is so heavy that it is doubtful if any modern state could be persuaded or forced to carry through the full programme of self-sufficiency to the end, except by the most complete tyranny. The work of European capitalism in the nineteenth century cannot easily be undone. It has been the great internationalizing force of the modern world, and has tied the nations together in a nexus of credit and trade that can only be broken at a price. So far as concerns the advanced industrial countries, it is doubtful whether their existing huge populations can be maintained in the absence of the great international trade in dependence upon which they grew up. Self-sufficiency may be merely another way of spelling mass suicide.

Here again, however, we must refrain from dogmatism. By military pressure a dictatorship such as the German may gain economic control of a wide area with diversified products. Given not merely one state, but a large part of a Continent to exploit, the possibilities of economic totalitarianism become immensely greater; but what the future may hold in store for a new Continental System cannot be said.

Even allowing for this development, it must be admitted that the economic disadvantages of autarky so greatly overbalance the initial economic advantages given by dictatorship, that one had to ask why the sacrifice is demanded. With the answer we come to what is the fundamental drawback of dictatorship in the economic field. Economic distress may be a first cause of the rise of dictatorship, but economic improvement is not and cannot be its essential end. The final motive of dictatorship is always political power. Faced with the choice between this and economic welfare, its own nature compels it to choose the former. If autarky seems necessary to the dictator's political ambitions, however great the economic sacrifices it involves, they will perforce be accepted.

It still remains, however, the *sine qua non* of dictatorship that it must continually produce results to justify its existence and keep the support of a sufficient proportion of its people: if economic facts are stubborn, then other motives must be appealed to. We have therefore to pass back from the economic into the political field, only now it is to foreign and not domestic politics that we must turn. If a dictator cannot command prosperity, he may at least strive after glory. The wars which result from this motive, such as the Mexican expedition of Louis Napoleon or the Abyssinian campaign of Mussolini, are sometimes represented as resulting from the need for economic gains; a mere balance-sheet should be sufficient to expose this as a piece of rationalization: the real aim is glory, prestige, for the sake of the internal strengthening of the regime. The willingness of nations to accept foreign triumphs in place of domestic prosperity, and to sacrifice their interests to their vanity, may surprise us, but cannot be questioned. Thus the force to which we are brought back as the true basis for dictatorship is once again the spirit of aggressive nationalism.

It is increasingly evident that in their latest developments nationalism and dictatorship have become essential allies. This is what Spengler has realized, though in saying that nationalism is only the first step towards Cæsarism, he makes the former subsidiary to the latter.[1] The dictator may have obtained power through his capacity to profit by the political and economic difficulties of the country, but the foregoing analysis of the political and economic tendencies of dictatorship suggests that these cannot by themselves maintain the dictator in power for more than a limited period, especially since the more successful he is in his initial tasks, the more unnecessary he renders himself. Moreover, every government requires some emotional basis if it is to last.

[1] O. Spengler, *The Hour of Decision*, p. 194.

Nationalism, in its new totalitarian form, provides such a basis for dictatorship: through nationalism the dictator may hope to change what was at first only a temporary expedient into a more lasting form of government. This is a return to government by faith: nationalism is the new religion, and the dictator is Pope and Emperor rolled into one. If we wish to know what force from within will overthrow him, we must ask what force, in the modern world, is stronger than nationalism.

§ 4 THE CRISIS OF WESTERN CIVILIZATION

Nationalism, then, provides the real basis for modern dictatorial government, and it is a strong one — though, if the irresistible tendency of dictatorial regimes is to war, one cannot pretend that even this offers any guarantee of permanence. The first unsuccessful war will bring revolution. In this way have fallen most dictatorships in the past. Apart from nationalism, it must be confessed, we have seen little reason to discriminate between the ordinary dictatorship of the past and totalitarianism, save in the colossal intensification of causes and effects in the latter. But we have left for final consideration what may be called the ideological aspect of modern dictatorship, connected with which are also its international consequences, for it is here if anywhere that the differentiation is likely to appear. Whereas dictatorship in the past has been a practical expedient, lacking any attempt at theoretical justification, behind the machinery of party bureaucracy and secret police, political armies and terrorism, there is a real spiritual principle in modern dictatorship, which makes it something more than a mere technique of government. The new totalitarian dictatorship is powerful not because it rules men's bodies, but because it controls their minds. Its essential aim is, in fact, as we have suggested above, the identification of Church and State.

The struggle initiated by the French revolutionaries against the Church's spiritual authority is being carried on to-day by the totalitarian dictatorships with much more deadly effect. The state has waged war with religion so many times, and has so often been defeated, or at best fought a drawn battle, that we have come to believe, almost without questioning, that every attempt to unite the two heads of the eagle must end in the same way. But this is to forget the gradual withdrawal of the churches from one sphere of activity after another. The secular state has won its most striking victories not in a sensational manner but by a slow and unremitting pressure, which has prepared the way for the final assault of totalitarianism. If the churches are finally defeated in this way, however, it will not mean the disappearance of religion so much as the rise of a new kind of religion, which can only be the religion of the state — *raison d'état*.

So long as there has been a state, *raison d'état* has been the standing rule of politics. Totalitarianism did not invent it. The really significant change has been in the idea of the state. *Raison d'état* may not have changed in principle, but when the state has become co-terminous with the whole life of the individual and society, the principle is extended so greatly in scope as to be practically different in kind. Machiavelli wrote the *Prince* as a handbook to politics: he made no pretence at being a teacher of morality or religion. It remained for our own time to moralize Machiavelli and make *raison d'état* into a religion.

This development of totalitarianism is notable in the policies of Italy and Russia, though in these countries there has been little attempt to systematize it. Moreover, as Croce points out,[1] idealism or absolute morality is one of the postulates of socialism, which has not been abandoned in theory in Russia, however it may have been interpreted in practice. In Germany, however, *raison d'état* has been given its fullest extension, in theory as well as in practice. It is frankly recognized that this involves a radical breach with what the Germans call Western thought, and it is applauded for that very reason. Liberalism — if under that head we include ideas such as liberal individualism, utilitarianism, parliamentarism, pacifism, humanitarianism, and the like — had apparently defeated the Central Empires in 1918, but let a German bear witness to the effect of that victory. 'The defeat of 1918 was inflicted upon us under the banner of liberal ideas. For fourteen years we lived under the banner of those ideas. The world tried to persuade us that we could only become a useful nation worthy of incorporation in the human community if we adopted those ideas. The world failed to discern that these ideas had been permanently compromised by the result of the war.'[2] He might have added, even more by the subsequent policy of the victorious states. 'Germany's subjugation has been effected

[1] B. Croce, *Historical Materialism and the Economics of Karl Marx*, trans. C. M. Meredith, 1914, p. 25.

[2] F. Sieburg, *Germany, my Country*, trans. 1933, p. 16.

by laying down a system of moral values and denouncing any attempt at self-assertion on her part as an attack on those values'.[1] Little wonder, then, if 'liberalism abandoned its position in Germany almost without a struggle'.[2]

The only criticism we would have to make of this interpretation of the spiritual evolution of post-war Germany would arise from the reflection that the cleavage between Germany and the West is not, after all, the work of merely the last twenty years. Germany as a whole has never been properly integrated into Western civilization. Such portents as the German mystics of the later Middle Ages, Luther and Leibnitz, indicate a peculiarity of German thought, which becomes fully manifest in the Romantic writers of the early nineteenth century. According to Hegel the characteristic of the German people is its sense of National Totality, of Heart — *Gemüt* — a quality with no particular aim, 'concerned with no objective condition, but with the entire condition of the soul'.[3] This element in the national character, which perhaps found its highest and most lucid expression in music, has unfortunately been introduced during the nineteenth century and at the present day into the realm of politics, in which it is peculiarly inappropriate and dangerous. The result has been to produce a widening chasm between Germany and the West.

Troeltsch, in a brilliant essay, translated by Professor Barker, has established the contradiction between Western thought, believing in the existence of universal

[1] F. Sieburg, *Germany, my Country*, trans. 1933, p. 125.
[2] id., p. 120.
[3] Hegel, *Lectures on the Philosophy of History*, trans. 1884, p. 364.

standards of right and wrong, in an eternal law of nature and in the brotherhood of man — a religious conception at root, whose existence gives what meaning it has to the word Christendom — and the thought of German Romanticism, which, he says, 'is directed to the particular, the positive: to what is eternally productive of new variety, constructive, spiritually organic: to plastic and super-personal creative forces, which build from time to time, out of the material of particular individuals, a spiritual whole, and on the basis of that whole proceed from time to time to create the particular political and social institutions which embody and incarnate its significance'.[1]

On the surface this view is not without its attraction. But consider for a moment its application. What it does is to complete the achievement of the autonomy of the community by carrying it one stage farther than had Sieyès. Surely, it will be said, this cannot be true, for it is impossible? Already Sieyès and the revolutionaries had emancipated the community from all human authority other than its own will. Of human authority this is true, but what of divine? What of the rights of nature implanted in every man's bosom, rights so sacred that the Jacobins did not hesitate to erect revolution into a constitutional principle in their defence? These too are rejected from German thought, and with them goes the last safeguard for the individual in the state and the last link joining the nations of the earth together. The result, in the words of Troeltsch, can only be in the end amoralism, cynicism, and a belief in force alone. German thought bifurcates

[1] E. TROELTSCH, *The Ideas of Natural Law and Humanity in World Politics*, trans. E. Barker in *Natural Law and the Theory of Society*, pp. 210-11.

in mid-nineteenth century. One line leads through Marx to Lenin and the other culminates in Hitler: but both bear, though locked in deadly combat, the unmistakable signs of their parentage and their kinship.

In contemporary Germany, above all, law is the will of the people, which in its turn is discovered by its incarnation in a leader, who is the embodiment of the spirit of the race, and through whom the German people turns its back on the basic principles of Western thought. 'Ultimately', writes the prophet of the gospel of Racialism, 'the instinct of self-preservation triumphs eternally over that pretended humanity, which is a blend of stupidity, cowardice and self-conceited pedantry.'[1] This does not differ so greatly from Nietzsche and Treitschke, after all. The acknowledged rejection of all universal standards of morality is the peculiarly German contribution to the development of the ideology of modern dictatorship, and with it dictatorship ceases to be a mere form of government and becomes a revolutionary challenge to the whole foundations of Western thought.

In what we have just said we must not, of course, be interpreted as in any way taking it upon ourselves to pass judgment on this development. To do so would be to overstep the limitations we have set ourselves, for here totalitarian dictatorship is no longer in the field of the political scientist. Any verdict one expressed would have to be founded on ethical or even religious considerations. If we permit ourselves a quotation which has bearing on this point, it must be with full recognition of the fact that we have no right here to endorse the verdict it passes. Lord Eustace Percy writes, in a lecture entitled *The Study*

[1] A. HITLER, *Mein Kampf*, (ed. 1935), vol. 1, ch. 4, p. 148.

of History, that, 'In the measure to which any State has succeeded in a complete identification between political dominion and the moral order, in the same measure has society decayed and dissolved . . . To-day, as throughout the history of European civilization, the success or failure of human societies depends upon the maintenance of a balanced dualism. Human progress — to adhere for the time being to that unsatisfactory term, one of the first for which the philosophical historian must find a substitute — human progress does not depend, except in a wholly subsidiary way, on political processes, that is to say, on the sort of combined action which can be taken by large bodies of men under the unifying force of compulsion. It depends on a force, the existence of which the historian must note and describe, but which he cannot explain, the force of the free movement of the individual human spirit . . . The State exists, above all, and especially in its moral aspect, to guarantee this freedom. Such freedom is, in fact, its life. The State which restricts this freedom or seeks to express the spirit of man exclusively through political processes — that is to say, through the processes of mass compulsion — loses its own power of self-renewal. If it succeeds in such an attempt, the society which it represents must decay; if it is unsuccessful, the force which it has tried to dam back will disrupt it.'[1]

One example of a state which tried the experiment here criticized, and accepted a thorough-going totalitarian system is worth recalling. The so-called Lycurgan reform of about 600 B.C. in Sparta achieved from the political point of view remarkable success, though, of

[1] LORD EUSTACE PERCY, *The Study of History*, 17th Earl Grey Memorial Lecture, 1935, pp. 18-19.

course, the government it established was an aristocracy, or oligarchy, not a dictatorship. It is only fair to note its political success, if at the same time we recall the fact that among its consequences was an annihilation of cultural activities so complete that men almost forgot that there ever had been a Spartan culture. Yet in earlier days the civilization of the Spartans seems to have possessed unusual charm. Now, in the words of the *Cambridge Ancient History*, 'The city, where life had been as beautiful as anywhere in Greece, became a barracks: there are no more Spartan poets after Tyrtaeus, no more artists . . . There was no more building after 550, and the pottery declines, and the little offerings to Orthia become steadily poorer'.[1] However illuminating this may seem, it is not safe to draw conclusions from a single historical example.

At this point our book should end, and indeed with a previous quotation we have already strayed beyond the strict province of the historian and the political scientist. Yet it is hard to resist a final glance towards the future, with particular reference to the international consequences, since with totalitarian dictatorship is bound up the whole fate of the Western world. While the political scientist is not a moralist, the historian is no prophet; but without passing judgment on the past, or prophesying the events of the future, we may perhaps be permitted a brief attempt to summarize the present situation and to indicate the logical consequences that seem to follow from it.

What future, we must ask, does totalitarian dictatorship promise for itself and for the Western world? If the totalitarian state lived in a world unencumbered by other states, if there were no rival and incompatible principles

[1] *Camb. Anc. Hist.*, vol. III, pp. 564-5.

at work in Western civilization, then, although by periodic revolutions the state might pass from the hands of one dictator to those of another, there would be no reason, except ultimate exhaustion, why this system of government should ever come to an end. The struggle between principles and states provides a complicating element which leaves the whole issue still completely open.

In forming a considered opinion on this conflict, it is important to remember that dictatorship, and even totalitarianism, are no sudden and strange reversals of the whole trend of modern history. On the contrary, the intellectual and political development of Western Europe has been preparing the way for them during the last four centuries. Forces that now seem to be their bitterest opponents, such as democracy and socialism, appear on the contrary, at least in so far as they embody the ideas of the sovereignty of the people and the class war, also contributory factors in their growth. Simple interpretations of the contemporary situation as a struggle of communism against fascism, or dictatorship against democracy, do not do justice to the complexity of the historic forces that have made our world and are still operative in it. This it is essential to keep in mind, for it is hardly likely that totalitarian dictatorship will be defeated by a continuance of the precise forces that helped to create it.

If the world does not wish totalitarianism and dictatorship to become its dominant political forces, it will have to turn aside from the way that has led up to them. It cannot reject the sum, while retaining the parts.

As they arise from nationalism and encourage the antagonism of states, so their opponents will have to rely on the principle of association between states, whether in a federal or any other form.[1] As nationalism leads up to imperialism, so in place of the latter will be required a recognition of the principle of free commonwealths. As totalitarianism insists on the union of the political and spiritual principles in the state, so the opposition will have to revert to a strict dualism or even pluralism, acknowledging a multiplicity of authorities, each in its own sphere. As dictatorship is authoritarian in the extreme, so those who dislike it must strive to preserve the liberties of the subject. As it relies on mass movements and the appeal of the demagogue, so they must exalt the individual; as the dictator appeals to the passions of the day, so they must rely on reason and on the more permanent emotions that outlive passion. As dictatorship aims above all at power, so they must place first of all welfare. As dictatorship arises out of the economic struggle in society which is bound up with the conception of the class war, so any effort to avoid it must be based on a subordination of economic to ethical principles, a maintenance of the moral unity of society and an acceptance of the principles of social justice. The tendency, unfortunately, is for those with power, place or wealth to expect others to recognize the ethical unity of society, while they themselves behave on the assumptions of the class war. Finally, as *raison d'état* is the very principle of dictatorship, so above all its opponents must fight against this principle, for its destruction would be the greatest revolution of all.

[1] The alternatives, Proudhon said, in a long polemic against nationalism, written in the middle of the nineteenth century, at a time when a realization of its potentialities showed great insight, are federalism and Cæsarism. 'Instead of pushing the peoples in the path of federation, which is that of all political and economic liberty, they are being intoxicated with gigantic Utopias and directed towards the sham of Cæsarism.' P.-J. PROUDHON, *Du principe fédératif*, 1863, pp. 189-90.

'The true revolution', wrote Proudhon, 'will be that which, putting conscience above all other mundane considerations, will abolish in politics and in all social relations the frightful principle of *raison d'état*, which, under the pretext of order, honour, public welfare, or morals, sometimes allows one to commit oneself, and sometimes excuses in others the most evident and patent crimes.'[1]

It must be admitted that all or any of these changes would involve for the modern state a breach with some of its most deeply imbedded traditions. They amount in fact to a moral revolution greater than any our age has seen, greater than anything that has happened since the decline of the Middle Ages. Whether the Western world is willing to recognize how fundamental a revolution in the basis of its political life is necessary may be doubted. A foolish optimism, relying on a sentimental attachment to traditions and policies that have proved inadequate, is a more probable reaction, and one which will lead, unless the conditions of the problem are entirely altered by the emergence of some unexpected factor, to the triumph of the totalitarian idea.

The condition we are postulating here is, it must frankly be recognized, the abolition of the sovereign state as we know it. The modern state has made much of what is called progress possible; without it the political stability necessary for intellectual and industrial advance could not have existed. But now Leviathan has undergone a metamorphosis and assumed the character of a Frankenstein's monster; its craving for power has swollen far beyond its capacity for service; soon, if the Western world does not abolish the state, the state will abolish it.

[1] PROUDHON, id., p. 283*n*.

Let us examine this a little more closely. When we say that the state must be abolished, we mean the state as an end in itself, and a system of morality based upon *raison d'état*. But *raison d'état* is an intellectual principle, and we have seen that the real motive power behind it is provided by the emotional force of nationalism, and on this in the last resort the totalitarian state depends. No nationalism, one can say, no totalitarianism. This is the crucial point in the struggle.

Nationalism must not, of course, be confused with nationality. Nations existed before nationalism was invented, and will exist after its career of war and devastation has worked itself out, whether by the triumph of peaceful progress or by exhaustion. The conception of the nation as a cultural, historic or linguistic unit, with its own local self-government, is in itself a useful and workable one. The crisis of present day Europe has come from the union of this idea with the idea of the absolute sovereignty of the state, in the form of that political monism which the French Revolution inherited from the benevolent despots; and since the sovereign state recognizes no external limits, it is only a step from nationalism to imperialism. In a sense, modern nationalism is the work of the French Revolution; and it is no far cry from the *nation*, *une et indivisible* to *ein Reich*, *ein Volk*, *ein Führer*.

It may seem — certainly, not many years ago it would have been considered — most unprogressive to criticize the principle of nationalism. In the nineteenth century it was opposed for the most part only by the reactionary supporters of the absolute monarchies; still, the pertinent comments of two thinkers, who refused to be carried away by the wave of nationalist sentiment, may profitably be recalled. P.-J. Proudhon had too original and independent a mind to be acceptable to any of the disciplined schools of socialist thought, but his ideas have stood the test of time better than those of many of his contemporaries, and he saw very clearly where nationalism was leading the nations of Europe. 'The plan of Garibaldi', he wrote, 'had for base of operations the principle of nationality, turned into a synonym of the principle of UNITY . . . For the Italians, who already were loudly claiming their former possessions, Corsica, Ticino, the Tyrol, Trieste, and Dalmatia, nationality means the re-establishment of imperial and papal Italy . . . For the Greeks . . . nationality consists in the restoration of the old schismatic Empire, with its capital at Constantinople . . . For the Poles, to whom would first be given back their limits of 1772, an area of 38,000 square leagues, including a crowd of populations which never had anything Polish about them except the title, nationality must end in the formation of a Slav empire, which would have extended as far as Moscow and Petersburg. . . .'[1]

From a different point of view, a similar warning was issued by the great historian, Lord Acton. 'Nationalism', he said, 'is a chimera. The settlement it aims at is impossible.'[2] His condemnation of nationalism is above all on moral grounds. 'Christianity', he wrote, 'rejoices in the mixture of races, as paganism identifies itself with their differences.'[3] 'The combination of different nations in one State is as necessary a condition of civilized life as

[1] P.-J. PROUDHON, *Du principe fédératif*, pp. 186-7.
[2] ACTON, *History of Freedom*, IX, *Nationality*, p. 298
[3] id., p. 291.

the combination of men in society.'[1] 'The co-existence of several nations under the same State is a test, as well as the best security of its freedom.'[2] Finally, 'Nationality does not aim either at liberty or prosperity, both of which it sacrifices to the imperative necessity of making the nation the mould and measure of the State. Its course will be marked with material as well as moral ruin, in order that a new invention may prevail over the works of God and the interests of mankind.'[3]

Such isolated protests went for nothing. The wave of nationalism swept on and mounted ever higher, and indeed nationalism is so potent a force that one is bound to ask whether in the form of the totalitarian state it is not irresistible. The last war is not without its lesson in this respect. The aggressive national spirit of Germany gathered against that country most of the remaining states of the world; and in the end the small nationalities, supported by a non-national state, or group of states, the British Commonwealth of Nations, and the United States of America, which is a nation of a new kind, were overwhelmingly victorious. On the same side, it is true, were Russia, Italy and France, but of these the first two are from the military point of view to be reckoned among the defeated countries; while the nationalism of France, apparently triumphant in 1918, had within the next two decades brought the nation to the verge of disaster.

Nationalism dictated the conditions of the Treaty of Versailles and may now seem the dominant force in politics, but we must remember that the same was true of absolutism in the Treaty of Vienna and the age of

[1] ACTON, *History of Freedom*, IX, *Nationality*, p. 290.
[2] id., p. 290. [3] id., p. 299.

Metternich. If we regard recent history as foretelling a continued triumphant onrush of nationalism and totalitarian dictatorship, we may be mis-reading the world situation. Not many countries, after all, are in precisely the right condition for totalitarianism. Where constitutional monarchy has retained some hold on the loyalty of the people, the wave of authoritarianism, instead of sweeping a dictator to power, has manifestly brought about a revival of monarchical sentiment, sometimes in the most unexpected quarters. This development is to be seen in Great Britain, in the Scandinavian countries, and in Belgium and Holland; while signs of a similar tendency are not absent from the Balkan States.

Even among the nominal dictatorships one must draw distinctions. South American dictatorships for the most part have not yet reached the phase of totalitarianism. Again, a dictator such as Kemal Ataturk, perhaps the greatest of contemporary rulers, occupied a position differing in important respects from that of the dictator as we have described him. Perhaps the most important distinction separating dictatorships such as the South American or the Turkish from totalitarian dictatorship, is that the former are practical developments and lack the ideological substructure of the great European dictatorships.

The onrush of totalitarianism in the post-war years is of course undeniable. It may well be attributed to the effects of that colossal disturbance upon domestic stability in every country in the world, but this does not mean that we must necessarily endorse the pessimistic conclusion to which the great French historian, Élie Halévy, found himself forced in the essay, *L'Ère des tyrannies*, which was his testament to the historical world. Halévy's view was that the modern age of tyranny dated from August 1914, because he believed that the inevitable consequence of the war was economic and intellectual *étatisme*, in which was implied totalitarian dictatorship.[1] That the war provided many lessons in the technique of *étatisme*, and revealed hitherto unimagined possibilities, especially in the use of propaganda, cannot be questioned. But it does not seem to us that it added any new factor in European history. Every element in the post-war development was already there in 1914. Nor did the war produce totalitarianism or dictatorship in most of the countries that took part in it. Only where the degeneration of the domestic situation and the setting up of stresses in society had reached a point amounting to civil war did dictatorship emerge. Elsewhere the forces in Western civilization with which it is incompatible have successfully held it in check: we have not yet to say, with Halévy, *Finis libertatis*.

The pyramid of tyrannies now being erected in Europe is more imposing in appearance than well-founded in reality. Their moral and psychological inter-dependence is the strength of the weaker ones, but the weakness of the stronger. Knock away even one stone and the whole edifice may come clattering down in war and revolution: 1848 is a date to bear in mind.

In certain respects the future is not entirely without promise. The changing policies of the so-called socialist parties in Western countries, together with the general acceptance of the necessity for social improvement and an advance towards social equality, have rendered the class

[1] E. HALVEY, *L. Ère des tyrannies*, 1938, p. 214.

struggle rather less acute in some countries: a state such as Sweden seems to have made a certain progress towards eliminating it altogether. The consciousness of the pressure exerted from outside by the dictatorial powers is not without its influence on this process. Democracy and socialism in the non-totalitarian states, now that the menace of totalitarianism has been revealed, are shedding some of the features through which they contributed to its rise. Further, the great increase in industrial productivity which has marked the post-war years in the West, accompanied as it has been by a considerable fall in the rate of growth of the population, would afford considerable prospect, if it were not for the menace of war and the armaments race, of a fairly rapid amelioration of the economic situation. On the other hand, the continuance of great wars, possibly even an armaments race by itself, is likely to produce economic conditions that, because they prohibit any real solution of the social problem, will therefore promote the development of an internal class struggle out of which dictatorship must arise. Unless the economic tension can be sufficiently relieved, at least to prevent the development of a real class war, there will be no alternative but totalitarianism in one form or another.

The triumph of totalitarianism will itself produce an intensification, not a solution, of the problems confronting humanity. The modern world, despite Spengler, is not in the position of the Roman world when Augustus laid the foundations for the *pax Romana* of the Empire, and the modern dictator is a Catiline not a Cæsar. For two effective reasons he cannot found a new Empire, like the Roman, based on the principle of universal law and peace. The first obstacle lies in the very nature of the dictatorial idea, which itself involves a definite and conscious rejection of these principles. A universal state cannot be founded on the principle of nationalism, which is itself a denial of universality; a general peace cannot be established by a system of government which regards states or races or nations as necessarily hostile to one another. Secondly, there is in the world of to-day no conceivable possibility of the establishment of a universal empire by any single state.

Dictatorship offers to the world, then, and can offer to it, only an intensification of the state of war. Carried out to the logical end it would make the condition of the world approximate to that described by Hobbes as the 'state of nature', and the life of man 'nasty, brutish and short'. But in this lies the last possibility of the avoidance of catastrophe. Man is, after all, partly a utilitarian animal, and he may prove unwilling to sacrifice all the best hopes of civilization for the sake of this new political creed. Dictatorship is in the beginning born of fear — the fear of anarchy in the state. But in the world of to-day the consequences of war between great states have become so appalling that the ordinary man and woman has acquired what may prove in the end to be a greater fear. If Hobbesian psychology, tracing the origin of political authority in the state to the motive of fear, has a certain degree of validity, why, it may be asked, should it not apply also in wider political relations?

In the past the consequences of war on ordinary life do not seem, except in the case of civil war, to have called the motive of fear so extensively into play. One cannot say how many demonstrations will be required before it becomes effective at the present day, but if it is realized that dictatorship is leading the nations towards a series of new and infinitely more destructive world wars, fear may conceivably produce, if not a revolution, then a state of passive hostility to war, which would in fact prevent it from being waged. Dictatorship would then, baulked of its natural development, be thrown back on its internal resources; and instead of a sweeping revolution resulting from military defeat, a slower and possibly more peaceful crumbling of the regime might be looked for.

On the other hand, that this motive is more likely to be effective in non-dictatorial than in dictatorial states has already been shown so far as concerns the governments of those countries. Dictators are used to taking risks and have no scruples about employing force to secure their ends. The lawyers, business men and trade unionists, who have taken the place of the old governing classes in the parliamentary states, are not normally capable of bold action and great schemes, whether for good or for evil. The pacifist and humanitarian sentiments associated in theory — though it is true that the association is not always conspicuous in practice — with liberalism and parliamentary government, are a further barrier against war. When these two tendencies are united in support of a policy of peace they are very powerful.

Unfortunately, however, it does not always take two parties to make a war. Parliamentary governments may yield and yield again, but if there comes a point at which they stick, then the hostile dictatorship, inflated with its easy victories, conscious of its strong and energetic leadership, will plunge into war. And whereas the law-abiding populations of the non-dictatorial states enter upon war reluctantly and only in the last resort, if the propaganda of the dictatorship has been successful with its own subjects these will have been imbued with a bellicose spirit that should render them apt for war.[1]

This, of course, is to assume that totalitarian dictatorship, besides being exclusive and arbitrary, is also naturally aggressive. Is this necessarily so? Its supporters have argued that in so far as it rests on nationalism it cannot be, that a nation which asserts its own right to self-determination must logically recognize equal rights in all other nations. But, as Sieyès had said, the nations of the world should be conceived as existing in the state of nature — not the nature of the primitivist Utopians, but the state of nature of a Hobbes, in which the survival of the fittest is measured in terms of brute force. Mutual aid, the Benthamite principle of the natural identification of interests, do unto others as you would they should do unto you — these rules were not made for the greater carnivores or for great nations.

The bias of nationalism towards war is only too evident. Humanity, Hitler believes, has grown great by perpetual war: eternal peace would lead it to the grave. His words merely echo Treitschke who, from his academic arm-chair, pronounced, 'It is political idealism that demands war, and it is materialism that rejects war ... A man must sacrifice not only his life, but also the profoundly just and natural impulses of the human soul. He must renounce his whole ego for the sake of a great patriotic

[1] The events of September 1938 suggest that it may not be so easy to work up enthusiasm for a great war, even in totalitarian countries that are completely propaganda-ridden, as had been expected. The decline, all over Europe, of the old-fashioned popular enthusiasm for war, is one of the most significant facts of our time, but it is equally evident that this will not at present prevent a dictatorship from waging war.

ideal. Therein lies the moral sublimity of war'.[1] *Il Duce* carries on the same idea in his authoritative article on Fascism: 'War alone carries to its highest tension all human energy and sets the seal of nobility on the peoples who have the courage to face it'.[2]

Nor does the alliance of nationalism with dictatorship incline it in any other direction, for sooner or later, and generally sooner, the dictator, faced with economic difficulties, discovers the need to inflate empty stomachs with the vain wind of glory. A further motive for war is to be found in the fact that, since no nation can isolate itself absolutely from the rest of the world, and since liberty is a contagious disease, every state with freer institutions is a standing menace to those under dictatorship. Intervention is therefore inevitably the international principle of dictatorship. This is to be seen in the ancient world with the alliances between the tyrants against democratic or aristocratic states, in the history of the medieval Italian city states, in the career of Napoleon, and at the present day.

Finally, there is one argument of a psychological nature, which applies, more or less, to all modern states, but particularly to the dictatorships. The modern state has carried social discipline and the organization of individual life to a point inconceivable even under the most absolute despotisms of the past. The emotional outlets of the ordinary man have become more and more limited. Now it is quite arguable that war results to a certain extent from a psychological reaction against such undue regimentation and suppression of important

[1] TREITSCHKE, ed. Davis, p. 130.

[2] Article, *Fascismo* in *Enciclopedia Italiana*, 1932, vol. 14.

elements in human nature, because it provides an opportunity for letting loose the primitive emotions that have to be contained in the Great Society of which Graham Wallas wrote. Even without this last argument, however, the tendency of dictatorship to war is sufficiently plain, and with totalitarianism it becomes not merely a bias towards war, but a return to the age of tribal wars, just as nationalism is a return to tribal religions; and the revival of tribalism in the form of racialism strengthens the parallel.

The wars that arise in consequence will be no mere political struggles for power; they would be less furiously pursued and more easily settled if they were dictated by simple motives of self-interest. The dictator, when he fires the militant nationalism of a people, is letting loose a force that he cannot control, a force that is ready to plunge the whole state into absolute ruin rather than admit defeat. The new wars will be the 'total' wars, which require the totalitarian state to prepare for them and to wage them. This is what Julien Benda has said, 'If indeed one asks oneself whither humanity is going, when each group of it is burying itself more violently than ever in the consciousness of its own particular interests as such, and is told by its moralists that it is sublime in the degree in which it knows no other law than that interest, a child would find the answer: it is advancing towards the most total and perfect war that the world will have ever seen'.[1]

Nations are the dervishes of a new religion and are as little controlled by rational or humane considerations. The dictator himself is at the mercy of the passions he has aroused, for the association between nationalism and dictatorship has become the determining factor in the

[1] J. Benda, *La Trahison des clercs*, 1937, p. 223.

development of both. In the modern world dictatorship, by using nationalism, has become tied to its wheel, and is whirled onward at a pace it cannot control, through paths it never envisaged, to an end beyond imagination.

All this, of course, is admittedly speculative. In the course of history events are always unique, though patterns may be repeated; and in our age factors which are novel, the consequences of which are as yet unknown, the mere existence of which we ignore, may change drastically the whole trend of events. History is a drama which has no fifth act.

One thing we can say with assurance. The long peace in the quiet harbours of the past, the cautious coasting from one known point to another known point, is ended. Perhaps it was always an illusion. The Western world is adrift, and all humanity has cut from its anchors. Through what channels, and driven by what winds and tides, we came to this point, it is possible to see; and the attempt to understand some at least of the forces that have carried the Western world onward is not a profitless task, for the same winds have not ceased to blow. Only through a sounder comprehension of the real social and political bases of our civilization can we hope to gain any effective control over its course, and to the attempt at a clearer understanding of one very important group among these is this book dedicated.

APPENDIX I

DICTATORSHIP IN EARLIER PERIODS

§ I MEDIEVAL ITALIAN TYRANTS

THE history of modern dictatorship provides fairly extensive material from which to draw conclusions concerning its nature and functioning; and since all ages have their own peculiar characteristics, which determine the mode of operation in them of every kind of government, it would be dangerous to expect too much from a study of earlier periods. But the fact cannot be ignored that there have been previous waves of dictatorship; and there has been sufficient uniformity in the working of human nature in politics during the evolution of Western civilization to render an examination of these earlier manifestations of the type of government we have been studying not without utility. Our definition of dictatorship, of course, must be rigidly maintained; nor must we forget the alteration in the nature of the political community itself in modern times; though, the difference between the classical or the medieval city state and the modern nation state being granted, it is astonishing to observe how true dictatorship runs to type even in the most divergent settings.

The existence of dictatorship in any community presupposes the overthrow of traditional authorities, and for this reason it can only appear at a fairly late stage in political development. In the Middle Ages it was only in the Italian city states that conditions appeared in which dictatorship was possible, since elsewhere, feudal, sacerdotal and royal authorities remained too powerful to admit of such a development; but Italy was from the beginning an exception to many medieval rules. The transition from classical to medieval came less catastrophically there than in other parts of the Empire. The bureaucratic and military apparatus which had held the Roman world together had been no mere oriental despotism: the other side of the fabric of the Empire, though it does not enter into competition in history with the brilliance of the imperial purple, the glory and the shame of Rome, was the life of the *municipia*, in which classical civilization was kept alive and handed down from generation to generation. The Roman Empire has with some justification been described as a federation of largely self-governing municipalities, and that condition of local self-government was carried over by the Italian cities into the Middle Ages.

Feudalism never struck deep roots in Northern Italy. The struggle of Empire and Papacy prohibited the growth of monarchy, except in Naples and Sicily, where the Normans were able to build up the necessary bureaucratic machine. In the cities of the north, as conditions gradually became more settled, republican institutions soon appeared. Trade brought wealth, and wealth power. Feudal barons moved into the towns, where they had perforce to deal on terms of something like equality with the wealthy citizens: those who remained outside the city walls declined in importance. Government fell into the hands of a Patriciate of rich merchants, under whose rule the cities flourished.

The chief defect of the Patriciate, as of most aristocracies, was its liabilty to party strife. Well-established groups in the older trades fought against new ones rising to importance; and the tendency to conflict was accentuated by the struggle between Papacy and Empire, which gave it a sort of theoretical justification. Guelph and Ghibelline factions grew up in every city, though external and domestic influences were so intermingled that it would have been very difficult to provide any general description of either party as a whole. Unrest was added to by the struggle of the aristocracies of wealth and birth against rising democratic tendencies. Lacking any adequate constitutional machinery, the cities were subject to frequent revolutions, though these, it has been said, 'often had no more constitutional significance than a modern general election: they were . . . the natural means of expressing the popular will in communities which had failed to evolve a system of democratic representation'.[1]

In such conditions a state was incapable of facing a serious external menace. This was sometimes the last straw, which compelled the abandonment of the attempt at self-government, though the fundamental cause is still to be found in the internal situation. Despairing of securing unity among themselves by agreement, the citizens would call in a *Podesta*, to whom arbitrary authority would be given, and whose rule, if he were successful, was sometimes extended for life. But the *Podesta*, being the chosen of the ruling class, was always in the last resort

[1] M. V. CLARKE, *The Medieval City State*, 1926, p. 113. I am particularly indebted to this book for guidance in the earlier part of this section.

dependent upon it; however powerful, he was still a constitutional ruler, and from his rule tyranny, or dictatorship as we should call it, seldom developed. Another officer, to whom arbitrary power was sometimes granted, was the War Captain, but as his position was generally only temporary, and had no structural connection with the city politics, it was unlikely to develop into a real tyranny.[1]

It has been pointed out that a third officer played a much larger part in the growth of tyranny than either of these — the Captain of the People,[2] whose appointment was usually the result of popular pressure, and whose function it was to protect the people and counterbalance the wealth of the Patriciate. His appearance is a sign that the people have become a political force. The strength of popular feelings in the medieval Italian states is suggested by their tumultuous history, and the presence of democratic ideas is shown by such an observation as that of Salutati, writing in 1400: 'If the people be sovereign, neither having nor recognizing any superior, the will of the majority gives validity to their action.'[3] To this struggle of the populace in the various cities against the prevailing oligarchies the setting up of tyrants has been attributed.[4] Tyrannies arise, Machiavelli observes, because of 'the excessive love of the people for liberty, and the passionate eagerness of the nobles to govern'.[5] 'When a people is led to commit this error of lending its support

[1] M. V. Clarke, *The Medieval City State*, 1926, p. 125.

[2] id., p. 121.

[3] Salutati, *De Tyrannus* (1400), in E. Emerton, *Humanism and Tyranny*, 1925, p. 88.

[4] Clarke, op. cit., p. 107.

[5] Machiavelli, *Discourses on the first decade of Titus Livius*, trans. N. H. Thomson, 1883, Bk. I, ch. xl, p. 132.

to some one man, in order that he may attack those whom it holds in hatred, if he only be prudent he will inevitably become the tyrant of that city.'[1]

The opinion that tyranny was merely a political reflection of the wealth of the city states and the result of its concentration in the hands of a few families, is surely disproved by the facts. At the end of the twelfth century we find the house of Este rising to power in Ferrara. Tyranny became general in Northern Italy during the thirteenth century; in Central Italy it sprang up in the fourteenth century, during the Babylonish Captivity of the Papacy at Avignon. Florence fell to the Medicis in the fifteenth century; and only Venice was left standing out against the general trend. Thus many of the first cities to accept tyrannies were places of little economic importance. On the other hand, Florence, the centre of Italian finance, was one of the last states to yield to even a veiled tyranny; while Venice, the greatest merchant state of the medieval world, preserved its oligarchical constitution to the end.

The nature of tyrannical government in Italy is too well-known to require prolonged attention; and many of its features are obviously peculiar to Italian conditions in the later Middle Ages. One point is worth emphasizing, however. Even when he has inherited his position, the tyrant can hold it by virtue of his personal qualities alone, and those are summed up in the idea of *virtu* — strength of will plus a sense of artistry, but minus any moral scruples. Though many of the tyrants were members of aristocratic families, the career of a Francesco Sforza shows how little essential was high or even legitimate

[1] MACHIAVELLI, *Discourses on the first decade of Titus Livius*, trans. N. H. Thomson, 1883, Bk. I, ch. xl, p. 132.

birth. Nobility, says Dante, is a personal, not an inherited quality. The rise of tyranny is thus to be associated not only with the appearance of a popular party, but also with the emancipation of the individual from the chains of caste and custom. This is no mere coincidence, and it is a fact worth retaining from the history of medieval tyranny.

Any further analysis of the nature of the medieval tyrant would be superfluous, since the work has already been done by one who could study at least some of the tyrants at first hand. Machiavelli is all the more valuable as a witness because he is one of the few commentators on politics who have been able in their study of a political phenomenon to free themselves almost completely from moral prejudice. He describes the deeds of the tyrant, not with the object of arousing indignation or moral disapproval, but only for the purpose of showing 'how things are done', for rulers if they wish to succeed, or indeed merely to survive must 'do what is done, not what ought to be done'.[1] *Il Principe* being a study in the technique of government, the only criterion Machiavelli adopts is that of success or failure: his book is as much a gospel of success as the biography of a modern millionaire. Those acts which ordinary morality condemns are approved if they contribute to political success. To take only one example, 'A prince, who is wise and prudent, cannot or ought not to keep his word, when the keeping of it is to his prejudice, and the causes for which he promised removed'.[2] We would not suggest for one moment that Machiavelli gives other than a faithful picture of actual international morality in his own or subsequent times.

[1] MACHIAVELLI, *The Prince*, ch. xv.
[2] id., ch. xviii.

'Three centuries', said Acton, 'have borne enduring witness to his political veracity.'[1] But few have had the frankness to put down in black and white what most have practised.

The only concession Machiavelli makes to morals is the admission that the tyrant should counterfeit the virtues he lacks. 'It is of great consequence to disguise your intention, and to play the hypocrite well; and men are so simple in their temper and so submissive to their present necessities, that he that is neat and cleanly in his collusions, shall never want people to practice them upon . . . It is honourable to seem mild, and merciful, and courteous, and religious, and sincere, and indeed to be so, provided your mind be so rectified and prepared that you can act quite contrary upon occasion.'[2]

At the same time, it must be remembered that Machiavelli's acceptance, in the *Prince*, of tyranny as a normal form of government, flies in the face of the classical writers who were his natural mentors, as well as of most medieval traditions. Indeed it runs counter to his own deepest convictions. Any modern dictator, who has looked to the great Italian to give that air of respectability, which the approval of one who has been dead for several centuries can supply, and which dictatorship so sadly lacks, can have read but few of the master's writings.

For Machiavelli's true political principles we have to look at the *Discourses on the First Ten Books of Livy*, where, as one would expect from a child of the Renaissance, he turns for his inspiration to classical history, and finds his ideal in the ancient Roman Republic. He cannot speak

[1] ACTON, *History of Freedom and other essays*, 1907, p. 212.
[2] *The Prince*, ch. xviii.

too highly in praise of the Romans, whose patriotic virtue enabled them to maintain their free institutions for so long. If they were tumultuous, that was a sign of freedom.[1] 'I affirm', he writes, 'that a people is more prudent, more stable, and of better judgment than a prince. Nor is it without reason that the voice of the people has been likened to the voice of God.'[2] He condemns those who 'having it in their power to establish ... a commonwealth or kingdom, turn aside to create a tyranny'.[3] His especial bitterness is reserved for Cæsar, the dictator: 'Nor let anyone finding Cæsar celebrated by a crowd of writers, be misled by his glory; for those who praise him have been corrupted by his good fortune, and overawed by the greatness of that empire which, being governed in his name, would not suffer any to speak their minds openly concerning him. But let him who desires to know how historians would have written of Cæsar had they been free to declare their minds, mark what they say of Catiline, than whom Cæsar is more hateful, in proportion as he who does is more to be condemned than he who only desires to do evil.'[4]

If these are Machiavelli's true views, then, how are we to account for his justification of tyranny? The explanation is that the ancient Romans were in his opinion unique in their civic virtue. In modern times, 'They who lay the foundations of a state and furnish it with laws must ... assume that all men are bad, and will always, when they have free field, give loose to their evil inclinations'.[5] 'In general', he says in the *Prince*, 'men are ungrateful,

[1] *Discourses*, Bk. I, ch. iv.
[2] id., Bk. I, ch. lviii, pp. 177-8.
[3] id., Bk. I, ch. x, p. 46.
[4] id.,
[5] id., Bk. I, ch. iii, p. 19.

inconstant, hypocritical, fearful of danger, and covetous of gain.'[1] While a people like the Romans may be held in check by laws, the corrupt, cowardly populace of modern Italy required, he thought, an arbitrary government. 'No change', he wrote, 'however grave or violent, could ever restore freedom to Naples or Milan, because in these states the entire body of the people has grown corrupted.'[2]

In the conditions of the Italy of his own day Machiavelli is not to be blamed if he believed that there was no alternative to tyranny consistent with the safety of the state, and this, of course, is his ultimate criterion. 'When the entire safety of our country is at stake, no consideration of what is just or unjust, merciful or cruel, praiseworthy or shameful, must intervene.'[3] Not for Machiavelli the *fiat justitia, ruat coelum* of a Gregory VII, nor the belief that 'there are ways by which a good man would not even save the state', of a Burke. *Raison d'état* is his ultimate moral principle, and behind the state he acknowledges no higher law.

But Machiavelli at least sees farther than the petty, selfish ambitions of individual tyrants. His advocacy of tyranny goes beyond the localism of the Middle Ages and looks to a wider unit than the city state. He foreshadows the developments of the present day, because his appeal in the *Prince* is really for a super-tyrant, who will use the methods of dictatorship to build up the power and unity of a nation. The last chapter in the *Prince* portrays in eloquent language the evil conditions of Italy, torn by the feuds of a host of minor despots and delivered

[1] *The Prince*, ch. xvii.
[2] *Discourses*, Bk. I, ch. xvii, p. 72.
[3] id., Bk. III, ch. xli, p. 473.

helpless to the will of foreign aggressors. 'Free Italy', he pleads, 'from her daily sufferings, exterminate these monstrous wild beasts, that have nothing in common with man save voice and aspect.'[1] He calls for a greater tyranny to cleanse Italy of her lesser tyrants, as Cæsar Borgia freed the Romagna from its petty lordlings.

Yet Machiavelli, who had served and done his best to save the last free republic of Florence, was not unaware of the sacrifice he was making. The speech that, in his History, he puts in the mouth of the Florentine Ambassador, addressing one who had aimed at establishing a tyranny in that city, is eloquent of his deepest feelings. 'Have you considered', he writes, 'what it means to a city like ours, this name of liberty, and how unconquerable it is? Strength cannot tame it, time cannot consume it, and no other merit can make amends for its loss.'[2]

Medieval liberties, as he came to recognize, were doomed. His aspirations for a tyranny on a national basis were not to be fulfilled for another four centuries; and when fulfilment did come it was to be in the form of a regime that was the consequence and not the cause of Italian unity, the creation and not the creator of the national spirit. Machiavelli himself was to be the end and not the beginning of an epoch. Three centuries of tyranny had so enfeebled the moral fibre of the Italian states and weakened their powers of resistance, that they fell an easy prey to French and Spanish and Austrian invaders. Independence survived only in the single city where there had been no domestic tyrant to prepare the

[1] Letter to Guicciardini, 1526; quoted in E. JANNI, *Machiavelli*, trans. 1930, p. 104.

[2] MACHIAVELLI, *History of Florence*, Bk. II, ch. viii.

way for foreign ones, Venice. Elsewhere, corrupt and inefficient despotisms, bolstered up by foreign arms, laid their heavy yoke on Italy, and when independence eventually was won, it had to be under the leadership of an extra-Italian royal house, and a state whose traditions were monarchical and not tyrannic.

§ 2 THE GREEK TYRANTS

Dictatorship, or tyranny, as it appeared in the Italian city states, presents such a striking contrast to ordinary medieval ideas on government that one can only regard it as a 'freak'. In the history of classical Greece, however, tyranny is so often encountered, that if it is treated as an aberration from the normal this can only be in a philosophical and not in an historical sense. Although there were two specific periods of Greek tyranny, it was to be found in some city or other throughout classical times. It needs no saying, of course, that the Greek conception of tyranny fits exactly our definition of dictatorship. To understand the reasons why it has been regarded as an abnormal form of government we have to remember the sources from which our knowledge of it has mostly been obtained.

The orthodox picture of the Greek tyrant is derived from two sources — the works of the great tragedians, and the conclusions and illustrations given by Aristotle in the *Politics*. Now the tradition of Attic drama was established in the great days of Athenian democracy and under the influence of ideas strongly hostile to tyranny. Again, Aristotle, although disillusioned with democracy, writes as one who has judged tyranny on moral grounds and found it the worst of all possible governments. Such ethical considerations must be disregarded here; but apart from these hostile sources our detailed knowledge of Greek tyranny is inadequate. What we can discover, however, strikingly confirms the general picture of dictatorial government that has emerged from a study of its development in modern times.

One further preliminary warning must be given. A group of figures, among whom Solon is the most conspicuous, have been termed 'elective tyrants'.[1] The adjective need not alarm us, because, after all, most modern tyrants have been elective in their fashion, but in our sense the term tyrant is not really applicable to them. A statesman such as Solon, nominated by the unfettered choice of the republic, establishing a rule of law, instead of an arbitrary government, and retiring when he has laid down a sound constitution, is to be regarded as an *aesymnetes* or a lawgiver, and not as a tyrant.

Even excluding these it is difficult to generalize on the origins or nature of Greek tyranny, especially if we include the later as well as the earlier phases. One theory, which has been presented very forcefully and with much scholarship, demands notice. It is the opinion of Professor Ure that, 'the seventh and sixth century Greek tyrants were the first men in their various cities to realize the political possibilities of the new conditions created by the introduction of the new coinage, and that to a large extent they owed their position as tyrants to a financial or commercial supremacy which they had already established before they attained the supreme political power in their several

[1] HALLIDAY, *The Growth of the City State*, 1923, p. 106.

states'.[1] While we have not the qualifications for discussing this theory in detail, it must be said that it does not seem to have won general acceptance; and indeed the evidence adduced seems to suggest that this is an over-simplification.

In a modified form, it has been suggested that the early tyrant was the leader in a class war, being the representative of a class of *nouveaux riches*, striving to wrest political power from existing aristocracies. Tyranny arises, it is said, when such a man manages to put himself at the head of a discontented populace, winning their confidence by encouraging their hatred of the wealthy and notables.[2] Thus Peisistratus is alleged to have led the 'democrats' of the Hill, whom Ure identifies with the silver miners.[3] But the aristocracies do not seem to have been as exclusive as this theory implies; and indeed practically all the tyrants of whom we know anything were themselves aristocrats.

On the other hand, it is true that the aristocracies were the natural enemies of any ambitious man, whether from within or without their own ranks, who desired to make himself a tyrant; and hence it was very likely that the would-be tyrant would look for support to the inferior orders in the state, favouring them, for instance, by handing over to them the property of his opponents. It is also not an accident that, as Aristotle remarked, tyrannies arose at a time when increasing wealth had produced a dangerous cleavage between the richer and the poorer citizens in many states, which often resulted in a condi-

[1] R. N. Ure, *The Origin of Tyranny*, 1922, p. 2.

[2] J. B. Bury, *A History of Greece*, 2nd ed., 1913, p. 146; cf. Aristotle, *Politics*, ed. H. W. C. Davis, 1908, pp. 200, 216 (v, 5, 10).

[3] Ure, op. cit., p. 291.

tion of suppressed or overt class warfare.[1] Tyranny is to be found mainly in the cities along the great trade routes; in the more backward areas, such as Arcadia, Bœtia and Thessaly, where such tension had not arisen, for the most part tyrannies did not appear. It must not be concluded from this that the tyrant inevitably plays the part of champion of the suppressed classes. On the other hand, the more fashionable explanation, that he was, as some modern dictators are supposed to have been, the defender of a decaying order, is equally untenable in view of the marked hostility of the aristocracies to the dominance of any single man. Indeed, the one statement we can safely make is that the tyrant had his opportunity wherever the social fabric was unstable.

One further general statement we may permit ourselves, however. Tyranny does not appear until the traditional monarchic and aristocratic authorities have either disappeared or are so weakened as to have lost their effective hold on the state. The republican principle, with its ideal of equality among members of the citizen body, must have been accepted, or at least have become strong enough to challenge the traditional hereditary rulers, before tyranny is possible. Only after citizenship has been extended to a fairly large body does tyranny raise its head: it is an alternative to republicanism, not to monarchy. This conclusion naturally follows from our earlier argument tracing the rise of tyranny to social instability. The collapse of the prestige of monarchy allows the conflict of interest between the different classes of society to develop into a real class war; party strife becomes acute, and the opportunity then exists for ambitious politicians

[1] *Politics*, p. 169 (IV, 11).

to build up their own power, by putting themselves at the head of one faction, or by making use of the general discontent.

Concerning the fall of tyrannies we know rather more than of their rise. The first phase of tyranny comes to an end when the great age of Greece begins. Various reasons may be found for the fall of individual tyrannies. Probably most did not last beyond the lifetime of their founder; it was as a general rule unlikely that his political ability and craft would be inherited. Further, it is improbable that all the tyrants were good rulers. Doubtless the worst made the strongest impression, but certainly, judging by the reputations they left behind them, there were more than a few who were real tyrants in every sense of the word. Finally, the early tyrants were in many cases allied to Persia and dependent on foreign support: when the free city states, led by Sparta and Athens, had overthrown the Persian menace, petty tyrants who had been the clients of the Persians were not likely to be spared.

The tyrannies of the later period are somewhat different in nature. They arise because of renewed discontent with the working of republican institutions, but the source of the actual power of the tyrant is now partly external as well as internal. In Sicily tyranny was endemic, perhaps for reasons of defence: the 'disorderly democracy' of most Greek cities was not capable of defending them against a peril as formidable and as persistent as the Carthaginian. In Greece proper during the fourth century Philip of Macedon was responsible for setting up many tyrants, who, because they depended on his aid, were easy to control, and were at the same time less expensive to maintain than a Macedonian garrison. Most of the later tyrants were soldiers; they appeared when the civilization of the Greek city state was breaking up, and they relied more on mercenaries, as well as on foreign aid, than the early tyrants.

A detailed analysis of the methods of rule of the tyrants, both early and later, would take too long. Some general features are worth noting, however. The use of an armed cohort of supporters as a bodyguard was very common with the tyrants. Thus Peisistratus, even before he became a tyrant, had a bodyguard of men armed with staves. They also generally formed a faction of their supporters in the state, and rewarded these with official posts or out of confiscations. Spies and informers, secret police, hostages, mercenaries, are all part of the machinery of tyranny. Heavy taxation, to weaken the rich, is fairly generally found. Aristotle says that the object of the great building projects associated with ancient, as with modern tyranny, was to keep the people busy and poor.[1] Ure suggests that the aim was to build up 'an industrial army of employee subjects'.[2] We may be excused if modern parallels induce us to believe that the real objects of this policy might have been to give the people employment, to provide a stimulus to economic activity in the state, to promote prosperity, and at the same time to raise the prestige of the tyranny by its material accomplishments.

Aristotle notices the way in which tyrants are accustomed to play off the poor and the rich against one another, and maintain the pretence of defending each against

[1] *Politics*, p. 226 (v, 11).
[2] Ure, op. cit., p. 14.

the other.[1] He remarks on the kinship between democracy and tyranny[2] — the attacks on the notables,[3] the demagogic methods of the tyrant, the licence given to the ruffianly element in society,[4] and government by arbitrary decrees instead of by laws.[5] What the demagogue is to democracy, Aristotle says, the flatterer is to the tyrant.[6] The tyrant, also, is prone to war.[7] A good example of this is provided by Dionysius of Syracuse, whose rule was admittedly imperialistic, and who depended extensively on the Punic peril to make his own government necessary to the people. Indeed it has been alleged that on this account he rather maintained than destroyed his Carthagenian rivals in Sicily,[8] though this it is difficult to believe.

Although the historian can find traces of good works accomplished by the tyrants, the Greeks, who knew them rather better, returned with surprising unanimity an unfavourable verdict on their rule. The feature of tyranny that left the strongest impression was the violence it did to the legal order, and what the rule of law meant to the Greeks is shown in the Oresteia. The tyrant was an ordinary man placed above the laws and therefore raised to an extraordinary position: *hubris* — that pride which provoked the wrath of the gods and foretold a dreadful fate — was almost the necessary consequence. The Greeks did not believe that a man could be emancipated from the laws of the state and invested with supreme power without

[1] *Politics*, p. 231 (V, 11). [2] id., p. 222 (V, 10).
[3] id., p. 130 (III, 13), pp. 218, 225 (V, 10).
[4] id., p. 246 (VI, 4). [5] id., p. 157 (IV, 4).
[6] id., [7] id., p. 226 (V, 11).
[8] J. B. Bury, *A History of Greece*, 2nd ed., 1917, p. 655; *Camb. Anc. Hist.*, vol. VI, p. 126.

losing his sense of balance and moderation. Madness is the political as well as the poetic nemesis on the tyrant.

Aristotle, who had a host of examples on which to base his conclusions, declared that no form of government was so short-lived as tyranny.[1] He has in fact nothing to say in its favour: it is by definition a bad form of government, not a constitution but the reverse of one.[2] The good deeds of tyrants find no place in his account. He establishes once for all the evil connotation which the term, at first without ethical implications, had gained during the age which followed the early tyrannies.

One cannot but suspect that there was another side to the medal. To the brilliant courts of the early tyrants is attributed an important share in the development of Greek culture.[3] Under Peisistratus Athens had peace and prosperity, was freed from the party strife which was the curse of most of the big cities, and enjoyed economic progress and even a training in the forms of self-government which was to be valuable later. He surely deserves to be credited with a real desire to give the state good government, and with a genuine interest in its artistic and intellectual progress, as well as in its foreign prestige. Indeed, the Aristotelian *Constitution of Athens* admits that, 'His administration was temperate . . . and more like a constitutional government than a tyranny, in every respect humane and mild'. In fact the tyranny of Peisistratus, it adds, was called proverbially the age of gold.[4]

But this very example indicates Aristotle's justification. The tyrant, or as we should say, dictator, can establish

[1] *Politics*, p. 232-3 (V, 12). [2] id., p. 162 (IV, 7).

[3] *Camb. Anc. Hist.*, vol. III, p. 548.

[4] ARISTOTLE, *The Constitution of Athens*, ed. F. G. Kenyon, 1891, ch. xvi, pp. 27, 28.

himself and rule well, but only by going against his nature, by ceasing to be a tyrant and becoming more like a king,[1] especially by preserving the old forms of the constitution, as Peisistratus preserved the constitution of Solon. But a tyrant with the self-restraint and the statesmanship thus to wrap up his authority in tradition and so build up imperceptibly a permanent rule is hardly to be found until we pass from the Greek to the Roman world. Under Alexander and his successors, although republican institutions survived in the local self-government of the Greek cities, in the wider political units that were now appearing, the principle of monarchy was being reborn; while, farther west, Roman republicanism was made of stern stuff, and did not accommodate itself very easily with tyrants.

§ 3 THE RISE OF CAESARISM

Since the Greek word tyranny, though more appropriate, did not express quite the meaning modern advocates of tyrannical government wished to convey, it was from a Roman institution that the term dictatorship was borrowed. The Roman dictatorship was an honourable and universally respected constitutional device of the Republic for meeting a crisis during a war. In common with dictatorship as the word is used to-day it implied that supreme power was placed in the hands of one man. But the Roman dictator was constitutionally appointed, held office only for a limited term, and when he laid down his power was judged for his deeds while he had exercised it.

[1] *Politics*, pp. 228-30 (v, 11).

Signs of dictatorship in the modern sense do not appear in the Roman republic until after the end of the Punic wars, when Rome was already discovering the difficulty of combining republican government with Empire. They are associated, as earlier in the Greek cities, with the appearance of economic troubles. The freemen were declining in number because of the wars; for the same reason a large slave population had grown up, whose cheap labour was undermining the standard of life of the citizens. The yeomen farmers, overburdened with debt, were forced to sell their lands to members of the Senatorial and Equestrian orders, who were building up, in defiance of the Licinian law, extensive estates worked by slave labour. In the city of Rome itself a large and impoverished urban population was developing. Faced with the dual task of governing extensive conquests and solving a complex economic problem the old system of government broke down.

The proposals of the Gracchi represent the first attempt to cope with these problems. Fog, in the words of the *Cambridge Ancient History*, 'enshrouds the history of the Gracchan age'.[1] But evidently both Tiberius and Caius Gracchus were endeavouring to reform some of the worst abuses in the state, and were relying to some extent on the support of the populace of Rome in their struggle with the conservative Senatorial party. The measures they wished to force through seem to have been moderate and reasonable enough, but to overcome the resistance of the Senate they had to aim at making themselves permanent tribunes of the plebs; that is, they had to violate the constitution and obtain personal power. Caius Gracchus even

[1] *Camb. Anc. Hist.*, vol. IX, p. 45.

went so far as to form a bodyguard of his supporters. But the Senators were too experienced and too well entrenched in power to yield; Tiberius and Caius Gracchus were each in turn attacked and killed by their opponents. Neither was a dictator, nor even aimed at a dictatorship, but their history indicates that a situation out of which dictatorship might arise already existed in Rome.

A long step was taken towards dictatorship in the modern sense of the word during the next generation; it is summed up in the careers of the two great generals, Marius and Sulla, who although they led opposite factions reflect the same political tendency in the state. The political struggle which had begun in the time of the Gracchi, was now becoming clarified. It was one between those who desired more efficient and less corrupt government, and who were at the same time not uninfluenced by a desire to share in the perquisites of Empire themselves, and the clique of Senatorial families, claiming a monopoly of the consulship, and an hereditary right to loot the Empire; for the biggest prizes that went with Senatorial rule were the corrupt provincial governorships. In the struggle the new men, trying to break into the Senatorial monopoly, called in the assistance of more popular elements in the state, but they must not for that reason be regarded as democrats.

However, Marius, a new man, who by his military ability had climbed into the consulship, which he held for five successive years (104—100 B.C.), reduced the property qualification for membership of the legions and enlisted large numbers of *proletarii* in them. It has plausibly been argued that this was the most decisive step in the whole history of the declining republic. The citizens who had filled the ranks of the legions in the earlier days of the republic, and who, when peace was declared, anxious to return to their farms and businesses, had insisted on demobilization, no longer served the state in war. The proletarians who now flocked behind the standards were prepared, so long as they received pay and booty, to remain permanently under arms. They became a standing army whose chief loyalty was to their general, and this was the force that henceforth could be flung into the struggle, and that was eventually to dominate the political system of Rome.

The existence of this standing army was in itself an invitation to would-be tyrants; added to the rivalry between the Senatorial class and the new men, and the evident insufficiency of the republican system of administration, it made the tendency towards dictatorship irresistible. Not only did the party hostile to the Senate put up as a potential dictator a far more extreme politician than either of the Gracchi, in the person of Marius, but the need for strong personal leadership was felt even by the Senate, which in self-defence accepted first Sulla as its champion, and then Pompey, although neither of these was in a position to be an effective dictator. Their function was to bolster up existing institutions, not to refashion the state: a real dictator could only come from the anti-Senatorial side.

He appeared when Julius Caesar rose to power as the representative of the Marian party. By alternating politics in Rome with war in the provinces, Caesar built up an army devoted to himself in the field and a large body of political supporters in the capital. The Senate had no better recourse against him than to call on a counter-dictator, Pompey. The defeat and death of Pompey settled the issue and the Senate accepted its master, heaped offices on Caesar, made him dictator for life, gave him forty-eight lictors, a seat in the Senate between the two consuls, and the right of expressing his opinion there first — perhaps to give the Senators warning as to the opinion they themselves should express. He had made himself chief pontiff at a comparatively early stage in his career; he controlled the composition of the Senate, had in practice the gift of state contracts, exercised the judicial functions of the prætors when it served his purpose, and was even voted a statue and the title of demi-god.[1]

Caesar was truly a dictator, and not in the old Roman sense. A dictator in some sense or other Rome certainly needed: only an absolute ruler could put down the misrule of the Senatorial cliques. Moreover, Caesar was far from being a mere tyrannical general. As well as military power, political authority in Rome had been equally necessary to him, and he had built it up skilfully from the nucleus provided by the remnants of the Marian party. In early days he had acted as prosecutor against two corrupt provincial governors — not so much from a love of the old republican virtue, as because the prosecutions enabled him to put himself forward as an opponent of Senatorial corruption, while their failure would show that no remedy was to be expected from Senatorial juries.[2] He made a reputation for himself as the 'general refuge of men in trouble',[3] and even while he was absent from the

[1] cf. W. E. Heitland, *The Roman Republic*, 2nd imp., 1923. As well as the specific references I have given, I must acknowledge my general indebtedness to Heitland on the career of Caesar.

[2] id., vol. III, p. 6. [3] id., vol. III, pp. 247, 265.

capital provided games and public holidays to please the 'mongrel mob' which had taken the place of the *populus Romanus*, borrowing money on a huge scale to finance these activities.

Once in power Caesar showed himself a genuine administrative reformer and began to introduce changes on a grand scale; he planned great public works — roads through Italy and buildings in Rome; marshes were to be drained, new cities founded for the legionaries, libraries established, a new digest of the law planned, and, with all this, a degree of financial stability was restored in the republic.

On the other hand, we must not neglect the steps he took to complete the degradation of the Senate, packing it with new men, including even sons of freedmen and provincials, levelling downwards as well as upwards, and encouraging members of the upper classes to disgrace themselves.[1] But the aristocracy had not yet lost all sense of shame, nor, in spite of their corruptions, had the memory of their ancient traditions entirely deserted them. Intellectually, and in executive ability, in the tasks of peace as well as in those of war, and even in practical political morality, Caesar stood head and shoulders above the whole Senatorial class. He represented efficient personal government against the inefficient and corrupt anarchy which was the only result of Senatorial rule. Yet in spite of all this he had made a mistake in despising his opponents, just as he had made a mistake in thinking that he could either win them over by a somewhat contemptuous patronage or else, who knows, rule the Empire

[1] cf. W. E. HEITLAND, *The Roman Republic*, 2nd imp., 1923, vol. III, pp. 337, 360.

without them. For the Senators still possessed the administrative tradition that was needed for the task of government, and they were still too imbued with the republican spirit to accept permanently Caesar's open dictatorship. In 49 B.C. he crossed the Rubicon, and in effect staked out his claim as dictator. After five years of civil strife he overcame all opposing forces; he triumphed in 45 B.C., in 44 became dictator for life, and in the same year fell beneath the daggers of Senatorial conspirators in the Forum at Rome.

The Empire plunged into a second, and even more violent and prolonged civil war, which ended in the triumph of Octavian, the heir to Caesar. Lacking, perhaps, the genius and the personal fascination of Julius, he was a more cautious, and in the end a more successful statesman. He claimed no dictatorial powers, but merely concentrated the normal republican offices in his own person; taking for himself the tribunician powers, he refrained from being made a tribune. Dictator, King or Emperor were not titles he envied, the most he would allow himself to be called was *princeps* — first citizen of the republic. The highest office he reserved for himself was that of high priest, *pontifex maximus* — not unaware that though the Roman state religion was a mockery to the smart society of Rome, it was acquiring significance in the provinces, and conscious that the old Roman *pietas* was still needed if a government was to be respected as well as obeyed. Wherever the religion of Rome spread, the name, and in the end the worship of Augustus spread with it. Not that he relied altogether on spiritual forces: by keeping the appointment of the proconsuls of the frontier provinces in his own hands, Augustus preserved his control of the armies, while the government of the peaceful inner provinces was left as a sop to the vanity and a bribe to the pockets of the Senate.

In effect Augustus was all that Caesar had been, and more, but his tyranny was a concealed one; it preserved the republican decencies; it showed that profound respect for existing forms which was part of the Roman genius for government. Where Julius had degraded the Senate, Augustus restored to it the dignity it had lost, purged it of the low-born or barbarian elements, assisted the Senators with loans to maintain their status, and in appearance shared his power with them fairly. The truth, of course, was that the Senators were little better than puppets in the hands of the Princeps: they were of use to him, but he was their master. And whereas Julius had died under the daggers of a score of assassins, Augustus lived to old age, revered and obeyed, the unquestioned master of the Roman world, passed on his authority peacefully to his successor, and laid down a structure of Empire that was to last with modifications for some four or five hundred years — the one dictator in the whole of our records to found a government which so far as human history goes can be called permanent.

A few generations later Seneca can hold him up to his promising young pupil, Nero, as a shining example of the virtues which distinguish a king from a tyrant.[1] The Principate at Rome may still seem to us more like a tyranny than a monarchy: but in the Empire it had already acquired the divinity that hedges a king. Augustus had achieved what, according to Aristotle, should be the aim of every tyrant. He had so concealed

[1] SENECA, *De Clementia*, I, II, 12.

the arbitrary nature of his authority, and exercised his power with such moderation, that in Rome the transition from a Republic to an Empire seemed but a natural, constitutional growth, and in the provinces the power and prestige surrounding Emperor and Imperial City alike, replaced government on a basis sanctioned by religious awe.

APPENDIX II

THE THEORY OF DICTATORSHIP OF CARL SCHMITT

It seems desirable to devote some pages in this book to a consideration of the only modern attempt at a general theory of dictatorship with which we are acquainted — that of Dr. Carl Schmitt in his book *Die Diktatur*. Dr. Schmitt does not give a formal definition of dictatorship, but he clearly regards it as involving the setting up of an exceptional regime, that is, of one which breaks away from some established norm, which may be either an existing constitution or an accepted political ideal. In contradiction with our treatment, he does not confine the term to the rule of one man: this he regards as only a terminological point. Indeed, the arbitrary rule of a single man, corresponding to no legal conception, is, he says, not dictatorship, but a mere objectless despotism.[1] Dictatorship is for him not absolute power in itself, but power put into operation for some specific purpose.[2] If dictatorship is a form of government which interests the legal philosopher — and Dr. Schmitt assumes that it is — then, he argues, it must have some basis in right; if it suppresses an accepted system of political rights it must be in the interests of some greater right; or, as he puts it, there must be a possibility of drawing the line between *Recht* and *Rechtsverwirklung*, right and the

[1] Carl Schmitt, *Die Diktatur*, 2nd ed., 1928, pp. v, viii.
[2] id., p. 136.

realization of right. 'The justification of dictatorship', to quote Schmitt, 'lies herein, that it ignores right, but only for the sake of its realization.'[1] Again, 'to every dictator appertains a commission'.[2] Thus the Roman dictator was given the right to override the law, but only in the interests of its ultimate preservation, and particularly to safeguard the existing rights of the aristocracy from the attacks of the plebs.[3]

Schmitt rightly separates this constitutional dictatorship from the tyranny of Sulla and Caesar, and the difference provides him with the distinction on which his theory is based — that between the *kommissarische* and the *souveräne Diktatur*.[4] The *kommissarische Diktatur* is appointed constitutionally and the task to which his power corresponds is the maintenance or restoration of an accepted consitutional norm.[5] Chapter II of *Die Diktatur* shows the use made of such an officer by the German princes in the seventeenth century when they adopted the practice of appointing commissioners with arbitrary powers. But this use of 'dictatorial' commissioners under an absolute prince is too familiar to need discussion. Nor need we pause over a lengthy discussion of the extent to which the idea of dictatorship is to be found in the writings of various seventeenth- and eighteenth-century political thinkers.

The real appearance of sovereign dictatorship in the modern world is in the French Revolution; but before proceeding to this, Schmitt has to deal with the one pre-revolutionary ruler who seems to fall into this category — Oliver Cromwell, and his analysis of the Cromwellian

[1] CARL SCHMITT, *Die Diktatnr*, 2nd ed., 1928, pp. viii, ix.
[2] id., p. 137. [3] id., p. 2. [4] id. [5] id., p. 137.

rule serves to clarify his conception of the sovereign dictator. Cromwell, he admits, possessed sovereign power; he was a military autocrat and the major generals who ruled under him can be considered as holders of 'dictatorship by commission'. This does not, however, amount to claiming that Cromwell himself was a sovereign dictator, for while the *kommissarische* dictator exists to preserve the constitution as it stands, the sovereign dictator is called into being to create the conditions in which a new constitution is possible.[1]

Schmitt does not agree with the saying that the dictator is *ein wunder*, one who suspends the laws of the state as a miracle suspends the laws of nature. On the contrary, he is the representative of law, but it is of new law in process of being born; he embodies the breaking through of what is rightful for the founding of a new regime.[2] One might be tempted to ask whether this description could not reasonably be applied to Cromwell: but here a further element in Schmitt's theory appears. It is implied in the argument with which he excludes Cromwell from the category of sovereign dictators. The fundamental source from which Cromwell derives his power is the will of God; whereas for Schmitt the sovereign dictator must essentially derive his commission from the people.[3]

It is thus natural that sovereign dictatorship should not appear until the French Revolution links the idea of sovereignty with the idea of the people in the theory of popular sovereignty. In this point our own view bears out that of Schmitt, though we do not follow him in his subsequent remarks. Concurrently with this develop-

[1] CARL SCHMITT, *Die Diktatur*, 2nd ed., 1928, p. 137.
[2] id., pp. 138-9. [3] id., p. 138.

ment, he says, comes a change in the whole basis of political ideas. The individualistic, rationalistic political theory of the eighteenth century is dropped and a new and more vital idea of the people or the nation appears. The people, says Schmitt, is now revealed as the inexhaustible source of new constitutional forms, with an eternal right to re-fashion its institutions to suit the new needs of new ages as they are born.[1] Out of this innate power or right residing in the people emerges the sovereign dictatorship.[2] Thus we are brought to the revolutionary assemblies, which exercise a dictatorial authority in the name of the people. At this point, when we are just about to approach what in our study we have taken to be the first modern dictatorship, Schmitt unexpectedly stops, with a brief glance into the possible change in political conditions produced by the rise of the proletariat, and a suggestion of the reappearance to-day of conditions in which the nation must reassert its constitution-making capacity through a sovereign dictatorship.

It will be seen that the development traced above is mainly a theoretical one. Schmitt is interested not in the actual exercise of dictatorship but in the theory behind it. Writing as a legal philosopher, rather than as a historian or a political scientist, his interest is not in the mode of operation of the arbitrary authority implied in dictatorship but in the problem of finding a means of justifying it juridically. The *kommissarische Diktatur* can be fitted into normal legal categories without difficulty, as a temporary suspension of the rule of law, made under legal conditions and for the preservation of the legal

[1] CARL SCHMITT, *Die Diktatur*, 2nd ed., 1928, p. 142.
[2] id., p. 145.

constitution. The stoutest upholders of the rule of law have accepted the justifiability of its temporary suspension in a national crisis; and the republican constitution of Rome has been regarded as strengthened rather than weakened by the institution of dictatorship. But the attempt to justify what Schmitt calls sovereign dictatorship by treating it as an analogous institution is much more questionable, because it subsumes under the category of law that which, it seems to us, in the nature of things is outside it. This, which at bottom is the whole effort of Schmitt's book, we cannot help regarding as a logical impossibility.

In the attempt to discover a respectable ancestry for his theory of dictatorship, he turns to Rousseau's definition of the legislator,[1] and Mably's statement that during a revolution the representatives of the people have the right to assume full control of public affairs and subordinate the executive to themselves.[2] But in fact he does not really produce a single pre-revolutionary writer who supports his conception. Rousseau, whom he uses as the last link in his chain, was a bitter enemy of the idea of personal dictatorship, and passionately devoted to the principle of the rule of law. Mably with almost equal firmness maintains the same idea. About the same time in England Burke was stating the case against dictatorship of any kind in magisterial fashion. For the real origins of the revolutionary dictatorship we have to turn, as we have suggested, not to theorists but to practical developments during the Revolution. But history cannot provide moral justification; so Schmitt has in the end to

[1] CARL SCHMITT, p. 127.
[2] id., pp. 115-16.

fall back on the theoretical arguments he himself can provide.

What is his problem? 'The content of the activity of the legislator', he says, 'is right, but lacking rightful power this is right without might; the dictator is all powerful but lawless — might without right.'[1] His aim is to unite these two, 'to give to the legislator the might of the dictator'. 'When a legislator has been given the power of a dictator and a constitution-making dictatorship has been set up', he writes, 'the transition from the *kommissarische* to the *souveräne* dictatorship has been effected.'[2]

These ideas obviously require further analysis. One cannot but suspect that the argument is not entirely free from the confusion involved in the use of the term *Recht* to mean both right and law. Thus when Schmitt says that the activity of the legislator is *Recht*, one is inclined to translate the word as law rather than right; but the dictator, by arrogating to himself the power of making laws, does not endow himself with any added right. His right may be derived from the source of his power, or from the object for which it is being exercised, but to call him a legislator as well as a dictator does not in itself contribute anything to his justification.

Schmitt, however, claims that the power of the constitution-making or sovereign dictatorship is rightful, first, because it derives from the inexhaustible capacity of the people or nation for creating ever new organs through which to exercise its power, and secondly, because its activity is determined by its end, which is the erection

[1] Carl Schmitt, pp. 128-29.
[2] id., p. 129.

of a new legal norm or constitutional system. His justification of dictatorship is thus based primarily upon the principle that all power comes from the people. He may be said to uphold dictatorship because he is a believer in the principle of democracy, which, he writes elsewhere, 'means the identity of sovereign and subject, of the government and the governed'.[1] When it is really this it is justifiable: the trouble is that the parliamentary system involves government by elected representatives, who substitute their will for the will of the nation: a dictator may be a truer representative of the people than an elected body.

Behind these arguments, we must insist, is the fundamental presupposition that all political right is an emanation from the will of the people, or the nation, against which no rival authority can stand.[2] Now this principle, while generally accepted by German thinkers, runs counter to the secular trend of Western thought. The laws of God, or the law of nature, or, by whatever name it be known, some oecumenical law, has normally been conceived as the true foundation of all local laws. Even if this be regarded merely as a principle of morality or justice, it still provides a criterion higher than the *pouvoir constituant* emanating from the nation, and by it the rights of dictatorship as well as of every other form of government, have been judged. The first point to be noted about Schmitt's theory is that he definitely breaks with this tradition.

A second basic feature of Schmitt's theory that requires comment is his use of the term *Diktatur* to cover all

[1] C. SCHMITT, *Verfassungslehre*, 1928, p. 234.
[2] *Die Diktatur*, p. 142.

arbitrary government, whether it be in the hands of a single individual or not. On the other hand, dictatorship, in the sense in which we have used the word, definitely implies the rule of one man — Caesarism. In pure juristic theory it may seem the better plan to group all arbitrary governments together as dictatorial, but if we pass from the theoretical basis to the practical, there will appear, as every political scientist since Aristotle has recognized, all the difference in the world between a government of one man, of a few, or of many. Any of these might be a dictatorship in Schmitt's sense of the word. For the jurist the nature of the sovereignty exercised and not the number of persons exercising it may be the significant fact; but for the student of actual governments the Aristotelian principle of division is sounder.

A third difficulty exists in the very nature of the criterion which Schmitt uses to distinguish between constitutional government and dictatorship. The former embodies a certain norm, which may be either an existing constitution or a political ideal.[1] Dictatorship can be regarded as an exception to either or both of these, though only for the purpose of setting up a new constitutional or ideal norm. According to this definition dictatorship is essentially a transitional regime, called into being when an existing constitutional norm has been destroyed, for the sake of creating a new one. It follows that as soon as it has made the new constitution which the nation demands, the task of the dictatorship is ended and it must relinquish the power it has only rightfully held while the task remained incomplete. But does this occur in fact?

[1] *Die Diktatur*, p. vi.

Between 1789 and 1804 the *pouvoir constituant* in France passed from one hand to another, but at what point did the government cease to be a rightful dictatorship? And when Napoleon had cemented his authority in the from of imperial institutions on France, was his rule then no longer dictatorial? These are the kind of practical questions to which Schmitt provides no answer. In fact, even if he can get us into a dictatorial form of government without sacrificing juristic right, can he show us how to get out of it?

Fourthly and finally, we are bound to ask whether Schmitt's justification of sovereign dictatorship is logically tenable. The dictatorship exists, he says, because the nation is passing through a crisis: the existing constitution has ceased to respond to the needs of the time and the new constitution has yet to be made. But what criterion have we of the existence of such a time of transition? Nations, in the course of history, have their periods of distress, or even crises, without necessarily requiring each time a remoulding of the whole political fabric. The only proof Schmitt can give that a dictatorship is necessary at any given time is that it exists; and its very existence provides it with an automatic justification. The conclusion is that dictatorship is always juridically justifiable if it can be successfully established. Once again, success is made the criterion of right, and history has to provide its own justification.

One cannot but suspect that to a certain extent *Die Diktatur*, although a very learned work, was a *livre de circonstance*, and that the author was perhaps mainly concerned with the conditions in Germany at the time when he wrote. His dominant preoccupation was evidently, as an appendix of some fifty pages indicates, with the famous Article 48 of the Weimar Constitution, giving the President the right in the interests of the state to override the legal authorities. Such presidential activity would obviously fall into Schmitt's category of the *kommissarische* dictatorship. But one wonders whether the author were not also looking forward to what he regards as a higher exercise of dictatorial power, to an arbitrary re-fashioning of the state in its entirety by a sovereign dictator. If such a possibility were in his mind — and given the political conditions in Germany the supposition is not unreasonable — it would explain his attempt to connect the *kommissarische* with the sovereign dictator and to justify the latter on arguments derived from a study of the former. We may take his book as providing useful evidence of some of the ideas behind dictatorship at the present day; but in none of the four fundamental points which we have just enumerated does his view seem to us theoretically sound. These considerations should be sufficient to show why we have not been able to accept Schmitt's general theory of dictatorship as the basis of our own study.

INDEX

INDEX

INDEX

INDEX

INDEX

INDEX